MW00460908

Lewis Carroll.

The Agony
of
Lewis Carroll

Richard Wallace

To my family.

Copyright © 1990 by Richard Wallace.

All rights reserved. No part of this book may be reproduced or utilized in any form or by any means, electronic or mechanical, including photocopying, recording, or by any information storage and retrieval system, without permission in writing from the publisher.

Cataloging data:
Biography, psychology.
Illustrations, Notes, Bibliography, Index.

First Edition 1990
Gemini Press, P. O. Box 1088, Melrose, MA 02176

Printed in the United States of America.

International Standard Book Number: 0-9627195-5-2
Library of Congress Catalog Card Number: 90-90304

"Bluff a rough, sordid,
heathen world,
and cheat death."
Lewis Carroll

"Oh, when shall it finish,
when shall it sate —
lie down to sleep —
this fury-bound hate?"
Aeschylus

Table of Contents

Preface

This is a journey into the pain of another human being, not just any other human being, but one whose persona has taken on a near legendary existence — the author of *Alice's Adventures in Wonderland* and many other works — Charles Lutwidge Dodgson, better known by his pseudonym *Lewis Carroll*.

Some may ask, as I did for many months in trying to determine just if and how I would approach this book, whether anyone has a right to enter so deeply into another person's private inner world and whether one has a right to bring the pain found there to public awareness. In answering those questions, I gave a great deal of thought to the anger this work may raise in those who love him as they have found him through his life, works, and words — the descendents of the Dodgson family, the hundreds who have spent significant portions of their lives in research and literary criticism nearly as a labor of love, and the millions who love him for the pure enjoyment his works have given them as children and adults. I concluded that any book which delves into the pain which his nephew biographer Stuart Collingwood sensed but did not identify must develop goals beyond pure disclosure. The book is published under the assumption that in the final analysis, Dodgson was crying out through his works *"I hurt!"* — hoping desperately to be heard.

In making the choice to publish, I established several goals. Those familiar with readings in psychology and human behavior know that the knowledge we gain from the clinical study of those in great psychological distress gives us insight into the kinds of pain from which we all suffer, some in more tolerable doses, others terribly, silently, and alone. The first goal of this book is to bring to light a life lived in great distress and from which, hopefully, a great deal can be learned.

The second goal is to provide a focus for the impact of child abuse and societal hypocrisy on the lives of its victims. In *For Your Own Good* Alice Miller used the life of Adolph Hitler as an example of the kind of twisted adult that can evolve from a childhood filled with physical and psychic abuse. I hope the life of Charles Dodgson, a victim of parental coercion, institutionalized hypocrisy, and brutality provides a more sympathetic historical figure upon which to focus in the pursuit of bringing to public awareness the pervasiveness of these destructive forces in all their forms.

A third goal is to encourage parents to focus attention on allowing their children to be children so that the experiencing of childhood is not distorted by the pursuit of parental goals and expectations but is spent in the development of their own true selves, ready to fulfill their own directions as fruitful and happy adults.

A fourth goal is to bring to the awareness of those readers who recognize Dodgson's pain or identify with it themselves will come to see his efforts to strike back as the same kind of struggle endured by all who suffer, often in silent rage, as they attempt to live in a world where intolerance for difference reigns. Many will see him as a hero for expressing his rage, however secretly, and rejoice in the success he achieved getting the last laugh by fooling generations of readers and intellectuals with complex webs of deception.

All of these goals notwithstanding, there is the risk that empathic understanding for Dodgson the man will be lost in derision if his works become the basis of parlor games for idle prurient entertainment. I hope this will not occur, but have proceeded on the basis that using his life as another example in spreading critical messages for the benefit of both children and their parents outweighs the risk.

I have included two verses in the Epigraph. The first is drawn from material written in the hand of Charles Dodgson on a wood block discovered in 1954 beneath the floorboards of the Dodgson family nursery in Croft, Yorkshire, England. Its relevance is discussed in Chapter 3. The second consists of the closing lines from *The Libation Bearers*, the second of the *Orestes* plays by the Greek dramatist Aeschylus, as translated by Paul Roche. Its meaning becomes evident in Chapter 8.

As a journey of this type is wont to be, it was accompanied by a journey into my own inner world. For it was this pursuit which brought me quite accidently into Dodgson's published world and then deeply into his secret life. As a writer hurrying to release myself from the grip with which this pursuit has held me, I hope readers will find this effort more than adequately fair and complete. I do not intend it to be a definitive biography; but I do hope it will open new doors so that others may examine further the many facets in Dodgson's life and works and contribute their own knowledge and perspective.

Due to the nature of the material presented, both its potential to offend and the "trade secret" nature of its formulation, I allowed very few to share in its development. Special thanks are due my wife and three children for not giving up on me, but particularly to my wife, who endured many lonely hours of my physical presence in the face of thoughts and emotions obviously drifting elsewhere. I owe a great deal to my parents, who taught me very early that the imitation of God is not in judging, but in loving. Thanks are due my brother Allen for his support throughout and Peggy Wallace for her encouragement and assistance with the cover design.

Thanks are due Jennifer Locke and Robbie Tourse, Ph.D. for their early encouragement, Lois Brown who struggled to improve my writing style, Barbara Blum, LICSW, Arthur and Susan Bass, and Serge Blinder for their patient review of a not-quite-ready manuscript and other close friends who provided a welcome relief from the stresses of the task. Thanks are due the many biographers, scholars and writers who have provided the material for research; I hope they see my effort as an honest yet different kind of search and not as one intended to diminish their own efforts. Thanks are due Boston College and its Graduate School of Social Work for the program offered me in 1987-1989, during which this all began, for their fine facilities and resources, and for the assistance of the library staff, without whom the research effort would have been considerably more difficult. Also thanks are due the Public Libraries in Melrose, Peabody, and Brookline, Massachusetts, the British Library for allowing me access to Dodgson's diary manuscripts as well as their fine collection, and to Christ Church, Oxford, for providing access to the diaries of Thomas Vere Bayne. And lastly, thanks are due Barry Melnick, Ph.D. who helped on several occasions to bring me back from the depths of Dodgson's despair even as we explored what brought me there.

Richard Wallace, M.S.W.

PART I

INTRODUCTION

CHAPTER I

FOCUS OF THE SEARCH

Is All our Life, then, but a dream
Seen faintly in the golden gleam
Athwart Time's dark resistless stream?

Bowed to the earth with bitter woe,
Or laughing at some raree-show,
We flutter idly to and fro.

Man's little Day in haste we spend
And, from its merry noontide, send
No glance to meet the silent end.

    With this dedicatory acrostic poem to his child friend Isa Bowman (whose name can be seen reading down the first letter of each line and again taking the first three letters of each verse) Lewis Carroll opens his most ambitious yet critically forgetable two volume novel *Sylvie and Bruno*. Published when Carroll was fifty-seven this poem offers a reflection on the meaning of life, it seems of his life. There is a note of wishful melancholy, an emptiness of meaning, indeed, a questioning of the very reality of life.

    Whether attempting to interpret a writer's works as being reflective of his inner feelings or of using more objective events to infer inner states, the writer of biography is challenged inevitably by the need to balance evidence and interpretation in making inferences or drawing conclusions regarding the life of his subject. [1] Whether it be his actions and activities, the testimony of peers (friend or foe), published or unpublished writings, private diaries, or spoken words remembered, the inner world of the subject remains elusive. By gaining a level of intimacy during the research process and attempting to apply some consistent and reasonable bases for generalization, the biographer attempts to complete the inner portrait to complement the record of events. It will become evident to many that the choices made in the preparation of this work challenge that notion to its limits. When is evidence not evidence? How much evidence can and should be filtered out? What if the evidence seems to be the answer to a riddle posed by the subject? Or, the riddle itself? When can fiction be considered auto-biographical? Can nonsense fiction possibly be considered auto-biographical, not by inference, but by the attribution of intent? What if much of the visible evidence regarding a person's life appears to be a construct, a virtual charade created and sustained until it becomes all that others see? Is it possible to live a public charade for a lifetime without being detected? To what extent can someone keep his totally different inner life secret, hidden behind a looking-glass, with the only reflection allowed to escape that which he has chosen to make visible? What motivation would drive a person to attempt to do so and to do so in so public a way? What circumstances would create that wish or rather, the obsession, the total control, which would be required to sustain it?

Just as Carroll's most famous works were unique for their time — perhaps for all time for reasons that shall become evident — so is their author an enigma, a puzzlement which this work may only further reveal and certainly not fully resolve. A summary of the life of Charles Lutwidge Dodgson, the man behind the pseudonym "Lewis Carroll," reveals a birth in rural Victorian England in 1832, an upbringing within the large family of a cleric in the Anglican Church, education in the English public school system, completion with honors of degree requirements at Oxford University, then residency there as a bachelor don until his death at age 65. During that time he taught mathematics without inspiration or feelings of accomplishment until he finally abandoned teaching altogether, published with cleverness but without great creativity several works in Mathematics, published with some creativity in the field of logic, and wrote and published serious and nonsense poetry and novels under his pseudonym. It was from these literary works, primarily just two of them, that he derived nearly all of his fame and some fortune and emerged from what would otherwise have been a life of total obscurity. The biographical mystery has been: what unlocked the genius which created the standard for nonsense literature?

In his personal life he cultivated numerous and what appear to have been close emotional friendships with pre-adolescent girls from the Oxford community, those he met at the beach or as fellow railway passengers, and among friends associated with the London theater.

He was an inveterate letter writer, record keeper, diarist, walker, theater goer, and inventor of games and gadgets, a significant hobbyist in early Victorian photography and sometime preacher in his early and later years. Throughout his life he suffered from stuttering and insomnia, and in his middle and later years from a variety of migraine symptoms. While he seemed to exert some effort to maintain a distance from the fame and popularity accorded the mostly invisible "Lewis Carroll," he did take pride in the exposure his activities gave him with British royalty and other Victorian artists and notables. What is known about his inner life is taken from the testimony of those family and many friends who praise his great kindness and gentleness (despite reports to the contrary regarding some with whom he had intellectual or political disagreements, primarily within the Oxford community), and the inferences made by literary and psychological analysts attempting to understand the man through his works. Nearly all see a sadness in his life, many a sexual repression and some great pain of unknown origin but often suggested as an unrequited love, a pain he alluded to but never fully described.

Already the subject of nearly a dozen serious biographical works beginning in the year following his death in 1898, with the most recent published in 1979, Lewis Carroll remains as much a source of curiosity and wonder as do his classic nonsense stories, popularly known as "Alice in Wonderland" and its companion piece "Through the Looking-Glass." Of these biographies, the earliest written by his nephew Stuart Collingwood with the guidance of Dodgson's siblings, *The Life and Letters of Lewis Carroll*, depicts a generous and good man seeming to live under the "shadow of some disappointment" which he preferred and encouraged others to leave unexplored. Langford Reed's 1932 biography *The Life of Lewis Carroll* suggests a split personality with the nonsense works his outlet for releasing inner conflict; Florence Lennon's 1945 work *Victoria Through the Looking-Glass* detects a great deal of emotional suffering and bitterness with the nonsense writing representing efforts to escape some painful reality in his life, most likely the effects of a repressed sexuality. Roger Green, editor of the *Diaries* and Derek Hudson, author of the 1954 biography *Life of Lewis Carroll* both recognize a man living in pain. Hudson accepts the notion of a man fixated emotionally in childhood even as he and Green both reject the categorical "certainty" of the Freudian interpretations which point to repressed sexual expression as the underlying cause. Morton Cohen, editor of the *Letters* and nearly lifelong Carrollian researcher resists the psychological interpretations that are too certain (especially the Freudian) and focuses on the lighthearted nonsense so evident in his works and in his interactions with children. Anne Clark's 1979 biography *Lewis Carroll: A Biography* appears to be factually the most complete but her text avoids interpretation. A few critics and analysts (especially John Schilder (1938) along with some early reviewers) have seen the "Alice" books as quite violent and as more than just innocent and harmless Victorian parody. Others receive them with pure delight; and still others regard them as deeply symbolic religious or political commentary.

This work focuses on the nature, origins and manifestations of the sadness and great pain in Dodgson's life. For there was great emotional suffering. Since exploration of this part of his inner life is the goal, the factual incidental details of Dodgson's life are presented only as they round out a total picture of his personality, support interpretation, or in fact require re-interpretation in the face of new evidence.

Perhaps it is appropriate here to inform readers that many will find the material presented in this work offensive __ very offensive. This may be true because of its inherent content __ language and imagery which is explicitly sexual, violent, and demeaning __ or because it conflicts so much with what we all wish to believe about the author of the "Alice" books. This is unavoidable; only as much as I deemed necessary to provide a complete if at times ugly portrait of his inner life and rage is presented. In addition, every effort has been made to remain non-judgmental in the handling of content and the attribution of motivation. The human condition is filled with pain, with people struggling in the best way they know how to live their lives out as fully as they can, to keep going, sometimes at great cost to themselves and others. Charles Dodgson engaged in that struggle for a lifetime; hopefully we can learn from his effort.

An examination of Dodgson's writings reflects that he acknowledged having agonized throughout his life with the consequences of some unspecified bothersome thoughts or activities. This admission is dismissed by most biographers as reflective of excessive shame or guilt associated with normal yet undefined bachelor temptations founded in a repression of sexual expression. For he appears to have pursued the promised Christian redemption in which he had been raised in an exemplary way as he engaged in good works, especially the many hours spent delighting children with stories and games. He shared the royalties from his books with great generosity, wrote some very inspirational letters to troubled family, friends, and strangers, all of which activities created and sustained the image which has become the basis for what we have known or believed thus far of his life. In contrast to this image (yet not refuting that he appeared also as all of these) I believe strong evidence exists that Charles Dodgson struggled with the life of a homosexual in Victorian England, during a time when getting caught in homosexual activity was a criminal offense subject to capital punishment in his early years, lengthy incarceration later on, even though its existence was known and secretly institutionalized and tolerated. In a secret battle against hypocrisy and from his protected environment as an Oxford don, consumed with a nearly murderous rage aimed at both his family and Victorian society, he published works of nonsense literature, not only as "gifts" to children, but as constructs for hiding self disclosure along with explicit (primarily) homosexual erotic imagery, which focused on masturbatory, anal-erotic, and pederastic fantasies and practices. There is strong circumstantial evidence that Dodgson worked in collusion with at least one other person, but more likely two or more, for some of the time. But it was he, partially hidden behind his pseudonym, who became increasingly bold and walked the terrifying yet titillating tightrope of inevitable personal disgrace and annihilation should disclosure occur.

The extent to which his own incomplete public acknowledgement of the presence of these unnamed struggles represents part of an overall effort to create a self serving public deception or represents a true reflection of his inner search for wholeness will be discussed, though inconclusively. There is evidence that this public image served the primary or secondary purpose of hoodwinking a gullible public even as he "thumbed his nose" at the world of adults of his and future generations and distributed his written works to their children under the guise of children's literature, often "wrapping" these works in prologues and epilogues shaped in the form of personalized poems and exhortations with religious themes.

The creation of this extremely complex and disturbed man struggling between the extremes of good and evil, love and hate, is laid within the circumstances of Dodgson's childhood upbringing, with the available material pointing to significant parental insensitivity to the nature and limitations of the young boy. An already damaged youngster before he entered public school at age 12, Dodgson was further assaulted to the point of near destruction. The combination of this upbringing, his physical limitations, and the environmental demands of Victorian England caused a channeling of nearly all his psychic energies into the avoidance of annihilation of his own sense of self. This was accomplished by his engaging in a lifelong attack on what he saw as the hypocritical society in which he lived, even as he stretched that hypocrisy well beyond the limits deemed "acceptable" by Victorian society. His life task became the pursuit of revenge in such a way that he viewed himself virtually as God's chosen avenger. Arguments will be made that the original targets of his rage were his parents and family, none of whom ever seem to have been either aware of or participants in his lonely task.

For Charles Dodgson, life was not the happy dream often so evident in his works. It was a nightmare of constant inner turmoil on the verge of psychic destruction which was kept alive by an all consuming hate — a blind rage. We will explore the extent to which he was incapable of loving. By traveling into his "Wonderland" (a term which will take on new meaning) we will be entering the destructive world of coercive parenting, the violent world of the English public school system, the worlds of pornography and erotica, homosexuality, sexual perversions, of stuttering, migraines, and insomnia. We will enter the worlds of Greek myth, Victorian, and nonsense literature, and the world of games of which Dodgson was a master. Indeed, he made life itself a deadly game. We will enter the world of rage, of rage turned into revenge, of life become revenge, and of manipulation — manipulation of all those around him, adults and children. We will also enter the world of self-justification, shame, guilt, fear of being overwhelmed by parents and by a dangerous world, fear of annihilation in this world by public discovery, and finally fear of punishment for eternity in the next by an avenging God. And lastly, we will explore as the underlying theme of this work the world of child abuse in forms not usually thought about by well meaning and caring parents. For Dodgson's parents, like most, were but products of their own childhood, struggling to do their best. They were like many well-meaning parents who often repeat and intensify their own experiences, unaware that they themselves were damaged as children and pass on similar damage to the next generation.

Psychological interpretations as they appear reference a framework or model which focuses on the "self" and is appropriately called "Self-psychology." This was chosen for a number of reasons — its ease of understanding by the lay reader, its focus on both the intellectual and feeling life of the individual as a total being, and the fact that the issues involved in Dodgson's life were in many ways existential in nature, with Self-psychology very much an existential model. With dangerous brevity, a summary description of the framework is provided along with the definition of a few key terms.

Self-psychology identifies within a person a "Self" — an awareness or "feeling" one has about one's being, a wholeness, an integrity — physical, emotional, and intellectual — a feeling of oneself based on internal "criteria" as well as criteria established over time when comparing oneself to others in the environment. For the adult these feelings run the gamut from wonderfully cohesive to terribly fragmented with any of a host of adjectives to describe the different feelings which make up the spectrum of life even as precision may be difficult to achieve. They are feelings one has about one's self. For the infant without a vocabulary and but a rudimentary intellectual life, that feeling about self is nearly entirely based on physical and emotional comfort, both provided by the attention and confirmation of the primary parent, historically the mother, who must, for the infant's emotional development, mirror back the infant's preciousness to her. This person becomes the self-confirming outside object — selfobject, a wonderful word, coined by Heinz Kohut. For it implies in its structure that self-wholeness requires the fused presence of another person or object. For the neonate, his selfobject is his mother, as at this stage he is unaware that the mothering activities are not part of him. As the infant grows the number of ingredients which contribute to the "self" definition broaden, to include awareness that the "self" is separate from others outside who confirm and soothe and that some of the confirmation and soothing will now have to be done from inside the self.

A "selfobject" is an object outside the self which the self sees as essential to its integrity or feeling of wholeness. From an infant totally dependent on the mother to soothe his every discomfort — physical or emotional — the "self" grows to be able to self-soothe as "taught" by the parents. This teaching takes place at the felt level, not the intellectual level, by the success or failure of the caregiver to understand and respond to the infant with empathy. Failure to respond empathically — with understanding-in-action — to the child's needs as he perceives them, produces frustration in the child, frustration for which the child is not equipped to self-soothe. This frustration which is felt but not articulated or understood "feels bad" and inhibits emotional growth, creates further frustration, and creates alienation and distortions in his emerging adult personality and his relationship with people based on the early experience that people cannot be trusted. Aware of his dependence on these adults, however, the child will learn to adapt by compromising his own self, if necessary, in order to achieve feelings of wholeness, acceptance, and oneness with parents whom he knows he needs.

These empathic failures represent child upbringing strategies or personality characteristics in the parents which cause them, despite their good intentions, to ignore the needs of the child in the interest of their own needs or plans. This effectively forces the child to adapt to external needs and expectations — those of the parents — rather than responding to his own inner needs. Having totally committed development years to adapting to the wishes of others at his own expense, the child becomes an adult alienated from his true self. The result is a young adult who does not know who he is, just as he begins facing the world alone. In its worst form, as Dodgson's life will show us, this forced total denial of the self in favor of the needs of primary caregivers creates significant distortions in personality which create a lifelong internal struggle if not in some way corrected.

Such a damaged person develops an inappropriate emotional need for external soothing selfobjects throughout life as the skills to self-soothe are inadequate. The individual turns to things — people as things, money, power, sexual activities, work — whose presence in excess is essential to attain or maintain a feeling of well being. Sexual activity is a most potent candidate as a selfobject because it involves a real or perceived, hungered for or avoided, human contact which replicates many aspects of the earliest selfobject and because it can create strong physical feelings to change the total feeling state of a depleted and empty self. A "transitional object," such as a child's favorite blanket, is a perfect example of a selfobject which serves to soothe because it accepts passively whatever the child does with it and is then discarded when the soothing skill is learned. The emotionally damaged child filled with emptiness or frustration, rather than graduating away from the healthy need for transitional objects continues with a pathological need for them, with serious implications if carried into the emotionally stressful pubertal and adolescent periods. In the worst cases of emotional damage and isolation, children never make use of transitional objects and in the process never experience or learn the legitimate use of others to help in extremely emotional situations. The result is a life lived in great emptiness and isolation.

An essential presence for a pre-pubertal child who as a developmental task is acquiring goals and values is that of a model, a person he can idealize and whom he perceives as possessing qualities that are achievable for him. Failure to experience this presence and relationship which can tolerate difference, in combination with earlier inappropriate confirming experiences which destroy or distort self-confidence, create the adult without goals, with values which are too negotiable. This in turn leads to a life of frustration and emptiness especially for one who has intellectual skills but no perceived constructive outlet for expression and recognition.

Rage develops early from the frustration caused by a sense that needs are being neglected by those the child depends on, and then later either when as an adolescent or an adult he realizes the magnitude of how he has been cheated. Or, if he is faced with a traumatic emotional experience such as abandonment, fears of annihilation, or enormous loss it further destroys any sense of self that remains. For such a person may suddenly realize that primary caregivers or "society" as their surrogates are directly or indirectly responsible for his situation due to their failure to provide either coping skills or an environment in which the woefully inadequate learned skills "work." Rage expression can take many forms, including an explosive behavioral outburst, self-abuse, or a calculated vengeful act or series of acts executed with utmost cunning. But even in circumstances where the self is placed in danger, including suicide, the damaged self is seeking to restore a feeling of integrity for the uncomfortable feeling state that is being experienced.

For those wishing more detail on these areas, three Appendices are offered. Appendix 1 summarizes the origins and expressions of rage. Appendix 2 reviews the subject of sexual perversions from the framework of Self-psychology. And Appendix 3 presents a review of the literature on homosexuality.

I have also included in the Bibliography a number of works on many aspects of these subjects, all of which are relevant to our understanding of Charles Dodgson and the other goals of the work. Of special meaning are the works of Heinz Kohut, "father" of Self-psychology, Alice Miller, who is very readable, on the many forms of child-rearing abuse, Miller and Kohut on the nature and expression of rage, and Masud Khan on sexual perversions as self-restoring efforts. John Boswell's work on homosexuality is excellent, with theories as to causation numerous and inconclusive, and, importantly, which rarely fully consider the impact of societal rejection and alienation as contributing causes to self-destructive and alienating homosexual activities.

Since this work represents a journey in which I invite the reader to participate, it is written in the first person. The book is comprised of four parts. Part I consists of this chapter, which establishes the hypothesis to be proven, along with some essential concepts regarding the approach, and serves as an introduction. I made it a separate chapter in order to emphasize its importance in understanding both the work and the life presented. Part II explores Dodgson's world of unreality and attempts to make it real, indeed to give it the quality of evidence upon which a complete re-assessment of his life may be based. Due to the complexity of his life and the material presented, the structure of Part II is disconcerting, as much material is raised with full exploration left to subsequent chapters. This section is intended to re-orient those very familiar with his life and works to a new technique and perspective with which to approach his biography;

for those totally unfamiliar with Dodgson, it introduces a facet of his
life heretofore not recognized or written about before proceeding on
with the more biographical presentation of his life. Part III presents
the biographical material itself with new interpretations provided in
light of the inferences drawn from the material in the earlier chapters
as well as new material and interpretations presented from his life and
works. Part IV invites readers to participate in relating the material
to issues which affect child rearing, child abuse, human development,
and societal hypocrisy. It represents an effort to suggest that little has
really changed from the Victorian environment — that Dodgson's
experience and response is not unique but is seen replicated with
regularity in today's alienating environment.

What are the sources of material from which these very different
hypotheses are explored and conclusions derived? We return to the
opening issue regarding the balance of evidence and interpretation.
With the exception of the handwritten diary manuscripts of Dodgson
and his friend Thomas Vere Bayne (both of which I examined well
after the research for this work was "finished") the evidence from
which interpretation is made comes from previously published material
— either by Dodgson under his own name or that of "Lewis Carroll" or
by other writers who had access to original material made available
over the years by the Dodgson family and estate. A review of some of
the interpretations of others is done, but is generally avoided for two
reasons. Firstly, I often found myself turning from agreement to
disagreement in mid-sentence. Secondly, I do not wish to focus on who
may have been tricked by the game-playing Dodgson.

Due to the nature of the work, there seemed no forthright way to
approach copyright holders for permission to quote extensively from
works about Charles Dodgson still under copyright protection.
Therefore, despite the benefits such reproduction of protected poems,
letters and diaries would lend to the task and to the understanding of
readers, I have done very little direct quotation. Fortunately,
Collingwood's biography — the first — was published in 1898 and is
therefore no longer subject to such protection; it contains many letters
which provide a good sampling and greatly supports the purposes of
this work. This is also true of the biography by Belle Moses, which
contains some useful letters though it is a really inferior work
compared to the others.

The most difficult part of this effort was the search for meaning
in the nonsense, a virtual contradiction in concept, but a task I
concluded would not be fruitless, having sensed a great deal of psychic
pain and bitterness beneath the parody and nonsense. Much of the
research task became a search for and identification of hints and clues

left in the games Dodgson came to play with his audience, my awareness of which slowly evolved. One such clue appears in a letter to a child friend, Agnes Argles, dated November 28, 1867, in which Dodgson, responding to a question of when Lewis Carroll would be writing another book, refers to his earlier "Alice" work as being about "malice". [2] We will come to understand why he responded as he did, and explore why this and other hidden things are present in letters whose form and content would make them sound wonderfully nonsensical to their recipients as well as future readers and researchers.

Presented in its entirety is another clue, heretofore seen as just the delightful poem it is. However, for reasons that will become clear it may also elicit a quite different reaction. The poem has the Latin title "Poeta Fit non Nascitur" which means "Poets are made, not born" and is from his collection *Phantasmagoria and Other Poems,* published when Dodgson was thirty-seven although written when he was thirty-one, three years before *Alice's Adventures in Wonderland* was completed.

"Poeta Fit, non Nascitur"

"How shall I be a poet?
  How shall I write in rhyme:
You told me once `the very wish
  Partook of the sublime.´
Then tell me how! Don't put me off
  With your `another time´!"

The old man smiled to see him,
  To hear his sudden sally;
He liked the lad to speak his mind
  Enthusiastically;
And thought "There's no hum-drum in him,
  Nor any shilly-shally."

"And would you be a poet
  Before you've been to school?
Ah, well! I hardly thought you
  So absolute a fool.
First learn to be spasmodic —
  A very simple rule.

"For first you write a sentence,
  And then you chop it small;
Then mix the bits, and sort them out
  Just as they chance to fall:
The order of the phrases makes
  No difference at all.

"Then, if you'd be impressive,
  Remember what I say,
That abstract qualities begin
  With capitals alway:
The True, the Good, the Beautiful —
  Those are the things that pay!

"Next, when you are describing
  A shape, or sound, or tint;
Don't state the matter plainly,
  But put it in a hint;
And learn to look at all things
  With a sort of mental squint."

"For instance, if I wished, Sir,
  Of mutton-pies to tell,
Should I say `dreams of fleecy flocks
  Pent in a wheaten cell´?
"Why, yes," the old man said: "that phrase
  Would answer very well.

"Then fourthly, there are epithets
  That suit with any word —
As well as Harvey's Reading Sauce
  With fish, or flesh, or bird —
Of these, `wild,´ `lonely,´ `weary,´ `strange,´
  Are much to be preferred."

"And will it do, O will it do
  To take them in a lump —
As `the wild man went his weary way
  To a strange and lonely pump´?"
Nay, nay! You must not hastily
  To such conclusions jump.

"Such epithets, like pepper,
　Give zest to what you write;
And, if you strew them sparely,
　They whet the appetite:
But if you lay them on too thick,
　You spoil the matter quite!

"Last, as to the arrangement:
　Your reader, you should show him,
Must take what information he
　Can get, and look for no im-
mature disclosure of the drift
　And purpose of your poem.

"Therefore, to test his patience —
　How much he can endure —
Mention no places, names, or dates,
　And evermore be sure
Throughout the poem to be found
　Consistently obscure.

"First fix upon the limit
　To which it shall extend:
Then fill it up with `Padding´
　(Beg some of any friend):
Your great SENSATION-STANZA
　You place towards the end."

"And what is a Sensation,
　Grandfather, tell me, pray?
I think I never heard the word
　So used before to-day:
Be kind enough to mention one
　`Exempli gratiâ.´"

And the old man, looking sadly
　Across the garden-lawn,
Where here and there a dew-drop
　Yet glittered in the dawn,
Said "Go to the Adelphi,
　And see the `Colleen Bawn.´

"The word is due to Boucicault —
  The theory is his,
Where Life becomes a Spasm,
  And History a Whiz:
If that is not Sensation,
  I don't know what it is.

"Now try your hand, ere Fancy
  Have lost its present glow — "
"And then," his grandson added,
  "We'll publish it, you know:
Green cloth — gold-lettered at the back —
  In duodecimo!"

Then proudly smiled that old man
  To see the eager lad
Rush madly for his pen and ink
  And for his blotting-pad —
But, when he thought of *publishing*,
  His face grew stern and sad.

PART II

A WEALTH OF EVIDENCE

CHAPTER 2

SEARCH FOR DIRECT EVIDENCE

Analyzing the works of Charles Dodgson as others have done leads one in many directions because he built a complex web of real meaning within a structure of nonsense. Several of these themes, along with new ones and new interpretations, will be explored in later chapters. The primary source of new evidence upon which to interpret his life lies hidden within two word games which he wove into his published works. After extensive research, I believe these have escaped discovery since being written. In his *Language and Lewis Carroll* [1] Robert Sutherland isolated several suggestive puns in *Sylvie and Bruno*, but he did not explore deeply enough to find the wealth beneath. The first of these word games is Anagrams, which Dodgson played often with his child and adult friends; and he has been recognized universally as an undisputed master. The second was Doublets, a word conversion game explored in Chapter 5.

Even that acknowledgement, however, represents an understatement, as with increasing sophistication he was able to blend anagrams into the content of his early stories, while creating complex hidden sub-plots in his final works. Whether one listens to the "sound and sense" of words in order to get their meaning as suggested by the Queen of Hearts in *Alice's Adventures in Wonderland*, Humpty Dumpty's argument over who will be master of the use and meaning of words in *Through the Looking-Glass and What Alice Found There*, or whether one is amused by the twiddling of the eyes of the fairy Bruno as he makes the word "live" out of "evil" in *Sylvie and Bruno*, Dodgson challenges us to look very closely at his works, and to rearrange them down to the letter if necessary in order to find all their meaning. "For first you write a sentence, /And then you chop it small. . . ."

For readers unfamiliar with the word game it consists of rearranging the letters of one or more words into new words. Two examples of Dodgson's published anagrams are presented in order to provide a sense of how he thought and worked. Derek Hudson provides us with a note from Dodgson to a Francis Paget which refers to Edward Vaughan Kenealy, a later disbarred defense counsel, and the anagram that Dodgson had thought out after retiring to bed. By rearranging the letters in the name he derived the statement "Ah! We dread an ugly knave!" which uses all the letters and keeps the sense of the story behind the name in reflecting some dubious behavior leading to disbarment. [2]

A second example comes from Dodgson's diary entry for November 25, 1868 [3] which notes three valid anagrams (the first of which he reports having sent to the [London] *Times*) for the name of the British political leader of the day William Ewart Gladstone: "Wilt tear down *all* images". When he later heard of another one: "I, wise Mr. G. want to lead all", he responded with an anagram on the political leader Disraeli: "I lead, Sir!" Later he thought of another for Gladstone: "Wild agitator! Means well." Sutherland [4] notes another on Gladstone: "A wild man will go at trees," as well as one on "Florence Nightingale": "Flit on, cheering angel." As can be seen, the best are sentences, some exclamations, and some simply provide a coherent image.

Upon discovering the first anagram in Dodgson's epic poem *The Hunting of the Snark: An Agony in Eight Fits,* and suspecting the presence of many more, I deemed it necessary, due to its content, and implicitly to the themes becoming evident, to establish several rules before proceeding on a search of his works. It became increasingly clear that the evidence to support the emerging hypothesis regarding Dodgson's inner life would depend on anagrams and would be accepted by serious scholars and a lay public only if the effort was disciplined and lacking in arbitrariness.

The first rule established was that it would be essential in creating an anagram to use all of the letters from the selected segment; no partial anagrams would suffice. Secondly, in selecting segments from the original works for examination, only those which comprised complete sentences, or which were bound in quotation marks or dashes, or which were printed in italics would be chosen. No arbitrarily "convenient" strings of words would be used. Thirdly, the sources for valid words must reflect Victorian or earlier usage; for it is clear from biographical material that Dodgson was a master of the meanings of words, particularly the multiple meanings words can take during their development and usage. Four sources were selected: *The Oxford English Dictionary*, 1989 edition, which dates examples from literature of the evolving usages, *Dictionary of the Vulgar Tongue*, published in 1811, *A Dictionary of Slang and Unconventional English*, 1967 edition, and excerpts from Victorian pornographic literature as published in *The Other Victorians*. Later in the process a confirming reference was found in the British Library's Private Collection — *Cythera's Hymnal*, a short book of pornographic and blasphemous but high quality poems, ditties, and nursery rhymes printed privately in 1852 but attributed to "Oxford University Press." It represented a truly confirming reference work for vocabulary-in-context — including time and place. Ronald Pearsall suggests the work is up to the quality of Lewis Carroll [5]; he does not, nor can such an attribution be drawn, despite the fact that anagrams of the type we will find hidden in Dodgson's work can be derived from the title.

Fourthly, if possible, a "best" anagram must be sought in each situation, one that appears to tie into his life or works. The production of a mere sequence of unrelated words would not suffice, nor would a valid sentence that did not seem to make "sense" or have relevancy; wherever possible a complete sentence which related in meaning to the original material should be found, with partial sentences accepted only if they reflected a coherent thought or image. As it turns out, this was a characteristic of the earlier works. In fact, several of the most important anagrams involving self disclosure appear clearly to have been constructed with this "purity" in mind, with the sense of the original being reflected in the anagrammatic restructuring. Lastly, if there were any anagrams which required a relaxation of these rules (of which there are some) the exceptions would be carefully identified.

Before considering any disclosure in publication, I determined there must be an overwhelming weight of evidence. It became clear that there were too many anagrams in the works to solve, many of which led only to repetitions of the same erotic imagery. Therefore I made a decision to include only some of them in this work, with a detailed analysis of small portions of selected works sufficing to "prove the case" as being more than coincidental and to demonstrate

Dodgson's breadth of mastery. The attribution of motivation on Dodgson's part is founded primarily in the presence of clue patterns, and the consistency of theme, imagery, and style. I found the task of identifying suspected phrases and then the solving of anagrams extremely time consuming and mentally taxing, with "only another" erotic image being something less than the productive use of time and energy. In attempting to identify when during his life the anagrams were created, the dates of publication are used, unless the date of authorship was found in the sources. Up until the date of publication, it is assumed that he could have changed his mind and withdrawn the material. Thus, we get a sense of how his state of mind may have changed over time, when he began, and if he stopped. It does not appear that he ever stopped, and the sophistication, boldness and self disclosure increased as he aged.

Before proceeding to identify significant anagrams from his works, a word should be said about the psychic process involved in anagrammatic problem solving, particularly true because of the use being made of them. There is no question that a projective process is involved, whereby the problem solver, viewing the sequence of letters as letters rather than words, rearranges them and "creates" words, then forms them into sentences which produce a coherent thought or image. Clearly a group of letters could be arranged into a number of words from which no coherent sentence "sense" could be derived. Likewise a group of words could be arranged into more than one sentence, with meanings not only varying, but contradicting, merely by the location of a word such as "not". The creation of words and the arrangement into sentences becomes a two step task — word creation and word arrangement — buried within the overall task of theme development. It was a task which began without inferential assumptions, but which gradually looked for themes, as common themes seemed to emerge.

One could argue that the inner world of the solver is laid bare during the process of thematic construction, and infer that the *original* writer's inner world is not reflected in the rearrangement at all, but only the solver's. This notion is not unlike the Thematic Apperception Test administered during some psychological evaluations; this test involves a process in which a number of pictures are shown to the patient who is asked to construct a story relating to each picture as he perceives it. The patient continually responds to the question: "What do you think is happening here?" From the themes of the "created" story, the psychologist draws inferences about the inner world of the patient as part of a number of clues for diagnosis and treatment planning.   Those inferences are given credence because of the training of the psychologist, who recognizes common patterns and themes which reflect deeper feelings and motivations. Pending confirmation in the appearance of other more objective evidence in expressed thought or behavior, initial hypotheses can be made. Story themes might reflect sadness, bitterness, anger, shame, guilt, dependency, or any of a number of feelings that comprise the human condition.

The potential that a normally subjective and projective process becomes the foundation for "objective" conclusions may be considered at this point the Achilles heel of this work; yet I would ask that judgement be withheld until the weight of evidence is presented. The "story" creation in these anagrammatic solutions represents the culmination of a building process from the known facts of Dodgson's life, the identification and interpretation of various clues, and the likelihood that certain themes follow others based on accepted theories of human development, thought, and behavior. A weight of evidence can only move us further along a continuum from "ridiculous" or "absolutely coincidental" to "absolutely intentional," with "highly likely" being an optimal conclusion with the circumstantial evidence involved. I hope readers will reach the conclusion that I did — that these anagrams represent a very clever and sophisticated means of self-disclosure in an unsafe environment as well as the safely hidden and contained explosion of inner rage. I also believe that Dodgson was fully aware of all of the anagrammatic possibilities, particularly those having multiple and at times contradictory solutions, and that his inclusion of them was intentional, driven by his own motives.

To begin, let us take a momentary look "with a sort of mental squint" at the lengthy clue which ended Chapter 1: "Poeta Fit, non Nascitur". Dodgson writes of the need to include a "SENSATION STANZA" yet follows with decidedly bland if somewhat lyrical lines, in which the grandfather is reflecting at the end of the poem, for some unstated reason, a reluctance to publish:

> And the old man, looking sadly
>   Across the garden-lawn,
> Where here and there a dew-drop
>   Yet glittered in the dawn,

> Said "Go to the Adelphi,
> And see the `Colleen Bawn.´

"Go to the Adelphi, and see the `Colleen Bawn´" is a poetic sounding anagram for the anal erotic sentence "*Go to lap the hide, and clean the bowel seen.*" This is surely a better example of Victorian sensation than the line as written, more likely to reflect a reluctance to publish, and provides a better introduction to the verse that follows:

> The word is due to Boucicault —
> The theory is his,
> Where Life becomes a Spasm,
> And History a Whiz:
> If that is not Sensation,
> I don't know what it is.

Boucicault is most likely a contemporary — Dion Boucicault (1820-1890), Irish playwright, director, and actor in Irish, English, and American theater — who wrote and produced "The Colleen Bawn" ["The Fairhaired Girl"] in 1860, two years before "Poeta fit. . ." was written. This play is thematically risque, as is his "Forbidden Fruit," but no evidence could be found regarding a theory toward life or history consistent with the anagrammatic theme. In his work *The Victorian Theatre 1792-1914: A Survey* George Rowell describes Boucicault's plays as featuring a "sensation scene" which made dramatic and spectacular use of the Victorian theatrical resources. [6] In "The Colleen Bawn" the forcible drowning of the heroine on the shore of the lake is such a scene, spectacular, violent, yet expertly integrated into the flow of the play. In his Introduction to *Collected Plays of Dion Boucicault* Andrew Parkin writes that Boucicault's contemporaries "revelled in his sensation scenes" even as they "condemned him for creating vulgar theatricality and pandering to the contemporary taste for it." [7]

Perhaps Dodgson is playing on Boucicault's first name, shortened from Dionysius (in Greek, Dionysos), the Greek "effeminate young stranger with long hair" [8] from Euripides play *Bakkhai*, whose own homosexual, heterosexual, and bestial activities and those of his followers and worshipers are fully explored in Arthur Evans' *The God of Ecstasy* (Chapter I) in which he includes the inference from a graphic Latin source that Dionysos used a "wooden phallus as a dildo in anal masturbation." [9] *Adelphi* is most likely the theater in London where "The Colleen Bawn" was presented. So, we have here, as it were, one of many "Class A" anagrams where the original line and the anagrammatic re-working "fit" the reference material.

The title of the volume of poems containing "Poeta Fit, non Nascitur" ― *Phantasmagoria and Other Poems* ― yields the anagrammatic solution "*Ah! Pants and orgasm hero poet am I!*" with sounds and sense providing clues to solution, and, as it turns out, themes to be found in some of the poems within the work.

> . . . "We'll publish it, you know:
>   Green cloth ― gold-lettered
> at the back ―
> In duodecimo!"

Dodgson presented his handwritten version of *Alice's Adventures Under Ground*, covered with green leather, to Alice Liddell two and a half years later, in 1864; her personalized version of *Alice's Adventures in Wonderland* was published in white vellum, with gold letters; the public's version was covered with red cloth with gold lettering.

While we shall return to the "Alice" work shortly, the strongest evidence of the nature of Dodgson's publications under the name "Lewis Carroll" along with numerous self disclosure comes from clues provided many years later in his own Preface to *Sylvie and Bruno*:

> It was in 1874, I believe, that the idea first occurred to me of making it ["Bruno's Revenge," a Chapter in *Sylvie and Bruno* but published in 1867 as a short story in *Aunt Judy's Magazine*] the nucleus of a longer story. As the years went on, I jotted down, at odd moments, all sorts of odd ideas, and fragments of dialogue, that occurred to me ― who knows how? ― with a transitory suddenness that left me no choice but either to record them then and there, or to abandon them to oblivion. Sometimes one could trace to their source these random flashes of thought ― as being suggested by the book one was reading, or struck out from the `flint´ of one's own mind by the `steel´ of a friend's chance remark ― but they had also a way of their own, of occurring, *à propos* of nothing ― specimens of that hopelessly illogical

phenomenon, `an effect without a cause´ [This is an anagram for "*Caution: a few use the fact*."].    Such, for example, was the last line of `The Hunting of the Snark´ which came into my head... quite suddenly, during a solitary walk: and such, again, have been passages which occurred in *dreams*, and which I cannot trace to any antecedent cause whatever.   There are at least *two* instances of such dream-suggestions in this book — one, my Lady's remark, `it often runs in families, just as a love for pastry does´, at p. 88; the other, Eric Lindon's *badinage* about having been in domestic service, at p. 332....

The first of these is quite revealing. As we shall see here and elsewhere, the reader need not be familiar with the plot detail to solve anagrams, since plot is often just a construct for hiding them. In the first passage referenced, which appears in Chapter VII, Lady Muriel is responding to a statement made by "His Adiposity the Baron Doppelgeist," who has just said: "My ancestors were all famous for military genius." She responds, smiling graciously: "It often runs in families, just as a love for pastry does" implying a genetic transmission of sorts. After this, the subject is quickly changed by the Vice-Warden.

Lady Muriel's response is made, not only to the words as spoken, but to the anagrammatic re-working of the Baron's statement: "*I was a terror from all my incestuous family genes.*" It appears here that Dodgson is acknowledging that he was involved in something terrible and is placing at least part of the blame on his parents, who were first cousins. Although marriages of such close relatives were sanctioned at the time, Dodgson appears to be implying genetic defects from inbreeding as the cause or at least a contributor to his situation and consequent behavior, not yet defined except by the word *terror*.

Two short paragraphs later, however, he identifies the activity that made him a terror:

> ... the Vice-Warden had barely time to explain to my Lady that her remark about `a love for pastry´ was `unfortunate. You might have seen, with half an eye,´ he added, `that that's *his* [the Baron's] line. Military genius, indeed! Pooh!´

Her line about "a love for pastry" becomes "with half an eye" the Baron's line in the anagrammatic re-working: "*I stir for pederast unions just as often as family love.*"

And what of the Baron's full nonsensical title — "His Adiposity the Baron Doppelgeist"? "*O, I pity Dodgson, his path a rebel spite!*"

The second reference from the Preface is to the libertine Eric Lindon's badinage in Chapter XXII on page 332 of the original work. It involves a conversation in which Eric is describing to the child Bruno his lowly occupational past. Eric responds to Bruno's guess that he must have been a *servant* while Lady Muriel remains engrossed in a problem with her gloves, seemingly ignoring a delicate subject:

> `Lower than that, your Royal Highness! Years ago, I offered myself as a *slave* — as a `Confidential* Slave,´ I think it's called?´

He then turns to Lady Muriel for a reaction, but she has not heard his confession and the conversation goes on.

This ninety-five letter anagram is the longest found in Dodgson's works and again is very revealing as it also adheres to the sense of Eric's original statement: "*Lewis Carroll, suffered so as loyal fag love-slave, as an honest gay search, I think. Oh, say I intended it a family threat!*" The structure of this anagram is somewhat awkward as the honesty of the search or the intention as a family threat can both be placed in a way as to imply its preceding the other as the motivating force. Nothing that was found in the course of research clearly eliminates the ambiguity. In Part III which contains biographical material and a review of the public school experience at the time, awareness of the sexual services rendered to upper classmen by the younger boys (fags) will contribute to an understanding of this anagram, and, indeed, point to a likely pivotal experience in Dodgson's life. The anagram is consistent with psychological theory which identifies the suffering of trauma, followed by a self-defensive joining with the aggressor in the assaultive behavior as the means of psychic survival, with a rage response directed to other targets the only safe course.

The biggest problem we have with this anagram is the word *gay*. The dictionaries and excerpts from Victorian pornography support its use as a noun meaning "a loose female" with no allusion to its current use as applied to homosexual men and women. Partridge defines *gay* as an adjective meaning a person "leading an immoral or a harlot's life" without specifying the sex of the "gay" person. [10] *The Dictionary of the Vulgar Tongue* refers only to a "gaying instrument" as a penis. [11] Steven Marcus, in his *The Other Victorians* after quoting from an early Victorian pornographic work *My Secret Life* reflects that a prostitute considered herself "gay" because she "let men fuck you," penetration itself in any of the variety of ways being the *sine qua non* for gay behavior in that world. [12] John Boswell presents the fullest review when he indicates that the word was an English homosexual sub-culture password in the early twentieth century. [13] Vern Bullough supports the word as derived from its application to the immoral life of prostitutes, but dates it later than this period. [14]

What we may be seeing is an early use of a whispered word still in its process of definition, a word/concept whose public use certainly at that time could lead to violent attacks. It clearly implied loose moral behavior or had been moving toward a definition with male-based penetration following on the female-based definition. It should be noted that the word "homosexual" is a twentieth century word, appearing earliest in Havelock Ellis's works on the subject in the late 1890's, although he disliked it as hybrid. During Dodgson's time *Sodomite* was used to describe those who engaged in homosexual acts, without inferring sexual erotic preference, for the concept of such preference was still rudimentary. The words *Uranian* and *urning*, most likely derived from Plato's *Symposium*, were frequently used by nineteenth century gay writers. [15] *Urning* was coined by Karl Heinrichs Ulrichs (1825-1895) in his writings produced between 1865 and 1875 as he attempted to define, understand, and defend his own orientation. He presented it as a description of a homosexual male, with its appearance in this work consistent in time with its introduction during this period. [16] *Cythera's Hymnal* contains a single contextual reference to "gay" applying to a male (a churchman at that), but I cannot determine from the context whether the sexual behavior described is heterosexual or homosexual in nature. [17]

This whole issue is discussed in the literature on homosexuality which describes sexual roles and activities as being "passive" or "female" in nature. Passivity refers, not to "inactive" but in the participant being orally, anally, or genitally penetrated. Dodgson may have viewed his inner self image as feminine and he may have taken the feminine position in homosexual activities, a totally consistent possibility if he had been, as suspected, the victim of an attack, or rape as we would describe it today. In this sense, "gay" would imply engagement in masturbation, mutual masturbation, oral sex, and sodomy or anal intercourse, all of which fall within the realm of Victorian prostitution and, therefore "gay" behavior. There is no question that there was a *quid pro quo* for this activity among male prostitutes just as there was for women; but there is no direct evidence that Dodgson either paid or was paid for any activities in which he might have engaged.

Fortunately, none of the inferences from these anagrams is supported by a single anagram or erotic image. In order to establish the notion of intent versus coincidence as we move to further analyses of his works, I deemed it important to identify very promptly the only two instances found which Dodgson suggested readers examine closely. Interestingly, in the Preface to the second *Sylvie* volume published four years later Dodgson refers to two other puzzles in this Preface regarding the location of "padding" (extra text inserted to accommodate illustration placement) within the *Sylvie and Bruno* text. Though he provides solutions to those two puzzles, he makes no reference at all to these two "dreamlike" segments which I believe are anagrammatic puzzles.

The following resumes the Preface quotation above and can now be interpreted, not as just coy, but as a more cynical game Dodgson played with his audience:

> And thus it came to pass that I found myself at last in possession of a huge unwieldy mass of litterature — if the reader will kindly excuse the spelling — which only needed stringing together, upon the thread of a consecutive story, to constitute the book I hoped to write. Only! The task, at first, seemed absolutely hopeless, and gave me a far clearer idea, than I ever had before, of the meaning of the word `chaos´: and I think it must have been ten years, or more, before I had succeeded in classifying these odds-and-ends sufficiently to see what sort of story they indicated: for the story had to grow out of the incidents, not the incidents out of the story.

In short, the structure and content of the *Sylvie* books depended on the ability to string anagrammatic reconstructions of "litter" together into a story line. The "plot" became rather irrelevant. And while he succeeded, how well we shall see, the awkwardness that literary scholars and critics find, particularly in the adult conversations (perhaps making the works critically "forgetable") becomes a little more understandable.

With some crucial evidence now established that the presence of these anagrams is something less than coincidental, let us move on to explore other places within the whole body of his works in which they appear and further identify their content.

CHAPTER 3

SIGNIFICANT FINDINGS

The search for anagrams really began with an examination of the titles of Dodgson's major narrative and poetic nonsense works and then broadened to include the entire body of his writings. Until very late in the process, the serious poems were left untouched in the hope that the sentiments expressed could be taken at their face value. Tackling and finding anagrammatic structures in the serious poems and other writings brought on great disappointment and made even more difficult the effort to draw inferences as to the real status of his fragile personality. This chapter focuses on a number of the more significant findings in the nonsense.

The Hunting of the Snark

The first title examined was *The Hunting of the Snark: an Agony in Eight Fits*. Published when Dodgson was forty-four, this "epic" nonsense poem written in eight verses or "fits" tells of the journey of a ship, its captain, and its crew who sail in search of the Bandersnatch, a dangerous but undefined demon. I felt the presence of great anxiety beneath the surface of the nonsense, particularly in light of some biographical material which reflected that Dodgson suffered from insomnia and wrote his mathematical work *Pillow Problems* to ward off "unholy thoughts, blasphemous thoughts, skeptical thoughts," as he said in the Preface to the work, and religious doubts, as others have added. I sensed a disturbance not adequately explained by the "normal bachelor temptations" referred to by his biographers, who do not clearly define the problems but who were most likely referring to masturbation as a sexual tension release mechanism which Dodgson, as an unmarried man, might be expected to have struggled with or engaged in. *Pillow Problems* is a short volume of seventy-two problems in algebra, plane geometry, and trigonometry which Dodgson tells us he solved in his head while lying awake. He claimed to use this technique in an effort to keep his active mind more productively focused. He would wait until morning to record them. [1]

The first anagram found within this title was "*Hunt the king of hearts, a non-gay in fine tights.*" While it did not make a great deal of sense, a search through *Alice's Adventures in Wonderland* resulted in the location of a passage in the trial scene in Chapter XII where the King of Hearts puns on the word "fit" upon hearing the Queen of Hearts' vehement denial to his inquiry as to whether she suffered from fits. And the picture of the trial contains the King of Hearts dressed in "fine tights." Thus began the search for anagrams throughout Dodgson's works.

The *Oxford English Dictionary* (OED) lists "of uncertain gender" as a meaning for *fit* as well as "a sense of conflict," or "convulsions." Later more anagrams emerged: "*None hunt a king of hearts in the gay night fits*" with *gay* working equally well if placed before *king*. This anagram introduces us to the "Hearts" family, King, Queen, and Knave. Given the recurring "Off with their heads!" which falls repeatedly from the lips of the Queen of Hearts, along with Dodgson's acknowledged theme of that work, which is "malice", and this work, which is rage, *hearts* may very well mean *haters*. Several other anagrams, somewhat more contrived, make reference to "fag" and "sty", both of which bring us to the English public school experience and the recurring "pig" theme in his works as well as the anagrams. Two additional anagrams reflect the more contemporary words for *gay* — *Uranian, Onanite,* and *urning* — with "*They, the Uranian kings, often hit on night fags*" and "*The king of urnings hateth any Onanite fights,*" (a best solution among several variations of word placement as it implies that Dodgson as self-appointed leader dislikes fighting with others of like orientation). Of course, Dodgson was an established Greek scholar, undoubtedly aware of the words in their original Greek contexts.

In Dodgson's Preface to the *Snark*, he begins immediately with double meanings and anagrams:

If — and the thing is wildly possible — the charge of writing nonsense were ever brought against the author of this brief but instructive poem, it would be based, I feel convinced, on the line,

`Then the bowsprit got mixed with the rudder sometimes.´

In view of this painful possibility, I will not (as I might) appeal indignantly to my other writings as a proof that I am incapable of such a deed: I will not (as I might) point to the strong moral purpose of this poem itself, to the arithmetical principles so cautiously inculcated in it, or to its noble teachings in Natural History — I will take the more prosaic course of simply explaining how it happened.

He then proceeds to explain in detail the function and care required of the ship's bowsprit.

Several biographers and writers have indicated that the line identified above is an expression of doubt regarding sexual identity. I believe it is, but also that, as usual, Dodgson had more in mind, more meaning packed into his written words. The *1811 Dictionary of the Vulgar Tongue* indicates that *bowsprit* referred to the most projecting part of the human face, i.e., the nose. Within this context, this statement harks us back to the imagery expressed in "Poeta Fit. . ." which placed the face near the "rudder". Or, Dodgson could be re-defining the most projecting part of the male anatomy. But even more poignantly, this statement is also an anagram which tells us very much about what is coming and who is the target of his rage: *"To Mother: Disturbed, I themed the worst pig sex with men."* (*Themed* is a valid Victorian verb.) There are others with alternative word placement, but I believe the one chosen is the best because it identifies Dodgson as considering himself disturbed (perhaps only in the sense of "angry") and identifies the target of the rage in a more rage-filled, cynical, dedicatory way.

Dodgson rejected the original rendering of the "Snark" which was drawn by his illustrator Henry Holiday. He claimed he wished to retain the mystery surrounding the monster, keeping it unfathomably horrible. But in light of the genital imagery already identified, particularly the focus on the penis, a not too thorough examination of that original illustration presents us with as close an approximation of the head of a penis one could imagine disguised and potentially presented in a children's book. I have no question that this was quite by accident on Holiday's part, but the closeness of the likeness may have been an additional reason for Dodgson's rejection of it.

Of interest in finding such themes in this work is the fact that Dodgson planned its publication for April 1, 1876, after missing his original (and usual) target, Christmas, of the preceding year. Just as it is today, April 1 was April-fool-day in 1876.

> [It is the day on which] it is the custom among the lower
> people, children, and servants, by dropping empty papers
> carefully doubled up, sending persons on absurd messages,
> and such like contrivances, to impose on everyone they can,
> and then to salute them with the title of April Fool. [2]

Although it was not his first choice, Dodgson indicated he could think
of no better day to have the work appear.

The publishing of this work seems to have been attended by an
elaborate charade. Six months before his planned publishing date,
Dodgson published on June 1, 1875, an article entitled "Some Popular
Fallacies About Vivisection" in *Fortnightly Review*. This article was
ostensibly an attack on the use and abuse of animals in medical
experimentation and was perhaps also written to ward off possible
criticism which might be aimed at his forthcoming book on "hunting,"
which he had also criticized in articles on "sport." His opening
paragraph sets the trap:

> At a time when this painful subject is engrossing so
> large a share of public attention, no apology, I trust, is
> needed for the following attempt to formulate and classify
> some of the many fallacies, as they seem to me, which I have
> met with in the writings of those who advocate the practice.
> No greater service can be rendered to the cause of truth, in
> this fiercely contested field, than to reduce these shadowy,
> impalpable phantoms into definite forms, which can be seen,
> which can be grappled with, and which, when once fairly
> *laid*, we shall not need to exercise a second time.

While Dodgson's argument is directed to the practice of vivisection and
its abuse of animals, his opening paragraph and hidden argument
responds to the anagram formed from the article's title, a defense of
bestiality: "*I crave lamb coitus, save up fellatio poison.*" The *Pall Mall
Gazette*, to whom Dodgson submitted the article and who had
published other things by him sensed something amiss; for as Dodgson
recorded in his diary, they declined publication, claiming that they did
not see any fallacies in the arguments being attacked as "fallacious."
Had Dodgson the logician been hoisted unknowingly on his own
petard?

Throughout this work, we will be faced with the question of
whether Dodgson practiced any of the imagery about which he wrote;
and we will have no answer. For like the Marquis De Sade, who wrote

his most explicit works while in prison, they, too were written as much to attack his persecutors as for his own enjoyment. However, Dodgson was known for his fifteen to twenty mile walks in the countryside, alone or with a close friend. A farm boy himself, he certainly had ample opportunities to satisfy any needs or wishes he may have had with the many animals to be found on neighboring farms. We shall return to the themes of the *Snark* shortly.

Through the Looking-Glass

The title from which the most information is gleaned is *Through the Looking-Glass and What Alice Found There*, popularly known by its shortened title *Through the Looking-Glass*. (As we can see, the shortening of titles causes the hidden material to disappear.) This work was published in 1872, when Dodgson was forty. According to Collingwood, the title itself was originally planned by Dodgson to be "Behind the Looking-Glass and What Alice Saw There". The final title was suggested by his fellow Oxford don, Dr. Henry Parry Liddon, [3] who was an immensely popular and erudite preacher at Oxford and later at St. Paul's Cathedral, London, where he served as Canon. This suggestion from Liddon represents the first of several possible clues that Dodgson was working in collusion with at least one other person. The original title "Behind the Looking Glass. . ." produces the anagram *"With glass look behind the new hat; see a caring lad."* Dodgson himself indicated that the story originally had Alice moving behind the mirror, not through it. Thus it appears that he changed the story to fit the anagram produced by the Liddon title and its picture-supported anagram: *"Look with a lens through the cute darling; he's a fag don."* This is a much more appropriate anagram, one which reflects some of the bitterness we have seen and will see in the relationship between Dodgson, Alice, and the "real" Alice — Alice Liddell.

Neither of these have much meaning unless we relate them to a picture by the book's illustrator, John Tenniel, political cartoonist for *Punch*, who was engaged by Dodgson to produce the pictures for this book as well as *Alice's Adventures in Wonderland*. The supporting illustration appears in Chapter III, entitled "Looking-Glass Insects."

Presented on the following page it depicts Alice in a railroad car, dressed in a new hat and sitting across from two characters while the railway guard examines her intensely through the carriage window "first through a telescope, then through a microscope, and then through an opera-glass." There is no explanation given in the story line for the guard peering at her head through what appear like large binoculars from a very close distance.

But

... At last he said `You're traveling the wrong way,´ and shut up the window and went away.

"You're traveling the wrong way" is an anagram for "*Wary nag whore: evil rotten guy*", one of a number of anagrams which just produce imagery. Shortly thereafter,

... a hoarse voice spoke next. `Change engines ___ ´ it said, and there it choked and was obliged to leave off.

"Change engines ___ " becomes "*Change genes in ___ ,*" at which point it choked.

On December 15, 1875, Dodgson wrote a letter to a child friend Magdalen Millard which contains a paragraph which describes an incident in which he "met" a wheelbarrow in which he could barely see the image of a person in the reflection; but with the assistance of a telescope, a microscope and a looking-glass he was able to make out those features as his own.It is the only letter known to have been signed "Lewis Carroll, and C. L. Dodgson." [4]

Through the Looking-Glass. . . also breaks down to *"Alice, how the king of hater's huge tool and glands hurt!"* This is a quite different attitude toward the recipient of the earlier work, his friend Alice Liddell, daughter of the Dean, than is usually attributed. *Tool* was common slang for a man's private parts, and more often specifically the penis. *Gland* is, of course, a secreting organ.

Sylvie and Bruno

In examining the titles of his last works *Sylvie and Bruno* and *Sylvie and Bruno Concluded* there is a note of sadness in the anagrammatic reconstruction: *"O, sly vain burden (concluded),"* a melancholy we have already seen in the dedicatory poem which opened his work and mine. This anagram also answers in part the comment of Phyllis Greenacre that "Bruno" was so un-English a name to use that one wondered why it was chosen. [5]

Dodgson's diaries reflect that he considered another title after making this his tentative choice. His alternative was *Four Seasons* [6] which becomes *"Our safe sons"*. Again the question arises as to whether he was working alone or with one or more fellow dons. For the anagram comments on the safe environment at Oxford from which he or they could live securely, with extremely modest work requirements, with no objective measures of performance, and freely engage in angry games with the world.

Alice's Adventures in Wonderland

The work for which Dodgson gained and retained fame was, of course, *Alice's Adventures in Wonderland*, which was published when he was thirty-three. The book represented nearly a doubling of the earlier *Alice's Adventures Under Ground*, which had been presented to his child friend Alice Liddell in hand-written form but was later published in facsimile when he was fifty-four. Several alternative titles were considered before the final selection was made because Dodgson stated that he felt the original title suggested the story might be about mines. These consisted of: *Alice's Adventures in Wonderland* and alternate titles: "Alice Among the Elves"; "Alice Among the Goblins"; "Alice's Hour in Elfland"; "Alice's Doings in Elfland"; "Alice's Hour in Wonderland"; and "Alice's Doings in Wonderland".

The best anagram identified from the chosen title, and perhaps the best among the titles regarding his angry task is *"Censure an evil and stained world*", as strong a statement that hypocrisy was his target as he could make. Its theme will reappear shortly in an even more bizarre way. There are others, as usual; they include, with some word rearrangement possible: "*Dear unwed don, an evil silent scar*", etc.

Clark reports that Dodgson nearly removed the name *Alice* from the final title [7]; perhaps there were second thoughts to overcome regarding the association of the "Alice" character with Alice Liddell, perhaps in deference to her as many contemporaries knew of his close association with her, perhaps for fear that he was going too far.

Notwithstanding any last minute reservations and always prepared, Dodgson had anagrams for all of the other title alternatives. They were (in the order given above): "*Love a nice theme, gals?*" (*gal* slang for prostitute); "*Malice benign; goal shot*"; "*Hold ill Uranian feces*"; "*Dons feeling sin! Call aid!*"; "*No lad can hinder our Lewis*"; "*I scaled wandering don's lion.*" The word *lion* had a special meaning to Dodgson, that of penis or cock. We will learn in Chapter 8 why it had that meaning and why it is a recurring theme in his works.

The Nursery "Alice"

The Nursery "Alice" was a version of the story drawn from *Alice's Adventures in Wonderland* which Dodgson published in 1889 for children "from Nought to Five." The title forms several anagrams, with perhaps the most vicious "*Her cunt! Leer, I say!*" There are others which use the word *real* or *Lear*, with the latter use perhaps reflecting Dodgson's effort to attack posthumously a contemporary by the name of Edward Lear twenty years older than Dodgson, and who died the year before this book was published. A writer and illustrator of his own works and primarily known for his nonsense verse and limericks, Lear, too, was shy, timid, unmarried, and with an affinity for children. It is believed that he, like Dodgson and all nonsense writers, was harboring strong anger.

This completes the review of the titles to Dodgson's nonsense works. I have concluded that hidden meanings were deliberately incorporated and that their presence, therefore, is not mere coincidence. While the foregoing touched on anagrams within the works, the following expands on this aspect in order to further identify when the process began and to locate patterns which may have meaning.

The Number "42"

Scholars have been fascinated by the appearance of the number "42" throughout Dodgson's works. Though it does not appear in the source book presented to Alice Liddell, it appears in *Alice's Adventures in Wonderland* as "Rule Forty-two" in the Court Scene when the King of Hearts exclaims: "All persons more than a mile high to leave the court." Alice denies being a mile high but she has experienced increased growth and confidence as the trial has proceeded.

It appears again in the *Snark* within Carroll's Introduction to the work as:

Rule 42 of the Code: `No one shall speak to the man at the helm and the man at the helm shall speak to no one.´

It appears again in the *Snark* as 42 packages that belong to the Baker, one of the crew and long considered to represent Dodgson by interpreters of this work.

He had forty-two boxes, all carefully packed,
With his name painted clearly on each:
But, since he omitted to mention the fact,
They were all left behind on the beach.
Fit 2, v7

Some have made a hypothetical connection between Dodgson's age and that of the narrator in *Phantasmagoria*. However, Dodgson was thirty-seven at the time of the text's publication. There are forty-two Tenniel pictures in *Alice's Adventures in Wonderland* and there are twenty-four total chapters in the two "Alice" books, which Clark points out is the reverse of forty-two. [8]

Solving the phrases involved with the number 42 as anagrams results in the following: "All persons more than a mile high to leave the court", published in 1865 when Dodgson was thirty-three, becomes a quite different rule: "*Let not holier thoughts reveal cheap animal mores.*"

"No one shall speak to the man at the helm; and the man at the helm shall speak to no one", published in 1876, when he was forty-four, becomes: "*No one shall spanketh the hot male meat; and the hot male meat shall spanketh no one,*" *meat* a valid word for genitals and suggesting shared masturbatory fantasies which appear in many forms within the *Snark* and in other anagrammatic themes from other works.

From whence comes the fascination with the number 42? There is a risk of using writer's license in deriving this solution; for in order to solve this riddle, the rule established at the beginning that all letters must be used has to be broken. Partly due to the theme of this pivotal anagram, my sense is that this was a deceptive trick by Dodgson within his game play, a deliberate changing of the rules. This theme reappears as his fundamental attitude toward Victorian societal hypocrisy in general and is reflected in the bitter parody. I believe the appearance of this number is associated with the following, rather fortuitous occurrence. In 1950, nearly a hundred years after it was acquired by the Dodgson family, when the interior of the Croft Rectory was being remodeled, workmen found several items beneath the floor boards of the room used as a nursery during the Dodgson family residency — a left foot shoe, a thimble, a hair slide, and the following verse written on a wood block, reportedly in Dodgson's hand. Also found with the family items was a note from the workers: "This floor laid by Mr. Martin and Mr. Sutton June 19th, 1843.) The verse on the block reads:

> And we'll wander through
> the wide world and
> chase the buffalo. [9]

This verse has been used by several writers as an example of the work of a creative free spirit who at an early age began producing imaginative verse. The house was acquired by the family in 1843. Dodgson was eleven at the time and began attendance at Richmond Grammar School after the family's relocation here. Although Dodgson maintained a permanent residence at Oxford as an adult, he called Croft "home" until he was thirty six. It was then that the home was sold and the family moved to the "Chestnuts" in Guildford, south of London, following their father's death. This was well after he began using anagrams in his works.

There are fifty letters in the verse and with eight removed an anagram emerges which I believe represents a manifesto to the world, a manifesto of the rage he carried with him wherever he went as forty-two symbolic letters or boxes: "*Bluff a rough, sordid, heathen world and cheat death!*", his strategy for achieving immortality. Note the thematic affinity to "*Censure an evil and stained world.*" Did he put this in at age eleven when the floor was laid, or did he manage to slip it there in the intervening years?

There may be an answer to this question in *Alice's Adventures in Wonderland*. For immediately following the introduction of "Rule Forty-two", as the King of Hearts attempts to close the case against the Knave, a new piece of evidence is introduced:

`There's more evidence to come yet, please your Majesty,´ said the White Rabbit, jumping up in a great hurry: `this paper has just been picked up.´

`What's in it?´ said the Queen.

`I haven't opened it yet,´ said the White Rabbit; `but it seems to be a letter, written by the prisoner to __ somebody.´

`It must have been that,´ said the King, `unless it was written to nobody, which isn't usual, you know.´

`Who is it directed to?´ said one of the jurymen.

`It isn't directed at all,´ said the White Rabbit: `in fact, there's nothing written on the *outside*.´ He unfolded the paper as he spoke, and added `It isn't a letter, after all: it's a set of verses.´

`Are they in the prisoner's handwriting?´ asked another of the jurymen.

`No, they're not,´ said the White Rabbit, `and that's the queerest thing about it.´ (The jury all looked puzzled.)

`He must have imitated somebody else's hand,´ said the King. (The jury all brightened up again.)

`Please your Majesty,´ said the Knave, `I didn't write it, and they ca'n't prove that I did; there's no name signed at the end.´

`If you didn't sign it,´ said the King, `that only makes the matter worse. You *must* have meant some mischief, or else you'd have signed your name like an honest man.´

There was a general clapping of hands at this: it was the first really clever thing the King had said that day.

`That *proves* his guilt, of course,´ said the Queen: `so, off with____.´

As the scene continues, the White Rabbit reads a six verse poem commonly interpreted as a nonsensical screen for a search for identity. Except for the fact that it is written on paper in the story, the characteristics of the note fit the suggestion that the verse on the wood block was written by Dodgson as an adult. He could have imitated his youthful hand for purposes of fooling the public. It also could, in fact, represent the "evidence" for the motives behind his works.

Not only does the number 42 have meaning, but so do the numbers 50 and 46. There are 50 Tenniel illustrations in *Through the Looking-Glass*, though only 42 were planned originally. [10] There are 46 by Harry Furniss in each of *Sylvie and Bruno* and *Sylvie and Bruno Concluded* with the same additional one by "Miss Alice Havers" in each. Four of the eight unused letters from the block could make up the word "well" (*"Bluff well. . ."*) or perhaps another hint of collaboration (*"We'll bluff. . ."*). As we examine Dodgson's life and works in more detail, this theme becomes increasingly pivotal as the rage response of one intent on a life of revenge. It was for this reason that I chose it as the first quotation in the Epigraph. Did this wood block represent a "time capsule" for later discovery, very often a plotter's secret wish?

"Miss Alice Havers"

A second curious anagram appears to be a very elaborate construction, elaborate because it draws in the name of a "real" person. It involves the name of the artist who would do a single illustration which appeared in each of the *Sylvie* books.

`Miss Alice Havers´ was the pseudonym of an artist by the name of Mrs. Morgan, whose art shows Dodgson had attended and whose works he purchased. His diaries contain several references to her as Mrs Morgan, Miss Alice Havers, and `Miss Alice Havers´. Her illustration of the Magic Locket which appears on pages 77 and 409 (of the respective original works) contains the engraved words "Sylvie will love all" or, as the plot unfolds, "All will love Sylvie." Carroll's Preface to the work (with similar comments in *Concluded*) opens with:

> One little picture in this book, the Magic Locket at p. 77, was drawn by `Miss Alice Havers.´ I did not state this on the title-page, since it seemed only due, to the artist of all these (to my mind) *wonderful* pictures, that his name [Harry Furniss] should stand there alone.

Earlier, in a postscript to a letter dated July 5, 1888, to his friend Lucy Walters, he indicated that someone other than Lucy would be his artist, claiming that "Destiny" had spoken and would get her way. [11] The illustration itself is far inferior to those drawn by Furniss, even though it complies with Dodgson's lines-per-square-inch density requirement which Furniss described in *The Strand Magazine* of January, 1908. Dodgson would subject each square inch of illustration to a minute examination, counting the number of lines, and comparing the density with those done by Tenniel in the *Alice* books. At one point Furniss pretended he could deal with the don no longer, and wrote to Dodgson refusing to complete the work. [12] What other reason could Dodgson, the meticulous perfectionist and already a supporter of Mrs. Morgan's work by his purchase of her art, have had for insisting that this artist do the single illustration when it is clearly evident that the artist's work is inferior? It could only be that she fit into his game plan. . . destiny.

In this instance Dodgson violated one of his own rigid rules that protected his identity and separated Rev. Dodgson from "Lewis Carroll" when he identified Mrs. Morgan's pseudonym in quotes as not a real name. Is it an anagram, quotes and all, for "*I'm Alice's shavers*," thus identifying the presence of the feminine imago buried within the Dodgson/Carroll identity? Or did he choose it because it provided a host of additional anagrams, some with anal-erotic themes? For we can also derive: "*Miss has lice! Rave!*"; "*Raise vile chasms!*;" "*Vice missal! Share!*;" or several others. In conjunction with Bruno's eye twiddling which found *live* in *evil*, Dodgson suggests that readers look closer at the Magic Locket, whose engraved motto translates from its published sentence "All will love Sylvie" or "Sylvie will love all" to "*All sly low live evil*" and "*All low live sly evil*," or any of the following:

"*Evil love silly wall.*" (nonsense as mask)

"Silly will lave love." (foolish will cleanse love)
"Ally, evil! Love swill!"
"All sly ill view love." (voyeurism, although perhaps not
    Victorian appropriate)
"Sly ill wove all evil." (multiple participants?)

The Inimitable Riddle

In Chapter VII, "A Mad Tea Party," from *Alice's Adventures in Wonderland*, Alice is asked: "Why is a raven like a writing desk?" This riddle has confounded readers and nonsense scholars since it first appeared. Even Dodgson claimed to deny knowledge of its answer, though in response to readers' inquiries he did suggest one in the Preface to the sixth edition, written two years before his death:

> Enquiries have been so often addressed to me, as to whether any answer to the Hatter's Riddle can be imagined, that I may as well put on record here what seems to me to be a fairly appropriate answer, viz: `Because it can produce a few notes, though they are *very* flat: and it is never put with the wrong end in front!´ This, however is merely an afterthought: the Riddle, as originally invented, had no answer at all. [13]

When is the evidence the riddle itself? Perhaps Dodgson was again giving a clue: if there is no answer, examine the question more closely. Doing so we find: *"His kind Lewis a gay knave writer"* or *"Lewis his kind, a gay knave writer."* Dodgson's belated answer responds on two levels, with the first half ("notes" as letters) pointing to the riddle as written as well as the anagrammatic re-working, the second half ("wrong end in front") to the anagram, with the connotation of anal penetration evident.

An interesting alternative presents itself: *"I view kind Lewis gay, hater, Snark"*, or some combination thereof. If Dodgson were aware of this solution then the "Snark" was born in 1865 when this was published and not in 1874 when Dodgson claimed he began the epic poem with its last line as it came to him while on one of his long walks: "For the Snark *was* a Boojum, you see."

Early Works

Moving back in time, we can examine a short story entitled "The Walking Stick of Destiny," which appeared in the family publication *The Rectory Umbrella*. The story was published in 1850 when Dodgson was nineteen; and biographer Richard Kelly describes this as the first appearance of Dodgson's nonsense in story form. [14] Present in this nonsense text was the rage which was to last throughout his life, and it seethed with the immaturity of a young man. We must remember that at this point his parents were alive, and he was, until May 23 of 1850, living with the family at Croft just before moving on to Oxford. He had just completed the Rugby experience and was taking nearly two years to prepare for Oxford. While at home, as the children had always done, he was writing for and publishing this family publication with the assistance and support of his parents and siblings.

This title breaks down into: "*King licks soft, tiny, wet head.*" The entire story which is filled with mysterious nonsense appears to climax with the appearance of Dodgson's masturbatory fantasy (although not named or identified yet). It involves such characters as Baron Slogdod — (look at the arrogance!) "*Dodgson labor*", and Signor Blowski, "*I blow gross kin*" with *blow* meaning "to fume, storm, or speak angrily" in Partridge's work. No dictionary supports the 20th century meaning as a man's view of copulation (OED). The title *The Rectory Umbrella* is itself an anagram for "*Re Rectum/Ball Theory.*" (*Re*, without the colon, is correct Victorian usage.)

In 1954, a notebook collection of Dodgson's early works, produced "around 1845" when he was about 13 years of age, was released for publication by his niece Frances Menella Dodgson. He had called this collection of poems *Useful and Instructive Poetry*; the work contains a variety of short poems, some of which have been published in collected works. Several depict a strict and controlled childhood, and some end in a moral. One, entitled "My Fairy" appears to depict life as controlled by some outside force which directed the inhibition of all feeling, whether of happiness or sadness. Such lack of feeling in an adult is the a symptom of a self destroyed in childhood, where feelings, especially negative or "sinful" ones, and their expression were not tolerated unless approved by the parents. In this situation, the self-soothing skill that is taught for dealing with angry disagreeable feelings is suppression rather than venting and resolution. Another, "Rules and Regulations" represents a long of behaviors which must be either avoided or adhered to. Most of them prohibit a host of normal childhood behaviors, none with any of the moral implications one might expect.

While it appears that Dodgson was only beginning to test the edges of his word/image games, a rarely reproduced poem entitled "Clara," reflects a significant sophistication in anagrammatic construction. It is a key piece of evidence. The poem tells of Clara waiting at home in bed for her husband, when the vision of a "hoary monk" appears, encouraging her to have no fear about letting her husband "in" when he returns. She trembles in fear and anticipation of his arrival home drunk demanding he join her in bed.

The poem ends with the monk asserting: "He's only been drinking too much gin, /And got dead drunk!" [15] This final statement produces at least eight anagrams. Several of them apply to a period well beyond the purported date for the notebook, yet are explicit in pointing to a time in Dodgson's life which biographers know imprecisely, but from his own words know to have been painful — his years in public school, especially Rugby. Significantly, the solutions to six of them require the incorporation of "Rule 42 of the Code" — the elimination of two letters from the total of forty-four. We have:

> "*Rugby turned a keen Dodgson child into a demon king*"
> "*But kin and Richmond led keen Dodgson to gay urning.*"
>   Richmond was the first public school Dodgson attended,
>   at age 11, and where there is other evidence to suggest
>   pederast activities started.
> "*Stingy mother bore kind, nodding* (in obeisance), *angled
>   eunuch don.*" Dodgson was tall and angular, walking
>   with a backward tilt. His mother may have been
>   perceived as stingy as she managed a very tight family
>   income in the early years.
> "*Oh, Liddon, Bayne, Dodgson trick the game, nude urning.*"
>   The names may be interchangeable as object, but
>   Liddon and Bayne were three years older than Dodgson,
>   Liddon not a friend until Oxford. Thomas Vere Bayne
>   was his lifelong friend from childhood in Daresbury and
>   a fellow Oxford don, whose own daily diary is filled with
>   notations that he had "walked with Dodgson" and about
>   whom more will be said in Chapter 11.
> "*In drunk den night agony; mired don suckled hog bone.*"
>   Hog is supported only as a filthy person, not as a penis;
>   this may be an early use of a word as it appears again
>   several times in the latter context. Bone is slang for
>   penis.

"Bared urning don king mounted holy chaste don king."

Returning to the poem "Clara" itself, the ending "Moral: `Woo the yellow moon´" [16] (including the word *Moral*) becomes: *"The low moan room yell — OOW,"* adhering to the poem's theme of heterosexual intercourse in the bedroom. Is it coincidence that the title to one of the Slang references, *Cythera's Hymnal*, is also an anagram for *"Thy Clara's Hymen"*?

In his introduction to the collection, Derek Hudson agrees with other critics when he describes the notebook as representing the work of a very precocious child whose handwriting reflects a maturity he describes as "astonishing." [17] Perhaps, as suggested, not all the poems were produced at the same time. In any event, Dodgson, in 1845, had returned from his first two years of public school experience at Richmond, where he had lived in the Master's large house along with the family and other boys and where they may very well have roamed at night. Rugby was still in Dodgson's future.

The Pseudonym "Lewis Carroll"

Finally, we are confronted with the pseudonym Dodgson used for all except the earliest publications. He had written under two pseudonyms before settling on Lewis Carroll — "B.B.", and "R.W.G." The latter is presumably taken from the fourth letters of Charles Lutwidge Dodgson). I believe that "B.B." (unidentified in the literature on Dodgson) may have represented an early birth of "Bandersnatch-Boojum", the mysterious creature which emerges later in the *Snark* and other works.

When asked by his publisher to change his pseudonym, his first choice was "Dares", which we perhaps can now recognize as having an additional meaning than normally attributed — that of coming from his birthplace, Daresbury. When his publisher rejected it as being more appropriate for newspaper use, Dodgson promptly provided him with a list of four more from which to choose. In his diary entry of February 11, 1856, he made note of his proposed choices and a few days later recorded that "Lewis Carroll" was chosen. Dodgson claimed his proposed "Edgar Cuthwellis" and "Edgar U. C. Westhill" were "transformations" for "Charles Lutwidge"; and that "Louis Carroll" and "Lewis Carroll" were approximations of the Latin derivations *Carolus* for *Charles* and *Ludovic* for *Lutwidge*. [18]

Dodgson acknowledged that the first two of them were anagrams, or what he chose to refer to as "transformations," on his name.

However, all four are anagrams.   The first two have additional
solutions from those he presented. He would not be stopped!

Edgar Cuthwellis	-	*"Hide, cur! Wag tells!"*
Edgar U. C. Westhill	-	(ditto)
Louis Carroll	-	*"Roll! A cur soil!"*
Lewis Carroll	-	*"Role will scar."*
(ditto)	-	*"Lore will scar."*

CHAPTER 4

DENSITY OF EVIDENCE

The pursuit of anagrams continues and now focuses primarily on portions of *Alice's Adventures Under Ground* and *Sylvie and Bruno*, with brief but important stops at *Alice's Adventures in Wonderland*, *Through the Looking-Glass*, and *The Nursery "Alice"*. It is clear from an examination of these works, which represented Dodgson's first and last efforts that he specifically directed to children, that the anger so blatant and explicit in the first work only became more sophisticated and brazen in the latter. We shall see the density with which he could pack anagrams into his works and just how well nonsense serves as a mask.

Alice's Adventures Under Ground

This first of Dodgson's childrens' books was written in response to requests by the Liddell children, Alice particularly, to write down the story that Dodgson had told "extemporaneously" while on a boat trip with ten year old Alice, her younger sisters Lorina and Edith, and his Oxford friend Robinson Duckworth. Ironically, the trip occurred on a very specific day which everyone, including Dodgson, recalled as bright, warm and sunny, but which weather records tell us was cold and rainy. Within days, Dodgson began the process of putting his story to print and presented his handwritten manuscript containing thirty-seven hand-drawn pictures to Alice as a Christmas gift a year later in 1864. His own copy appears to have been lost or destroyed. Alice reported that it was written just as she remembered him telling it, a word-for-word rendering, as she recalled in later years. In 1886, several years after she had married, he requested and was granted permission to borrow her copy of the manuscript for publication in facsimile. He guarded it judiciously throughout the printing process, turning the pages himself, in order to insure that no damage should befall it and returned it to her upon completion. He had long since published *Alice's Adventures In Wonderland*, a version which used the original as a base, but to which he had added material which caused it to be nearly double the size of its source.

In the following analysis of the work, page references are to the hand written numbers as they appear in facsimile reproductions. The passages in question are surrounded by story-in-context in order to demonstrate the clues Dodgson left suggesting that the specific passage should be re-examined. All in-text quotation marks and italics are Dodgson's. His other works are referenced as they contribute to an understanding of this work.

On page 1 right at the beginning of the story, Alice saw a white rabbit run close to her:

> There was nothing very remarkable in that; nor did Alice think it so *very* much out of the way to hear the rabbit say to itself `dear, dear! I shall be too late!´ (when she thought it over afterwards, it occurred to her that she ought to have wondered at this, but at the time it all seemed quite natural); but, when the rabbit actually *took a watch out of its waistcoat-pocket*, looked at it, and then hurried on, Alice started to her feet, for it flashed across her mind that she had never before seen a rabbit with either a waistcoat-pocket or a watch to take out of it. . . .

There are two anagrams in this paragraph and the clues to their presence are the quotation marks or underlining (italics in printed copies). Also, both are followed by Alice's reactions which suggest something out of the ordinary. The device of incorporating the appropriate exaggerated response of children was frequently used by Dodgson and was in keeping with the nonsense character of the material, while also appropriate to the anagrammatic theme.

"dear, dear! I shall be too late" is an anagram for "*dear, dear! I eat tool, he balls.*" Dictionaries support *balls* in its current slang use as a noun, but not as a verb. The underlined phrase "*took a watch out of its waistcoat-pocket*" becomes "*O, oft I wait to wash, to pet, to suck at a cock.*"

On page 2 and the beginning of page 3, Alice, while falling down the rabbit hole, removes a jar which was labelled `Orange Marmalade´, but to her great disappointment it was empty. . . .

Again we have a Dodgson clue; the fact that the jar is empty suggests that we look at the label as a label, ignoring any contents it might point to. From "Orange Marmalade" several anagrams can be derived:

> *"Dream a male organ"*
> *"Or learn a mad game"*
> *"Or dream a male nag"*
> *"A mad male groaner"*
> *"An ogre male drama"*
> *"Or deal Mama anger."* "Mama" was the Dodgson children's
>   word for addressing their Mother.
> *"Mama: red anal ogre."*
> *"Lear! O, danger, Mama!"* Edward Lear was a contemporary
>   nonsense writer.
> *"Ram a mean ogre lad."*
> etc.

In his later years, when his nephew wished to sell family-made Orange Marmalade at Oxford, Dodgson placed an advertisement on the bulletin board addressed "To all lovers of Orange Marmalade. . ."

On pages 4 and 5 Alice wonders dreamily if "cats eat bats" or "bats eat cats". The *1811 Dictionary of the Vulgar Tongue* indicates that "bat" and "cat" were both slang words for "prostitute", with the oral behavior of prostitutes clearly suggested as possible however the question is posed.

Having already been introduced to the oral/anal nature of Dodgson's sexual imagery, the Freudian interpretations of Alice's alternating growth to enormous proportions and shrinking to ten inches or smaller, her face ("head") flushing in the process, from things she eats and drinks in response to "EAT ME" labels on cake and "DRINK ME" labels on bottles go beyond the usual interpretation as expressions of the unconscious. Dodgson seems to be writing directly to the erotic imagery, the whole purpose of the scenes described on pages 7 to 12 being to find a way through the "little door" next to the "tree" into the "garden." The suggestions that "Alice" is far better a description of Dodgson-as-phallus [1] rather than a fictionalized Alice Liddell, as several scholars have suggested, begins to gain increased credibility. This direction and the special meaning of *tree* culminates in *Sylvie and Bruno*, and its Magic Locket which is to be explained later in this chapter and an entirely new word game to be described in the next.

This allusion receives a different yet supportive twist as Dodgson uses the White Rabbit, another oft-considered self character, to lead Alice into this "Wonderland." In his *The Raven and the Writing Desk* Francis Huxley quotes scientific opinion from 1904 which did not deny the notion passed down from the days of Plutarch that hares were considered double-sexed, carrying in themselves both male and female, which roles they exchanged for purposes of copulation and generation. [2]

On page 12, Alice contemplates posting a present to her feet, now far below her head after her enormous growth, and suggests:

". . . And how odd her directions will look!"

> ALICE'S RIGHT FOOT, ESQ.
>   THE CARPET,
>   with ALICE'S LOVE.

This is followed by "oh dear! what nonsense I am talking!" Again we have the Dodgson clue.

While this posting address suggests also the curious use of the male "Esquire" following Alice's foot, the following anagram emerges:

> *"LEWIS CARROLL, ESQ.*
> *CAT VICE POET,*
> *I FIGHT SO THE HATE".* (or, "*I hate so the fight.*"

Perhaps Dodgson is expressing the struggle, the agony of shame and guilt he feels for what he is doing. My study of the original handwritten diary manuscripts identified many — very many — unpublished exhortations to God ". . . for Jesus Christ's sake. . ." to deliver him from his "hardness of heart" and unnamed activities and habits, prayers which were very frequent during the period when these *Alice* works were being written. One wonders if he slowly changed his mind, then took on the task with renewed fervor when he expanded the original work for publication, for he changed the address in *Alice's Adventures in Wonderland* to:

> Alice's Right Foot, Esq.
>   Hearthrug,
>   near the Fender,
>   (with Alice's love).

This modification allows for two anagrams, with sentiments different from those expressed in the original. The first is *"Watch Alice's gender fool the evil Queen of Hearts; her rat is right."* The story line describes Alice and the mouse, now rat size due to Alice's own shrinking, swimming in the pool created by Alice's tears. The rat approaches Alice, then quickly swims away. He is suspicious of her, and is frightened by her unintentional references to cats. This includes her attempt to communicate in French with "Ou est ma chatte?" (otherwise *"Out, chaste mate!"*) after which "The mouse gave a sudden jump in the pool, and seemed to quiver with fright. . . ." Perhaps the rat was aware of and wary of "cat" behavior as well as the innate fear of cats. On the other hand, the Queen of Hearts accepts Alice's statement that she is a little girl.

After extensive searching, the second anagram is the only one found which seems to reference Dodgson's father directly: *"Father, who loveth a gentler faith, raises grotesque ice children."* The use of *ice* for *cold* or *brittle* is an acceptable allusion in OED. Chapter 11 will focus on the overall warmth and relatedness of the Dodgson children, all except two of whom remained unmarried all their lives, despite coming from a large, and heretofore perceived nourishing, family environment. This was not a normal or desired path for Victorian women. It was rarely elected as women were trained for marriage and motherhood. In his *The Rectory Umbrella*, Dodgson referred to his siblings as "children of the North."

On page 39, the White Rabbit, searching for Alice, calls out incorrectly, "Mary Ann! Mary Ann!. . ." While Green identifies *Mary Ann* as meaning "Servant girl" [3], it is also an appropriate Victorian slang expression for a sodomite; and it appears also in *Alice's Adventures in Wonderland* and in *The Nursery "Alice"*.

On page 70, there is a procession of courtiers, Royal children, and the entire Queen's court that parades before Alice,

> . . . the Knave of Hearts, carrying the King's crown on a cushion, and, last of all this grand procession, came THE KING AND QUEEN OF HEARTS.

In *Alice's Adventures in Wonderland* the last words were changed to "THE KING AND THE QUEEN OF HEARTS", but this had little effect on the buried anagram: *"He, (the) quaint son, faketh gender."*

On page 74, the White Rabbit informs Alice that the Queen of Hearts is also the "Marchioness of Mock Turtles." Adhering to the sense of falseness and hypocrisy, the anagram *"O fuck mother's incest morals!*" emerges, with *fuck* a common word in Victorian pornography.

> "`What are *they*?´ said Alice, but there was no time for the answer, for they had reached the croquet-ground, and the game began instantly.

Page 75 contains the illustration drawn by Dodgson of the croquet grounds on which all the game participants are assembled. These participants include Alice, the King and Queen, playing-card wickets, and the flamingos and hedgehogs used as mallets and balls. Standing together are two courtiers, one kissing the other. The latter appears to have his tights turned down with his penis firmly in the grasp of the one being kissed. Martin Gardner comments at the end of the work's Introduction that Freudian interpreters have long had an interest in this and other pictures in this work. The interpretation and verification for this picture comes, I believe, in *Through the Looking-Glass* and may have been a major reason for Dodgson wanting this earlier work published in facsimile. Toward the end of the first Chapter of that work entitled "Looking-Glass House," the White King, a chess piece who had fallen into the fireplace ashes decided to make a memorandum of his feelings. While struggling to write in the book with an enormous pencil, he is unaware that Alice has grasped the end of it and is guiding him. He writes "*The White Knight is sliding down the poker. He balances very badly*" (Carroll's italics). The White Queen responds "That's not a memorandum of *your* feelings!" The illustration by Tenniel depicts the White Knight sliding down a fireplace poker handle. The underlined statement re-works to "*Ah, ye! When I slid down the lonely knave's tights I grabbed the prick.*" The 1811 slang dictionary supports the word *prick* as the slang for *penis* with OED supporting *Ah, ye!* as an early version of *My, my!*

In the trial scene the accusation against the Knave of Hearts was read from the parchment scroll, a verse familiar to most:

> `The Queen of Hearts she made some tarts
>   All on a summer day:
> The Knave of Hearts he stole those tarts,
>   And took them quite away!´

Quoting C. S. Lewis, Bullough writes that in the early Twentieth Century fags were known as "House Tarts": what he described as effeminate-looking boys who offered themselves in pederast service to upper classmen, not quite as slaves or prostitutes. [4] Both the use of "tarts" and the description of pederasty in the schools most certainly predates Lewis's writings. Effeminacy was seen as a characteristic suggestive in and of itself of homosexuality in mid-Victorian England. [5] While not found having earlier origins, the theme is consistent with those appearing in the anagrams. Within the verse, the origins derive from the "baking" process of the Queen of Hearts, an allusion to which we shall return in Chapter 7 when we explore the various mother figures in Dodgson's nonsense.

Concluding the work, Dodgson focuses Alice on the "curious" and "wonderful" nature of the dream she has just experienced. And he placed his own drawing of Alice Liddell on the last page, but later covered it with a small photograph of her. Though he gave no reason at the time of publication in facsimile, he urged her emphatically to remove her photograph. She followed his advice.

Alice's Adventures in Wonderland

Although it is somewhat incomplete and unfair to only touch on this most famous of Dodgson's works, it does contain nearly all the anagrams reflected in the source work in addition to new ones. The characters at the Mad Tea Party all have names with anagrammatic solutions — March Hare as "*Reach harm*", Dormouse as "*Sure doom*," and the (Mad) Hatter as "*Threat.*" Beyond those, only a single additional anagrammatic situation is presented from the longer *Alice's Adventures in Wonderland*, solely because it again reflects Dodgson's skill at building a web of innocence. Best known for his nonsense poems within his works, when preparing "The Walrus and the Carpenter" Dodgson offered his illustrator Tenniel the option of drawing a carpenter, a baronet, or a butterfly, and indicated he could use any of them as the basis for rhyme and meter. While Tenniel told him *carpenter* would work better artistically, Dodgson was prepared to use whatever Tenniel chose for his anagrams.

> "The Walrus and the. . .
> Carpenter" - "*Repent! The death crawl's a run!*"
> Butterfly" - "*Wander! Butt at the hell's fury!*"
> Baronet" - "*Ah, hand, beware rotten lust!*"

Readers are asked to take a leap of faith that the work is filled with repetitions on the same themes, with no new themes found in the anagrams identified but not presented here.

Through the Looking-Glass

Considerable written commentary has focused on the chess game which Dodgson describes as being played in the movement of the characters within the story line of *Through the Looking-Glass*, whereby Alice moves along the "chess board" landscape to finally become a queen. It is clearly evident that this chess game, while a clever construct in itself, was intended primarily to provide an additional diversion from his real task, the burying of his explicit material. Dodgson was successful. Much has been written about the extent to which Alice's movements adhere to or violate the accepted rules of Chess.

In 1974, a chapter of what was more likely a segment of a chapter [6] in *Through the Looking-Glass* appeared at auction in London. Tenniel reported he was having difficulties drawing a wasp and Dodgson removed the segment at Tenniel's request. This segment was published in 1977 separately by its original title "The Wasp in a Wig," and depicts Alice coming upon a crotchety old Wasp with whom she converses briefly before she finally makes the final chess move of jumping the last brook to become queen. Two lines from this segment are very typical of the entire work. In his introduction Martin Gardner, aware of the way the remark just drops in without comment, suggests that Dodgson was acting nearly as a ventriloquist as the Wasp asserted: "Worrity, Worrity! There never was such a child. . . ." [7] The Wasp has just commented on how Alice prattles on and the line is followed by her offense at the Wasp's words. Again we have an anagrammatic clue, that of the inappropriately placed line, which just appears as though dropped in the text and is totally lacking in context. The Wasp's line re-works to *"Re-write! Thrive! Worthy Alice's word's raunchy!"* For the Wasp responded to the anagram deriving from Alice's inquiry as to whether he was cold [8], a question which reworks to: *"O, lay her or eat her red cunt!"*

Within *Through the Looking-Glass* itself lies "Jabberwocky" which is considered the greatest example of Nonsense poetry in the English Language. The body of this poem was first presented at an in-family "competition" as other members also made their own contributions. The opening verse which is repeated as the closing verse was added later, but changed slightly for publication. While the entire poem was intended to be presented in "mirror" writing — readable by holding it up to a mirror — Dodgson published only the first verse as such and then presented the whole poem in readable form. Accompanying the poem is a picture of a dragon-like creature being slain by a young boy with a sword, an illustration intended originally to be the frontispiece for the book. However, by sampling friends Dodgson determined that it might be too frightening for children and replaced it with the illustration of the bumbling Knight:

"Jabberwocky"

Twas brillig, and the slithy toves
  Did gyre and gimble in the wabe:
All mimsy were the borogoves,
  And the mome raths outgrabe.

`Beware the Jabberwock, my son!
  The jaws that bite, the claws that catch!
Beware the Jubjub bird, and shun
  The frumious Bandersnatch!´

He took his vorpal sword in hand:
  Long time the manxome foe he sought —
So rested he by the Tumtum tree,
  And stood awhile in thought.

And, as in uffish thought he stood,
  The Jabberwock, with eyes of flame,
Came whiffling through the tulgey wood,
  And burbled as it came!

One, two! One, two! And through and through
  The vorpal blade went snicker-snack!
He left it dead, and with its head
  He went galumphing back.

`And hast though slain the Jabberwock?
  Come to my arms, my beamish boy!
O frabjous day! Callooh! Callay!´
  He chortled in his joy.

Twas brillig, and the slithy toves
Did gyre and gimble in the wabe:
All mimsy were the borogoves,
And the mome raths outgrabe.

The story continues:

`It seems very pretty,´ she [Alice] said when she had
finished it, `but it's *rather* hard to understand!´ (You see
she didn't like to confess, even to herself, that she couldn't
make it out at all.) `Somehow it seems to fill my head with
ideas — only I don't exactly know what they are! However,
somebody killed *something*: that's clear, at any rate —´

Later on, Alice repeats the first verse to Humpty Dumpty, who
claims he knows the meaning of *all* words. He proceeds to give a
meaning to all the nonsense words. *Brillig* becomes "four o'clock in
the afternoon — the time when you begin *broiling* things for dinner."
Slithy is a portmanteau word, a single word carrying the combined
meaning of two words, in this case *lithe* and *slimy*. *Toves* are
"something like badgers — they're something like lizards — and
they're something like corkscrews." Humpty Dumpty continues and
attends to all the words. Eventually all coherent meaning is lost with
the poem becoming purely nonsensical. As Daniel Kirk points out in
his work *Charles Dodgson Semeiotician*, the nonsense words comprise
what appear to be nouns, adjectives and verbs and are surrounded by
connectives, which give the poem an obvious though, in this case
deceptive, sense of structure. [9] The sound of foreboding in the
opening and closing verse is evident.

The creation of a mask continues. As suspected, the poem
reflects Dodgson's masturbatory fantasies in story form with the final
slaying of "something", as Alice concluded. The opening verse "Twas
brillig and the slithy toves. . ." becomes, in anagrammatic
reconstruction, consistent with the illustration of the lad with sword as
he prepares to slay the Jabberwock (see page 166):

"Bet I beat my glands til,
With hand-sword I slay the evil gender.
A slimey theme; borrow gloves,
And masturbate the hog more!"

"Jabberwocky" is such an important poem in the entire set of Dodgson
works that its full meaning, beyond its being masturbatory in theme,

will be discussed more thoroughly in Chapter 8, after more groundwork is laid for relating the masturbatory imagery with the slaying of "the evil gender." Note, however, that the weapon can be changed from *sword* to *words,* with *hand* moved to describe *beat.*

Sylvie and Bruno

As indicated at the beginning of this chapter, *Sylvie and Bruno* is the last work to be examined in any detail. I have chosen to focus on the first chapters because other portions of the work appear only to represent variations on previously discussed themes. Before proceeding, however, a comment is in order regarding the manner in which Dodgson's sly humor is again so evident in the cross referenced index he places at the end of these novels. Most of the entries point to sections and themes worthy of further examination. While the notion of a work of fiction having an alphabetized subject index has long been considered humorous and a typical twist to a nonsense writer, its form and presence is curiously similar to the classic eleven volume Victorian pornographic "biography" of "Walter" entitled *My Secret Life* which also contains an alphabetic index of the names of each person conquered and another which provides the reader with the location of every possible combination of coupling or type of sexual activity described in the story.

Essentially, *Sylvie and Bruno* is a story which shifts, suddenly at times, among three of what Dodgson described as "eerie" states of consciousness. One depicts Sylvie at age ten and her brother Bruno, age five, living in Outland. A second "eerie" state depicts Sylvie and Bruno as fairies a few inches tall living in Fairyland. In a third state, the children are represented by their adult counterparts, Lady Muriel and Arthur Forrester who live in England. A narrator of the story observes and moves between states, in each of which live a host of other characters, including Prince Uggug, a fat pig-like boy who is about the same age as Sylvie and in the end is transformed into a prickly porcupine. Greenacre describes Uggug:

> ... whose repulsiveness is expressed in his name, which sounds like a combination of burp or gulp and the sound of fecal dropping, so similar to many of the neologistic words of Swift... [and] reminds one of the pig baby. [10]

Uggug is the son of the Sub-Warden in Outland. Among other characters is the nonsensical sounding "His Adiposity, the Baron Doppelgeist." What becomes apparent in the anagrammatic restructuring is a fourth "eerie" state in which Dodgson weaves his themes of pederast imagery and practices.

Within these early chapters, men from Outland are marching for "More __ bread __ Less __ taxes!" as they parade in what seems a sashaying movement through the streets. At times it seems the crowd has changed its chant to "Less __ bread __ More __ taxes!", but on closer listening, the first chant is heard. Later, after several efforts to quell the noise of the crowd. . .

The Lord Chancellor recovered himself with a great effort, and pointed to the open window. `If your High Excellency will listen for a moment to the shouts of the exasperated populace __´ (`of the exasperated populace!´ the Sub-Warden repeated in a louder tone, as the Lord Chancellor, being in a state of abject terror, had dropped almost into a whisper) `__ you will understand what it is they want.´

Again the cry "Less — bread — More — taxes!" is heard, then "More — bread — Less — taxes!", with a worried Warden repeating that he had already opened a new government bakery and abolished taxes; what could they possibly be looking for?

Within this extended scene the cry "of the exasperated populace" is really the "*axe of the pederast populace*," not calling out "More bread, Less taxes!" but "*Stable sex dares more!*" (which plays with both meanings of *stable*) or "*Stale sex dreams bore!*", or again "*Dare stable sex mores!*". Shortly thereafter the Sub-Warden is given the right to act as Vice-Warden, and the "vice" over which he governs runs for pages in passages of anagrams and statements with double meanings, including the plot theme of changing the Constitution and putting their child, the despicable Uggug, in place as heir to the throne instead of Bruno.

The following passage from Chapter II is worth quoting fully, as it provides, not only examples of anagram integration, but a statement of the goal Dodgson appears to have established for himself in this work: to create a single book which, by word and letter rearrangement, could elaborate on any subject ("grave and gay" as he said in his preface), and thus represent a universally applicable single work to replace all other books. The greatest value that any work derived from such a book would have is the one reduced so as to contain the greatest "intensity."

Struggling with unexplained embarrassment over a post script to a letter he had received: "Do you believe in Fate?" ("*You on a vile beef diet?*", with *beef* being slang for prostitute), "I" the narrator, is reassured by a lady overhearing the question that:

`. . . it was a case of what you Doctors call "unconscious cerebration?"´ ["*Nice curious note on crabs*," reflective of the Victorian pre-occupation with social disease]

`I am no Doctor,´ I replied. `Do I look so like one? Or what makes you think it?´

She pointed to the book I had been reading, which was so lying that its title, "Diseases of the Heart," was plainly visible.

`One needn't be a *Doctor*,´ I said, `to take an interest in medical books. There's another class of readers, who are yet more deeply interested ___´

`You mean the *Patients*?´ she interrupted, while a look of tender pity gave new sweetness to her face. `But,´ with an evident wish to avoid a possibly painful topic, `one needn't be *either*, to take an interest in books of *Science*.

Which contain the greatest amount of Science, do you think, the books or the minds?´

`Rather a profound question for a lady!´ I said to myself, holding, with the conceit so natural to Man, that Woman's intellect is essentially shallow. And I considered a minute before replying. `If you mean *living* minds, I don't think it's possible to decide. There is so much *written* Science that no living person has ever *read*: and there is so much *thought-out* Science that hasn't yet been *written*. But if you mean the whole human race, then I think the *minds* have it: everything, recorded in *books*, must have once been in some *mind*, you know.´

`Isn't that rather like one of the Rules in Algebra?´ my Lady enquired. ("*Algebra* too!" I thought with increasing wonder.) `I mean, if we consider thoughts as *factors* may we not say that the Least Common Multiple of all the *minds* contains that of all the *books*; but not the other way?´

`Certainly we may!´ I replied, delighted with the illustration. `And what a grand thing it would be,´ I went on dreamily, thinking aloud rather than talking, `if we could only *apply* that Rule to books! You know, in finding the Least Common Multiple, we strike out a quantity wherever it occurs, except in the term where it is raised to its highest power. So we should have to erase every recorded thought, except in the sentence where it is expressed with the greatest intensity.´

My Lady laughed merrily. `*Some* books would be reduced to blank paper, I'm afraid!´ she said.

`They would. Most libraries would be terribly diminished in *bulk*. But just think what they would gain in *quality*!´

`When will it be done?´ she eagerly asked. `If there's any chance of it in *my* time, I think I'll leave off reading, and wait for it!´

`Well, perhaps in another thousand years or so —´

Before examining the content in the passage, note the list of anagrams from words highlighted by the Dodgson. There are at least the following:

Patients - "*Pet stain!*"
Science - "*Ecce! Sin!*" with *Ecce* being Latin for *Behold*.

Algebra - (to which the reader's attention is drawn directly with "*Algebra,* too!" It becomes "*Bare gal!*" with *gal* a slang word for *harlot* after 1851 according to Partridge.

Factors - "*For cats!*"

While in his Preface to *Sylvie and Bruno Concluded* Dodgson denied reader suggestions that the words of any characters were his own, this passage clearly seems to describe the kind of book "constructs" he sought to build. In the Chapter 10 we will explore the reasons why Dodgson himself had such an interest in medical books, as is revealed by an examination of his private library sold at auction shortly after his death.

Later, in Chapter IV of *Sylvie and Bruno,* after hearing screams from the room to which the Chancellor and Uggug had retired, Lady Muriel begins:

> `Ah!´ said my Lady, graciously smiling on that high official. `Your Lordship has a very *taking* way with children! I doubt if any one could *gain the ear* of my darling Uggug so quickly as *you* can!´ For an entirely stupid woman, my Lady's remarks were curiously full of meaning, of which she herself was wholly unconscious.
>
> The Chancellor bowed, but with a very uneasy air. `I think the Warden was about to speak,´ he remarked, evidently anxious to change the subject.
>
> But my Lady would not be checked. `He is a clever boy,´ she continued with enthusiasm, `but he needs a man like your Lordship to *draw him out!*´
>
> The Chancellor bit his lip, and was silent. He evidently feared that, stupid as she looked, she understood what she said *this* time, and was having a joke at his expense. He might have spared himself all anxiety: whatever accidental meaning her *words* might have, she *herself* never meant anything at all.

Here we depart from one of the rules for anagram construction as I take non-contiguous italicized words, and only then because Dodgson highlights them as two sequences worthy of examination. In the first paragraph above which quotes My Lady, the italicized words *taking, gain the ear,* and *you* can be restructured to "*Oh, I take gay urning tea.*," with *tea* meaning *urine* in the Slang Dictionary. The italicized *draw him out* in her last words re-works to "*I'd mouth raw.*" All the while the Chancellor fears she is aware of what she is saying and fully aware of what he and Uggug were up to when alone in the room from which they had just both emerged, the Lord Chancellor "a little flushed and out of breath."

Another rather lengthy segment is worth examining because Dodgson pursues the nature and likely longevity of his own works, then moves into the subject of physiological inversion, the themes examined by J. A. Symonds and Havelock Ellis in their studies of homosexuality as sexual inversion in the late nineteenth and early twentieth centuries (see Appendix 3). In Chapter XVII, the narrator, Arthur, and Lady Muriel are attending a lecture by an art critic and are all examining a painting:

> `Do you observe?´ (such was the phrase with which the wretch began each sentence) `Do you observe the way in which that broken arch, at the very top of the ruin, stands out against the clear sky? It is placed *exactly* right: and there is *exactly* enough of it. A little more, or a little less, and all would be utterly spoiled!´
>
> `Oh gifted architect!´ [*Detect it, oh rich fag!*] murmured Arthur, inaudibly to all but Lady Muriel and myself. `Foreseeing the exact effect his work would have, when in ruins, centuries after his death!´
>
> `And do you observe, where those trees slope down the hill,´ (indicating them with a sweep of the hand, and with all the patronising air of the man who has himself arranged the landscape), `how the mists rising from the river fill up *exactly* those intervals where we *need* indistinctness, for artistic effect? Here, in the foreground, a few clear touches are not amiss: but a *back*-ground without mist, you know! It is simply barbarous! Yes, we *need* indistinctness!´
>
> The orator looked so pointedly at *me* as he uttered these words, that I felt bound to reply, by murmuring something to the effect that I hardly felt the need *myself* — and that I enjoyed looking at a thing, better, when I could *see* it.
>
> `Quite so!´ the great man sharply took me up. `From *your* point of view, that is correctly put. But for any one who has a soul for *Art*, such a view is preposterous. *Nature* is one thing. *Art* is another. *Nature* shows us the world as it *is*. But *Art* — as a Latin author tells us — *Art*, you know — the words have escaped my memory ——´
>
> `Ars est celare Naturam,´ Arthur interposed with a delightful promptitude.

`Quite so!´ the orator replied with an air of relief. `I thank you! *Ars est celare Naturam* — but that isn't it.´ And, for a few peaceful moments, the orator brooded, frowningly, over the quotation. The welcome opportunity was seized, and *another* voice struck into the silence.

... `You have studied Physiology, then?´ a certain young Doctor courteously enquired [responding to a comment by a young lady on the function of the Retina in distinguishing color].

`Oh, *yes*! Isn't it a *sweet* Science?´

Arthur slightly smiled. `It seems a paradox, does it not,´ he went on, `that the image formed on the Retina should be inverted?´

`It *is* puzzling,´ she candidly admitted. `Why is it we do not *see* things upside-down?´

`You have never heard the Theory, then, that the *Brain* also is inverted?´

`No *indeed*! What a *beautiful* fact! But how is it *proved*?´

`*Thus*,´ replied Arthur, with all the gravity of ten Professors rolled into one. `What we call the *vertex* of the Brain is really its *base*: and what we call its *base* is really its *vertex*: it is simply a question of *nomenclature*.´

This polysyllable settled the matter. `How truly delightful!´ the fair Scientist exclaimed with enthusiasm. `I shall ask our Physiological Lecturer why he never gave us that *exquisite* Theory!´

`I'd give something to be present when the question is asked!; Arthur whispered to me, as, at a signal from Lady Muriel, we moved on. ...

If we return to the "not quite right" Latin phrase "Ars est celare Naturam", Dodgson's variation on Horace's "Ars est celare Artim," we find it an anagram for *"Tear rectums, anal arse"*, with *arse* the correct Victorian word for *posterior* and the Latin phrase itself translating loosely to "The skill is to conceal one's true character." The "polysyllable" *nomenclature* which closes the discussion of brain inversion re-works to *"no mental cure"*, which we find an advanced notion in the history of homosexual studies. For it would not be until the late 1970's that the medically based psychiatric profession would remove homosexuality from their list of mental illnesses (though not all agree with that decision).

There appears a brief segment in Chapter XIX in *Sylvie and Bruno Concluded* in which planning is being done to encourage the treatment of dogs as pets. Included is a plan for the formation of a *"Charitable Association for supplying dogs with pockets"* [Dodgson's italics]. Playing on the large number of "cause" related Victorian organizations, many of them women's activities, Dodgson creates a title whose anagrammatic re-working reads: *"Pray stand, choose a cock, gulp frig poison, eat it with bliss."* *Frig* was another popular word in Victorian pornography.

Lastly, we will explore the meaning of the Magic Locket drawn especially by "Miss Alice Havers" and the etiology of the name "Bruno." The locket represents a central theme in the book. Eventually the children learn that it is not two lockets but one which appears red when looked at one way, and blue when looked at another way. As already noted the words on the locket "Sylvie will love all" or "All will love Sylvie" re-work to anagrams. Quoting now from Chapter VIII of *Sylvie and Bruno*:

> ... and here Sylvie drew the Magic Locket from its hiding-place, turned it over with a thoughtful air, and at last appealed to Bruno in a rather helpless way. `What *was* it we had to do with it, Bruno? It's all gone out of my head!´
>
> `Kiss it!´ was Bruno's invariable recipe in cases of doubt and difficulty. Sylvie kissed it, but no result followed.
>
> `Rub it the wrong way,´ was Bruno's next suggestion.
>
> `Which *is* the wrong way?´ Sylvie most reasonably enquired. The obvious plan was to try *both* ways.
>
> Rubbing from left to right had no visible effect whatever.
>
> From right to left — `Oh, stop, Sylvie!´ Bruno cried in sudden alarm. `Whatever *is* going to happen?´
>
> For a number of trees, on the neighbouring hillside, were moving slowly upwards, in solemn procession: while a mild little brook, that had been rippling at our feet a moment before, began to swell, and foam, and hiss, and bubble, in a truly alarming fashion.
>
> `Rub it some other way!´ cried Bruno, `Try up-and-down! Quick!´
>
> It was a happy thought. Up-and-down did it; and the landscape, which had been showing signs of mental aberration in various directions, returned to its normal condition of sobriety. ...

Again, in the mouths of his child characters, we are confronted with Dodgson's masturbatory fantasies, with the rubbed Magic Locket really being "*Me — a gilt cock*." And the sympathetic rising of trees on the hillside? By word conversion, we shall learn in the next chapter how *tree* becomes *cock*.

While the name "Bruno" appeared to have a purpose in the construction of the anagrammatic structure of the book's title, it also is an anagram, which relates to Bruno's suggestion that "rubbing" will solve the problem with the locket. For *Bruno* is an anagram for "*Rub on*." A clue for this is provided when the narrator, moving into the "eerie" state where fairies can be seen, comes upon the fairy Bruno in Chapter XIV:

> ... Then a little thrill of delight ran through me — for I noticed that the holes [in the leaves of the ground plants formed by a `leafcutter bee´ (my note)] were all arranged so as to form letters: there were three leaves side by side, with `B,´ `R,´ and `U´ marked on them [*RUB*], and after some search I found two more, which contained an `N´ and an `O´ [*ON*].
>
> And then, all in a moment, a flash of inner light seemed to illumine a part of my life that had all but faded into oblivion — the strange visions I had experienced during my journey to Elveston: and with a thrill of delight I thought `Those visions are destined to be linked with my waking life!´

The Nursery "Alice"

Only four anagrams are identified in this work, just to demonstrate that Dodgson's efforts to express his rage, even in this book for very young children and the parents who read to them was still seething. For, in this work he introduced anagrams which did not exist in the source book. The title of the dedicatory poem "A Nursery Darling" creates an interesting anagram which may have meaning undeterminable except in Dodgson's circle. For from it we derive "*Lear's a dry urning*" which may mean that Edward Lear was gay but also "not wet," i.e., not a participant in active sexual behavior. This is purely speculative as he could also be commenting on his feelings regarding the quality of Lear's nonsense. But since Lear's name may have been used twice in the anagrams, it is interesting to note that neither Dodgson nor Lear was able to avoid being attacked by dogs, including the otherwise very friendly household pets of his child friends. Dodgson avoided them totally. One wonders just what it was that dogs sensed that caused them to react that way without any reported provocation.

This same poem has as its first line a phrase used many times throughout Dodgson's poetry: "a mother's breast." It is most often used in a very sentimental context. The phrase is also an anagram for "a brother's meats." This is a most interesting anagrammatic coincidence, as the psychological references (especially Khan) suggest that in sexual perversions, the male genitals are psychological substitutes for the mother and the mother's breast as they become used in masturbation for self-soothing (see Appendix 2).

A third anagram appears in Chapter VII of The Nursery "Alice". In this work Dodgson added color to the Tenniel illustrations he chose to enlarge and use. In this case he changed the Caterpillar and its anagram "Ill cat raper" to a Blue Caterpillar and a new anagram "Pre-lubricate all," a notion frequent in the pornographic literature of the day and a reference to a lubricant sold by Father William in Alice's Adventures in Wonderland that analysts have questioned. In Chapter VI Dodgson introduced a birthday-treat of "oatmeal-porridge" [Dodgson's italics], from which a number of anagrams can be formed. These include:

> "Poor girl made tea."
> "Lo! Marriage opted!"
> "A poet mirage, Lord!"
> "O, dear! Girl atop me!"
> "O poet! Dream a girl!"
> "Ram leg a poor diet" with mutton slang for an aphrodisiac.
> "Married tool! Gape!"
> "O, pat me, Lord; I rage." etc.

There is one last segment which deserves attention. It does not involve anagrams, but plays on the naivete of his audience as they are directed to follow instructions. Near the end of Chapter VII we have:

And Alice said she would like to be just a *little* bit larger — three inches was such a *wretched* height to be! (Just mark off three inches on the wall, about the length of your middle finger, and you'll see what size she was.)

While the story is directed to children "nought to five" the finger movement directions, if followed for children to see and imitate, would cause the parent to present, outside of awareness, the universally recognized sign of contempt, with Dodgson most likely caring little as to whether it was directed to the child, or the parent as reader.

This completes the detailed focus on anagrammatic structures in the published works which Charles Dodgson wrote for and directed to his child-friends.   The themes are clearly evident and the self disclosures provide much biographical insight into his own inner thoughts and feelings and those with whom he seems to have worked. We shall return to anagrams in later chapters as these and new ones allow us to address those portions of his life thus far shrouded in mystery with new understanding.

CHAPTER 5

ANOTHER GAME AND CONCLUSION

Up to this point, the entire focus of search for Dodgson's hidden expression has been the anagram. Having clearly established the presence of this mode of communication and the nature of the messages and imagery, a far more subjective, projective, and subtle game can now be explored. Without reader acceptance that the anagrams already discussed are in fact objective evidence of Dodgson's intentional expression of some aspects of his inner world and preoccupations, the next game that I suggest he played with readers will be rejected. For in this next game, Dodgson created his own private dictionary which allowed him to not only write nonsense, whose nature requires incongruity in meaning and relationships, but to rhyme it and to hide his own private meaning within.

He introduced the game to the public in a letter to the editor of *Vanity Fair* in 1879 when he was forty-seven and which he signed "Lewis Carroll."

Dear Vanity:
    Just a year ago last Christmas two young ladies, smarting under that sorest scourge of feminine humanity, the having `nothing to do,´ besought me to send `some riddles.´ But riddles I had none at hand and therefore set myself to devise some other form of verbal torture which should serve the same purpose. The result of my meditations was a new kind of Puzzle, new at least to me, which now that it has been fairly tested by a year's experience, and commended by many friends, I offer to you as a newly gathered nut to be cracked by the omnivorous

teeth that have already masticated so many of your Double
Acrostics.

The rules of the Puzzle are simple enough. Two words
are proposed, of the same length; and the Puzzle consists in
linking these together by interposing other words, each of
which shall differ from the next word *in one letter only.* That
is to say, one letter may be changed in one of the given
words, then one letter in the word so obtained, and so on, till
we arrive at the other given word. The letters must not be
interchanged among themselves, but each must keep to its
own place. As an example, the word `head´ may be changed
into `tail´ by interposing the words `heal, teal, tell, tall.´ I
call the two given words `a Doublet,´ the interposed words
`Links,´ and the entire series `a Chain,´ of which I here
append an example:

> Head
> heal
> teal
> tell
> tall
> Tail

*It is perhaps needless to state that the links should be
English words, such as might be used in good society* [my
italics].

The easiest `Doublets´ are those in which the
consonants in one word answer to the consonants in the
other, and the vowels to vowels; `head´ and `tail´ constitute
a Doublet of this kind. Where this is not the case, as in
`head´ and `hare,´ the first thing to be done is to transform
one member of the Doublet into a word whose consonants
and vowels shall answer to those in the other member
(`head, herd, here´), after which there is seldom much
difficulty in completing the `Chain.´ . . .

`Lewis Carroll´ [1]

Continuing where Belle Moses left off, Dodgson ended the letter as
follows:

I am told that there is an American game involving a
similar principle. I have never seen it, and can only say of its
inventors, `pereant qui ante nos nostra dixerunt!´ [2]

The Latin translates to: "Those who speak before us will perish."

Via subsequent communications to the publication, Dodgson encouraged and participated in many contests which involved readers submitting their solutions to suggested conversions. The scoring method in the contests caused a deduction of points once the number of links exceeded the total number of letters in both Doublet words (head to tail would score 8), with the least number of links providing the highest score. [3]

In light of what we have already seen of Dodgson's flirtation with invincibility and danger, it is very possible that he introduced the game in the name of "Lewis Carroll" so that he might add further tension to the risk of disclosure by challenging current or future game participants to examine his works. Secondly, his suggestion that only "proper" words be used seems a diversion from his primary or secondary goal (in addition to creating poetic doublets for nonsense rhyming) in creating the game — to simultaneously lessen the tension he had just heightened.

Even though he introduced the game to the public long after producing his earlier works, I believe his earliest use of and suggestion of the game appears in *Alice's Adventures in Wonderland* when the Duchess' boy baby turns into a pig when placed in Alice's arms — BOY, bog, big, PIG.

The effect of this word conversion game was the creation of a private dictionary in which it was easy to hide a double meaning within the clear text. The presence of such words also provides some of the reasons for ambiguities in portions of the nonsense stories, as characters respond inappropriately to the textual word, but appropriately to the target word in a doublet conversion. This is another dimension to Sutherland's Chapter 8. It is not the intent here to explore all possibilities within the works, as the task becomes an endless game and can certainly be construed as projective of the inner world of the player, but a few examples will suffice, only to show that it can be done. The reader is left to draw any conclusions on the extent to which Dodgson used the technique.

Is it the Cheshire cat's grin that appears and disappears in *Alice's Adventures in Wonderland* or is it the grin of the Cheshire don (CAT cot dot DON) with its "cat that ate the canary" grin as Dodgson, born in County Cheshire, plays his word games with a gullible public? Or does it also reference the "cat-as-harlot" view of himself he appears to have had as he wrote of gay prostitute behavior?

The Duchess's moral "Oh, 'tis love, 'tis love, that makes the world go round!" in *Alice's Adventures in Wonderland* and the refrain from *Sylvie and Bruno* that critics have panned for its sweet "gurgling" "morass:" [4]

> For I think it is Love,
> For I feel it is Love,
> For I'm sure it is nothing but Love!

Or again the final words of *Sylvie and Bruno Concluded* "It is Love" all take on quite a different meaning if "love" is turned into "hate" using the Doublet conversion "LOVE lave late HATE." (It should be noted that by anagrammatic reconstruction, the last line above also become "O, 'tis evil.")

Is the Queen of Hearts' interminable cry "Off with their heads!" really the Queen of Haters command for castration? The ambiguity of the text which follows suggests a meaning other than the literal one:

> The executioner's argument was, that you couldn't cut off a head unless there was a body to cut if off from: that he had never had to do such a thing before, and he wasn't going to begin at *his* time of life. The King's argument was that anything that had a head could be beheaded, and that you weren't to talk nonsense.

What were the tarts that the Knave of Hearts stole? Did "Father William," with the anagrammatic solutions "*Fate, I will harm!*" and "*I will farm* [i.e., cultivate] *hate*" really balance an eel on the end of his nose, or was it a fag (don, man, boy, or gal) on the end of his cock? What limbs were to be kept supple using the ointment that Father William sold for "one shilling a box?" Was it to "pre-lubricate all?" The nonsense begins to disappear if one applies the same imagery using Doublet conversion as one finds in the anagrams. In fact, nearly any four letter word can be turned into "cock," including *tree* (TREE, thee, them, teem, seem, seam, ream, roam, room, rook, rock, COCK), which we saw rising in response to the rubbing of the "Magic Locket" in *Sylvie and Bruno*. Was it cocks (lock, lick, line, lime, LIMB) and not limbs that Father William was keeping supple?

And finally, when *Alice* can be turned into *Prick* (ALICE slice slick click crick PRICK), just as the Magic Locket was an anagrammatic restructure, all psychological interpretations arguing that Alice represented phallus in Dodgson's works improve in their acceptability. [5] But the imagery does not emerge from deep in his unconscious; rather, it was consciously designed on Dodgson's part.

In as open an example as was found in the works, taken from *Sylvie and Bruno*, the Vice-Warden considers holding an Election, asserting in the face of some doubt, that if the Court-Professor finds it awkward. . .

`Well, well! Then the Election shall be held without you.´ `Better so, than if it were held *within* me!´ the Professor murmured with a bewildered air, as if he hardly knew what he was saying. . . .

Doublets in the *Snark*

Little has been said thus far about *The Hunting of the Snark*, except brief comments on the general story. A crew of characters, whose names all begin with "B," search in the land of the Bandersnatch and Jubjub Bird for the frightening Snark. Fit the Eighth, the eighth and last stanza entitled "The Vanishing" is presented below, with the crew finally closing in on the Snark, the Baker vanishing when he finally confronts it.

The Vanishing

They sought it with thimbles, they sought it with care;
  They pursued it with forks and hope;
They threatened its life with a railway-share;
  They charmed it with smiles and soap.

They shuddered to think that the chase might fail,
  And the Beaver, excited at last,
Went bounding along on the tip of its tail,
  For the daylight was nearly past.

"There is Thingumbob shouting!" the Bellman said.
  "He is shouting like mad, only hark!
He is waving his hands, he is wagging his head,
  He has certainly found a Snark!"

They gazed in delight, while the Butcher exclaimed,
  "He was always a desperate wag!"
They beheld him — their Baker — their hero
      unnamed —
  On the top of a neighbouring crag,

Erect and sublime, for one moment of time.
  In the next, that wild figure they saw
(As if stung by a spasm) plunge into a chasm,
  While they waited and listened in awe.

"It's a Snark!" was the sound that first came to their
    ears,
  And seemed almost too good to be true.
Then followed a torrent of laughter and cheers:
  Then the ominous words, "It's a Boo—"

Then, silence. Some fancied they heard in the air
  A weary and wandering sigh
That sounded like "—jum!" but the others declare
  It was only a breeze that went by.

They hunted till darkness came on, but they found
  Not a button, or feather, or mark,
By which they could tell that they stood on the ground
  Where the Baker had met with the Snark.

In the midst of the word he was trying to say,
  In the midst of his laughter and glee,
He had softly and suddenly vanished away —
  For the Snark *was* a Boojum, you see.

Interpretations of this poem range from Greenacre's in which a too-early traumatic witnessing of the primal scene of parental intercourse is unconsciously re-enacted, resulting in the annihilation of the observing child [6]; to Gardner's view that it relates to existential agony and annihilation and his less convincing reference to the modern day existential threat of annihilation by the atomic bomb, which makes it a poem, as it were, for any age. [7] The changing of a few words in this ending, indeed, in the entire poem, by playing the Doublet game provides in ways a summary reinforcement of the primary themes of Dodgson's hidden words, which thus far have been anal erotic in their imagery. I think Gardner is correct but Dodgson defines explicitly the nature of his existential threat.

Beyond noting that the Butcher's description of the Baker "He was always a desperate wag!" re-works in anagrammatic form to "*He saw always a pederast wage!*" (pederast services were sold in Victorian England) readers are asked to re-examine the verses with the following Doublet conversions:

Snark to Prick - (stark, stack, stick slick, slice, slime, clime crime, prime, price)

Chasm to Cheek - (chase, cease, lease, least, beast, blast, blest, bleat, bleak, break, creak, creek)

Crag to Hole - (brag, brat, boat, goat, goad, good, hood, hold)

Bandersnatch to Genderswitch - (bander to gander, snatch to snitch)

Jub Jub to Tum Tum - (tub tub)

Bird to Tree - (bind, bend, tend, teed, feed, fled, flee, free)

Tree to Cock - (as shown above)

It becomes clearly possible (recall Humpty Dumpty's interpretation of "Jabberwocky" after the nonsense words are "defined") that the Prick lives in the land of the Genderswitch and Tum-Tum (Victorian childhood word for *Tummy*) Cock, and the Baker, after standing "erect and sublime", "as if stung by a spasm" (recalling "Poeta Fit. . ."), has the Prick plunged into his Cheeks and Hole and he vanished without a trace. Dodgson's constant fear of annihilation within the sexual imagery is here again acted out by his characters, and becomes far more explicit if his word games are played. (A re-examination of "Jabberwocky," which introduced many of the same words used in the *Snark*, reinforces the masturbatory interpretations of that work).

The Baker is commonly considered to represent Dodgson himself, with one rather explicit clue recognizable to readers already familiar with the family (covered more fully in Chapters 6 and 7). This clue comes from the line "'A dear uncle of mine (after whom I was named). . .'" (from Fit the Third — The Baker's Tale). While it seems more evident that Dodgson was given the name of his father, Charles, and that his middle name, Lutwidge, was derived from his mother's maiden name, Charles Lutwidge was the name of his maternal grandfather, who, due to the first-cousin relationship of his parents, was also his maternal great uncle.

The Bellman is considered by many to be the most serious character in the poem, representing "time" as he tolls his bell at presumably key points in the narrative. There also existed a position at Oxford for a bellman who tolled his bell to warn of the impending death of a member of the community. For those very familiar with the "Snark," the Doublet conversion of *bell* into *sand* makes the *Bellman* and his infernal bell ringing really the *Sandman* lulling us to distraction if not sleep, with *sandman* a valid Victorian allusion.

Doublets in *Sylvie and Bruno*

As our last example of the use of Doublets, we'll examine "The Pig Tale" from *Sylvie and Bruno Concluded*. This poem is filled with three and four letter words, which by substitution create quite different imagery than that presented if Doublet conversions are done. The Doublet conversion is most evident in the title itself as, in addition to *pig* conversions, *tale* is capable of easy conversion to *tail*, a frequently occurring word in Dodgson's works, most likely because *tail* can likewise become *cock*. Is it coincidence that the Latin word *penis* carries two meanings, both "tail," and "the male member?" For brevity in establishing the point, the "Little Bird" sequences intermingled with the poem are excluded:

The Pig Tale

There was a Pig that sat alone
  Beside a ruined Pump:
By day and night he made his moan —
It would have stirred a heart of stone
To see him wring his hoofs and groan,
  Because he could not jump.

A certain Camel heard him shout —
  A Camel with a hump.
"Oh, is it Grief, or is it Gout?
What is this bellowing about?"
That Pig replied, with quivering snout,
  "Because I cannot jump!"

That Camel scanned him, dreamy-eyed.
  "Methinks you are too plump.
I never knew a Pig so wide —
That wobbled so from side to side —
Who could, however much he tried,
  Do such a thing as *jump*!

Yet mark those trees, two miles away,
  All clustered in a clump:
If you could trot there twice a day,
Nor ever pause for rest or play,

In the far future — Who can say? —
 You may be fit to jump."

That Camel passed, and left him there,
 Beside the ruined Pump.
Oh, horrid was that Pig's despair!
His shrieks of anguish filled the air.
He wrung his hoofs, he rent his hair,
 Because he could not jump.

There was a Frog that wandered by —
 A sleek and shining lump:
Inspected him with fishy eye,
And said, "O Pig, what makes you cry?"
And bitter was that Pig's reply,
 "Because I cannot jump!"

That Frog he grinned a grin of glee,
 And hit his chest a thump.
"O Pig," he said, "be ruled by me,
And you shall see what you shall see.
This minute, for a trifling fee,
 I'll teach you how to jump!

"You may be faint from many a fall,
 And bruised by many a bump:
But, if you persevere through all,
And practice first on something small,
Concluding with a ten-foot wall,
 You'll find that you *can* jump!"

That Pig looked up with joyful start:
 "O Frog, you *are* a trump!
Your words have healed my inward smart —
Come, name your fee and do your part:
Bring comfort to a broken heart,
 By teaching me to jump!"

"My fee shall be a mutton-chop,
 My goal this ruined Pump.
Observe with what an airy flop
I plant myself upon the top!

Now bend your knees and take a hop,
  For that's the way to jump!"

Uprose that Pig, and rushed, full whack,
  Against the ruined Pump:
Rolled over like an empty sack,
And settled down upon his back,
While all his bones at once went "Crack!"
  It was a fatal jump.

. . . That Camel passed, as Day grew dim
  Around that ruined Pump.
"O broken heart! O broken limb!
It needs," that Camel said to him,
"Something more fairy-like and slim,
  To execute a jump!"

That Pig lay still as any stone,
  And could not stir a stump:
Nor ever, if the truth were known,
Was he again observed to moan,
Nor ever wring his hoofs and groan,
  Because he could not jump.

That Frog made no remark, for he
  Was dismal as a dump:
He knew the consequence must be
That he would never get his fee —
And still he sits, in miserie,
  Upon that ruined Pump!

Word substitutions for Pig, Pump (hump, once a fashionable word for copulation according to the *1811 Slang Dictionary*, if a verb, convertible to cock if a noun), Frog (pimp), trump (tramp), jump (hump also when desired), an examination of Dodgson's lifelong bout with grief and, in his later years, gout, the twice a day walking visits to the clustered trees, which we have already seen has special meaning, and the Frog's fee of a mutton-chop, as an aphrodisiac, all allow for an interpretation which conforms to the more prurient imagery already uncovered. Of course, any of these words can be converted to any words within any thematic construction the reader wishes, which is exactly the point of the exercise; Dodgson is telling us that words mean anything, or nothing.

In Dodgson's Introduction to his serious and probably best work, *Symbolic Logic*, he writes:

> ... I maintain that any writer of a book is fully authorised in attaching any meaning he likes to any word or phrase he intends to use. If I find an author saying, at the beginning of his book, `Let it be understood that by the word `black´ I shall always mean `white,´ and that by the word `white´ I shall always mean `black,´ I meekly accept his ruling, however injudicious I may think it.

In *Through the Looking-Glass*, Humpty Dumpty states the concept with a little more invective. We can recall that it was Humpty Dumpty who fell to pieces and disintegrated with neither all the Kings horses nor all the Kings men able to re-assemble him.

> `When I use a word,´ Humpty Dumpty said, in rather a scornful tone, `it means just what I choose it to mean — neither more nor less.´
> `The question is,´ said Alice, `whether you *can* make words mean so many different things.´
> `The question is,´ said Humpty Dumpty, `which is to be master — that's all.´

Dodgson's diary entry of May 11, 1885, notes that he had brought his list of seven letter words capable of Doublet conversion to over five hundred. [8]

Before concluding this chapter and with it Part II of this work, a curious incident that is reflected in Dodgson's diary entry for November 8, 1872, and appears in Collingwood is worth recording. After describing that most of Dodgson's ideas were ingenious, though many were entirely useless from a practical point of view, Collingwood quotes the passage:

> I wrote to Calverly, suggesting an idea (which I think occurred to me yesterday) of guessing well-known poems as acrostics, and making a collection of them to hoax the public. [9]

Roger Green noted that the entry was really made on December 26, 1872, as Dodgson often made entries for several weeks on one day and that "yesterday" would have been December 25 rather than November 7. While Green describes Dodgson as appearing to be "living backwards," [10] I believe the mistake in dates may have been evidence of a "Freudian slip," the emergence, due to anxiety, of unacknowledged and unconscious feelings which intrude and upset the smooth assembly of thought and speech and that reveal the presence of inner anxiety by causing the opposite of what is wished to be revealed to be said. Was the suggestion that Dodgson's own works might become the subject of detailed examination by players of word games momentarily too much for him? Charles Calverly, a peer and competitor in parody and word games, responded with the following letter:

> MY DEAR SIR, — I have been laid up (or laid down) for the last few days by acute lumbago, or I would have written before. It is rather absurd that I was on the point of propounding to you this identical idea. I realised, and I regret to add revealed to two girls, a fortnight ago, the truth that all existing poems were in fact acrostics; and I offered a small pecuniary reward to whichever would find out Gray's `Elegy´ within half an hour! But it never occurred to me to utilise the discovery, as it did to you. I see that it might be utilised, now you mention it — and I shall instruct these two young women not to publish the notion among their friends. [11]

Translations

A comment should be made regarding the numerous translations of Dodgson's nonsense works that were begun during his lifetime. The popularity of *Alice's Adventure in Wonderland* had reached such proportions in England that Dodgson himself studied French so that he could participate in the translation of the work. This was to be the first of many translations — into virtually all the world's major languages (with enormous difficulties encountered attempting "Jabberwocky"). How he must have been amused (or relieved) to see the anagrams and Doublets disappear, leaving just the nonsense literature.

Conclusion

Dodgson ends *Sylvie and Bruno Concluded*, his final work, with a scene which involves Eric Lindon, the avowed libertine struggling with the Christian message. Lindon (also considered a fictional "self" character) has just witnessed the power of Lady Muriel's prayer which has brought his friend Arthur Forrester out of the clutches of death. Though Eric acknowledges his own inability to accept Christian belief, he says in a broken voice: ". . . *there is a God that answers prayer!* I know it for certain now" [Carroll's italics]. The next task before us is that of re-assembling the reality of Dodgson's life and interpreting the meaning of the many religious themes on which he also wrote. As if to confound us he leaves us with at least two anagrams. Does he leave us with "*Gays, pederast warriors hate, then!*" which may be his final conclusion that rage is the cause of his behavior (a return to the "family threat" theme). Or is it a still veiled expression of hope for more aggressive assertiveness on the part of the homosexual community for acceptance which reads: "*The gay pederast warriors hasten!*" Either would allow for the response: "I know it for certain now."

As has been alluded to, the attempts of critics and biographers to analyze the life of Charles Dodgson have drawn increasingly on the characters and events within his works as representative of aspects of his character: the White Knight from *Through the Looking-Glass*, the White Rabbit from *Alice's Adventures in Wonderland*, Alice herself in both works, the Baker in the *Snark*, or Eric Lindon, the professor, as well as Bruno in the *Sylvie and Bruno* volumes. Likewise, writers have drawn inferences regarding the character of his father and mother from the generally weak male and dominant female figures in the works. This is a common practice in the appraisals of written works, fiction or not, which represent self expression of one's own experiences or impressions, whether real or imagined. These themes reflect beliefs, firmly held or casually explored. Therefore, they provide clues to the inner feelings and attitudes of the writer. Throughout the interpretive portions of this work, I will follow this practice, but for a reason somewhat different, and in ways more compelling than others have attempted to justify. I believe the material already presented, and that to come reflect the extremely fragile nature of Dodgson's psychological state. This inner world of his was almost entirely focused on himself and his relationships with family, child friends, and Oxford friends as the basis for psychic survival. Due to that fragility, I believe that all his nonsense works are intentionally and essentially autobiographical, constructed to be so by a man intent on and obsessed with telling his story, clearly by allusion, and coded in his anagrams. Other allusions written into the works represent an attempt to confuse and confound readers and critics with a web of seeming familiarity and meaning. But perhaps those from whom he felt most compelled to hide the truth as he saw it yet wanted to tell it, even if for its shock value, were his own surviving family members. Feeling he had no other alternative, he lived a Jekyll/Hyde existence, transferring fluidly from one to the other, but, unlike Dr. Jekyll, able to keep his Hyde from public awareness, even cheating death.

While *Sylvie and Bruno* closes with the impassioned plea "Look Eastward! Aye, look Eastward!" ("*Take low roads! Aye, take low roads!*"), we shall close this section by returning to the dedicatory acrostic poem which opened Chapter 1: "Is all our Life, then, but a dream. . . ." which displays the melancholy, and regret of a life coming to an end. This time, in an anagrammatic reconstruction of the original lines (I have chosen from several alternatives), we also see reflected a life filled with pain, hiding, loathing, targeted and untargeted rage, and hypocrisy lived and attacked, all finally coming to an end.

Mother abused all; life in a rut. [12]
Gay male don then felt glee in sin.
Mad, I thwart, resist tasteless remarks.

We were both bitter with death, too.
O, he, I arrange, show smut galore.
I duly dote, flatter, frown.

He will stand many a tested penis.
Don's friend not a remedy in storm.
To the silenced men. . . talent gone.

PART III

LIFE AND DEATH OF CHARLES DODGSON

CHAPTER 6

ENVIRONMENT AND EARLY YEARS

In Part III we explore many aspects of the life of Charles Dodgson with facts drawn from the several published biographies, analyses done by others as well as my own, and from his own writings — diaries, letters, poems and fiction. Only certain aspects of his life will be discussed, with a particular focus on his childhood. For it was during this period that the foundations were laid for the extreme distortions which produced a lifetime of revenge and its mode of expression. The full details of Dodgson's life have been well covered by others, especially Anne Clark. I will not duplicate that effort, for the details are of interest only as they fit within the broad themes we are exploring.

The areas of his life which are of particular interest for this work include his childhood at Daresbury and Croft, the family and Victorian culture in which he was reared, the character of his parents, his schooling, the nature of his emergent adult character and personality, the extent to which his health reflected his inner turmoil, child and adult relationships, hobbies, and finally, his struggles with religion and death. In short, the focus is on the extent to which Dodgson struggled to maintain psychological integrity and the experiences which led to the behaviors he found so necessary in that struggle.

Family and Cultural Roots

Charles Lutwidge Dodgson was born on January 27, 1832, in the family home in Daresbury, England. He was the third child and first son in a family of eleven children born over a seventeen year period. All the children survived, a rarity in Victorian England. [1] The names and nicknames Dodgson's siblings and his age at their birth are presented on the facing page. His maternal grandmother Elizabeth and paternal grandfather Charles were brother and sister, which made his parents Charles Dodgson and Frances Jane Lutwidge first cousins. Reflective of the family closeness Dodgson's mother married a cousin with the same name as her own father; they named their first daughter Frances Jane after Mrs. Dodgson; daughter Frances was called "Fanny" within the family, as was Mrs. Dodgson by at least Aunt Mary Smedley. [2] Their second daughter Elizabeth was named after the maternal grandmother. As already indicated, the name *Charles Lutwidge* could be construed as drawn from his maternal grandfather (and great uncle) or from his father's first and his mother's maiden name; nothing is known regarding the parental motivations in the choice. The two daughters born after Charles were given name variants of Charles — Caroline and Charlotte — although the latter name was also the name of the street on which his mother lived and in which house (whose address was Number One) she was married. [3]

On his father's side, in five generations, from his great-great-grandfather to his father, only his grandfather was not a churchman, having chosen a military career instead. [4] All of them were named Charles. While the heritage of naming children after family members reflects an effort to honor the memory of ancestors, it also presents to the child powerful suggestions of expectations for the modeling of behavior and achievement on the part of the parents, suggestions which can become or be perceived as subtle coercion totally contrary to the emerging adult's temperament and emotional and intellectual capabilities. The pattern of family closeness was repeated by the senior Dodgson's brother Hassard, who likewise married a cousin, and raised a large family of ten children.

In order to emphasize the tone of internal family communications I shall now revert to using the family nicknames when writing of the children. By Charlie's third birthday, two sisters had been added to the family, Caroline when he was a year old, Mary when he was three. These additions certainly increased the demands on his mother's attention and increased significantly the influence of the quantity and quality of her time spent with him. With such closely spaced siblings the process of parental abandonment can begin long before the child is able to soothe himself in the face of very normal frustrations, especially so if there has been undue attachment in the relationship to that point. Feelings of emptiness emerge with no outlet or resolution, accompanied by frustrating efforts to regain the lost attention by distorting the self to ways which seem to regain the notice

The Dodgson Children

(with nicknames and deviation from Charles' age)

Frances Jane (-4) - "Fanny" - same name and nickname as her mother.

Elizabeth Lucy (-2) - "Memy," later "Lizzie"

Charles Lutwidge - "Charlie"

Caroline Hume (+1)

Mary Charlotte (+3) - married Charles Collingwood, parents of biographer Stuart Dodgson Collingwood.

Skeffington Hume (+4) - "Skeff" - married, cleric in the model of his father.

Wilfred Longley (+6) - married, pursued career in commerce.

Louisa Fletcher (+8)

Margaret Anna Ashley (+9)

Henrietta Harrington (+11)

Edwin Heron (+14) - only child born at Croft rather than Daresbury, became a missionary.

of the lost parent. The "gift" so nicely described by Alice Miller in her *The Drama of the Gifted Child* begins to develop, as do the seeds for rage. [5]

Fanny would have been about five to eight during this period, with Memy three to six, both most likely providing much company for Charlie during the key development ages of one to four. Given the Victorian practice of training girls to be mothers or governesses, it is likely that sister Fanny was somewhat parentified and represented a surrogate mother for Charlie. The extent to which she may have modeled after Mama is not known, but it is highly likely. During Charlie's fifth year, a brother Skeff was born, presenting for the first time a male sibling to compete for his mother's attention.

Three boys later became clergyman, though Charles did not take final orders. Only one of the seven sisters ever married. Mary Charlotte chose a man with the same first name as her father, Charles Collingwood, a clergyman whose son Stuart Dodgson would become the family's choice to write the biography of Lewis Carroll within one year following his death. Of the four brothers, only Skeffington and Wilfred married. Edwin, five years old when his mother died, was the only child to leave the proximity of the family as an adult, when he became a missionary in Zanzibar. None of those who married did so prior to the death of both mother and father, putting the earliest age at marriage in the mid-thirties. All of the six unmarried sisters lived together in "The Chestnuts," the family home acquired after their father's death in 1868. Charles was the only one of the children to achieve any public recognition or distinction, and that through his nonsense fiction rather than scholastic achievements or academic contributions within the Oxford community. Except for Charles, all survived into the 20th Century, with Louise the last to die in 1930. [6] The family did not allow Green to publish the concerns Dodgson recorded in his diary in his late twenties that some of his sisters appeared to be shrinking into a kind of dwarfism, a process he also noted later when it appeared to stop. This is clear evidence that he was observant of the potential impact of his parents' consanguinity on his own life and will shortly support the notion that he viewed himself as somewhat of a freak.

It is clear that the ties that bind a family together were extremely strong within the Dodgson family. It is difficult to speculate on the bases for the apparent fusion between the Dodgson women after their parents' deaths, but by choice or chance they lived lives which depended on the close presence of one another for mutual support. In retrospective comments by later family members they have been referred to as an eccentric family. What is evident is that neither the experience of their own childhood nor their perception of the parental experience in a large and what is oft-presented happy family provided an example which the children chose to attempt to replicate in their adult lives. For those who did leave the family, the extent to which career and marriage choices represented safe patterned responses or truly independent choices is not known.

Within the parents' marriage there are several aspects of the Victorian family experience worthy of elaboration. The first is the extent to which parents of the time produced large families within a society which professed such avowed restrictions on all manifestations of sexual expression both within and without marriage. Janice Delaney, et al., provide much insight into the historical evolution of attitudes toward women and menses in their 1988 work *The Curse*. While by any current measurement such parents producing large families would most likely be considered "sexually active," the underlying knowledge level regarding menstruation, pregnancy and birth may very well have both limited sexual activity and led to the production of large families. Following very much the thinking of Aristotle (certainly no stranger to Mr. Dodgson, who was both a Latin and Greek scholar) and supported in the Christian tradition, the position of women in procreation was decidedly secondary. It was the male who contributed the soul which made man "human" and the woman produced the menses, nutrients for the body. Everything associated with menses was considered dirty and a source of venereal disease. (This preoccupation even appeared in the pornography, which also clearly assigned a single role to women — as objects for male sexual enjoyment.) In addition to this attitude, there was the belief that both the loss of semen and menses were seen as a depletion of vital bodily fluids having limited lifetime supplies; intercourse during menstruation was seen as providing a rejuvenating source of such fluids which benefitted the woman at the man's expense, and was therefore to be avoided. Consequently, both the experiencing of menstruation with all of its associated meanings and the pleasures-to-be denied in sexual intercourse could be best and safely avoided by pregnancy, a state which was believed to inhibit both activities for its duration. [7] These educated parents were doubtlessly aware of this "state of knowledge," which, combined with post-Puritanical moral strictures relating to sexual enjoyment, led them to present exemplary lives to their parishioners and neighbors by any contemporary standards.

The Victorian attitudes toward children and child-rearing also deserve comment. In a change from the 18th Century, the concept of a childhood-to-be-experienced had virtually disappeared, with children expected to assume adult behavior and attitudes promptly. The will of the child was to be "broken" early, to end his "obstinacy" and bring him quickly into conformity with adult behavior and expectations. [8] They were unprotected by minimum wage and hour laws until well after adults had gained them, with hard physical work seen as not only character-building but a fair use of children in an emerging industrial society. Children were depicted dressed or costumed as adults in Victorian art. That the mentally ill were given the status of children reflects a depreciation of the concept of childhood as something to be savored during its appropriate time, and suggests the need to hasten the growing-up process. Children were left unprotected from prisons and workhouses by the court system, with youngsters in their teens sometimes hanged for petty crimes. [9] The emergence of the industrial society with its attendant need for cheap labor from the poor and the redefinition of the needs to "achieve" for the middle and upper classes reinforced, if they did not cause, this perceived need to hurry the child to adulthood.

Victorian educators were moving from harsh discipline as the learning motivator; but they still believed "that the child could be molded into the desirable form by untiring direct pressure" with no more real sensitivity to the needs of the individual child than the whippings had provided. [10] Founded on religious grounds, the Church of their time and Charles' parents believed that children arrived in a state of Original Sin, a concept their son would question later, rather than Original Goodness and were therefore "beasts to be tamed", formed into the approved Christian and societal molds. The strategy for creating a loving, molded adult-child called for persistent exposure to and teaching of Christian principles, very often in practice a strategy of *teaching* love, which as Miller has pointed out, is not the way love is taught, for one reason because such teaching is often done within a modelling situation filled with hypocrisy.

The relationship of sons to their fathers in 18th Century England is very pertinent to understanding the life of Charles Dodgson due to the close family tradition from which his father emerged. Howard Wolf writes of the submissiveness of sons to the will of their fathers, who were seen as nearly God-like in their authority, sternness, and omnipotence. [11] While this view later became more generalized by being applied to mothers as well as fathers, it was known as psychological castration; [12] the child was never allowed to see the father's limitations; the father should "pretend to divine authority." The Victorian age saw an effort by sons to revolt against this positional relationship. John Stuart Mill was such a child, who as an adult could never recall his *not* knowing Greek, and blamed his father for not insuring as part of his upbringing that he would grow up with feelings. Mill's legacy includes, among many other things and very much a part of Western tradition, writings on liberty, the sources of which derived from his own personal quest.

Edmund Gosse (1849-1928), a British writer and translator of foreign fiction, may be best known for his self-liberating autobiography *Father and Son* in which he described his own struggles to overcome an over-controlling father. As a homosexual adult he could not recall a time when he did not understand that he would become a member of the clergy, following his father. Under such control, he escaped into fantasy and felt empty inside as he could not envision self-achievement given what he perceived to be a God-like idealized parent as his model. Supported by his mother's collusion, he was not allowed to see the humanness of his father, which created disillusionment when he finally did. This was followed by his successful revolt as he defined himself differently from his father's expectations which had also been supported by his mother. Such fathers did not allow their sons to experience an essential development task, that of merging with an idealized model, seen as having achievable qualities, but rather kept them in an inferior position. Thus the child was unable to establish a sense of achievable goals and values for himself, based on a model of openness which allowed the child to challenge the authority and adapt the parents' values to meet his own needs.

The position of women in Victorian society had already emerged by the time of the marriage of Mr. and Mrs. Dodgson. This position tended to place proper Victorian women on pedestals and make them virtually objects to be served and adored, with the woman herself prohibited by her culture from joining the struggles of life. Education for women, including the Dodgson daughters, was in the arts as preparation for making a good marital match and providing cultural exposure for children. Child-rearing and home management became the focus of feminine activities. These tasks were often accomplished with the assistance of nurses and governesses, if affordable, in order to provide burden relief and protect time needed for pedestal maintenance. In addition these practices provided, as it were, a display setting for the successful provider and husband. While this attitude is viewed today as demeaning of women, and certainly represents an inhibiting factor in the development of a true self for women, its cultural institutionalization created the potential for extreme entitlement distortions in women as their own grandiosity was inappropriately affirmed and as they mirrored themselves competitively against peers.

Entitlement is an attitudinal position regarding expectations about how one should be treated and perceived by others. It results from excessive mirroring (a confirming reflection) that continues either well beyond the appropriate development stage or reflects acceptance of only portions of the child's total self. In combination with really outreaching energy and "goodness" qualities, limited by societal restrictions (or personal inhibitions) on outward expression beyond the home and family, entitlement forms the seeds for well-meaning, unintentionally coercive, over-control and over-involvement in parenting, i. e., the potential for the "castrating" mother as well as wife to develop. Florence Nightingale represents a Victorian woman able to overcome societal restrictions regarding involvement outside the home. She turned her caretaking energies well beyond the constrictions of family to help in the Crimean War effort, becoming a legendary model of nursing and giving it a respectability not enjoyed in Victorian England, where nurses were viewed as "loose women." Dodgson wrote a poem in her honor entitled "The Path of Roses" in 1856. While at times the tone is maudlin, the recurring theme of his own wish to make a noticeable contribution of service can be seen, a theme always filled with regrets for his own lack of commitment. All of the signs of a product of entitlement, high expectations and recognition frustrated by the depleted self unable to make a commitment are evident in his references.

If there was a treasured personality characteristic during the Victorian period it was that of self-control, more correctly emotional control to the point of constriction. Psychological studies often refer to it as the Age of Anality, drawing on conclusions made by a man of that age, Sigmund Freud. He postulated the notion that the first significant childhood "willful" act of self control occurs over an issue of internal body function, that of bowel control, where conflict and outcome leave a developmental imprint which is then reflected in more or less severe emotional constriction. This attitudinal rigidity or obstinacy is then reflected in behaviors which bring about excessive control of self or others, or reflect degrees of greed, the pursuit of acquiring, possessing, and retaining "things" as the learned primary goal of self-achievement. This acquisitiveness was and is today commonly considered a successful and desired sublimation (turning a negative trait into a positive practice) in the then emerging and now current system of economic capitalism, which rewards acquiring and "having" at the expense of giving and sharing.

These then are the salient family and cultural conditions in which the Dodgson couple married and began the process of career pursuit and the building of a family. Intergenerational ties within the family structure were extremely strong. Religious beliefs were also strong and the pursuit of the clerical life of service was a deep-rooted family tradition. Victorian attitudes toward children encouraged forceful parenting and schooling, and were reinforced by the placement of Victorian women, including those women with high energy levels, in powerless, somewhat ornamental roles. It was a time in England's history when war was remote for most men, the Queen was good, and "English superiority seemed right and safe." [13]

From Daresbury to Croft

Biographers, particularly Anne Clark (1979) have written in some detail on the life of the Dodgson family at Daresbury, but, uncharacteristically for Victorian biography, Stuart Collingwood (1898) provides us with important insights. Prior to the arrival of the first child in 1828 Mr. Dodgson had been given a permanent assignment to the Daresbury parish, which provided him with a very small stipend along with a glebe farm on which he could live and augment his family and financial needs by growing and selling crops or leasing the farmland. The church used for services was located one and a half miles from the farm home, a trip which was made twice each Sunday by the entire family and household staff. He took a particular interest in establishing a ministry which addressed the religious needs of the partly transient population of boatmen and their families who worked the canal barges that passed through Daresbury, using a converted barge which a local benefactor provided as a chapel. The country village, still very much the same today as it was then, is very rural, covered with meadows and surrounded by flower-covered hedgerows. [14]   The farmhouse was more than adequate at the beginning for the growing family with ". . . seven bedrooms, two sitting rooms, two kitchens and a study [and] a schoolroom. . . ." [15] The farmland was adequate to raise livestock. In addition there was ". . . agricultural land stretching away as far as the eye could see. . . ." [16] Given its size, it was quite remote from traffic, with the appearance of any vehicle on the road considered an event worthy of the children's attention. With the approval of the Dodgson children who lived there, Collingwood described it as being in "complete seclusion from the world," [17] presenting, therefore an environment which provided feelings of complete security, with all knowledge of the outside world derived from books and learning, but not experience. Except for his friend Thomas Vere Bayne, whom he saw at church on Sunday, and occasional trips to visit relatives, Charlie's childhood was spent within the family unit of parents, siblings, and those hired to help with child-care and the demands of the farm. Typical of farm life, the workday started early and ended late at night except in winter, and was a hard life. [18] While hard work was seen as good for children at the time, with the Dodgson parents present to observe, there is no reason to believe that they were abused by hired staff.

All of the Dodgson children suffered from stammering, which most of them experienced throughout their adult lives. The meaning and etiology of stammering is covered later during discussion of Dodgson's health in order to develop its adult ramifications. But it appears highly likely that there was considerable "baby talk" in the household with perhaps a rather sudden demand for more mature speech once formal education began.

A letter written by Charlie to his nurse "Bun" at about age 5, his hand most likely guided by an adult, reflects word spelling which replicates "baby-talk" pronunciations. It contains words such as *kitt*, *twite*, *betause*, and *tan't* for *kiss*, *quite*, *because*, and *can't* respectively. [19] This letter reflects that the Dodgson household did have a nurse and that the five year old had an affectionate relationship with her. It also reflects someone's efforts to create a letter which would simulate the conversational style of the young boy for the benefit of the recipient, who was also sent a lock of hair from Charlie's head as a reminder of his presence. Later as an adult he would maintain the same practice with his child friends, requesting and receiving a lock of their hair. I believe it quite likely, as many do, that Bruno's baby-talk in the *Sylvie* books, found aggravating and unnecessary by most critics, is reflective of Dodgson's early speech experiences as he depicts Bruno as the ideally cute, albeit mischievous, self. Sylvie's reaction is always coquettishly accepting of it as cute. Within a family with many small children, it would not be difficult to imagine the lengthy presence of baby-talk, nor the influence of Fanny as she tried to or was assigned the task of being his mother-surrogate in fact as well as name. This would be an even bigger problem if the younger Memy tried to mother her younger siblings. And, as Greenacre notes [20], Fanny had the same age differential to Charlie as Sylvie does with Bruno, with Sylvie's behavior much as one would expect from an older, somewhat parentified sister, who in the story supervised Bruno's "lessons." There has been considerable discussion over the years in an effort to explain the many left-handed reversals in Dodgson's works. Of particular interest is whether his parents coerced him to right-handedness, a practice considered desirable at the time, and long thought to be a significant contributing cause of stammering. No evidence appears available to support such a hypothesis, although the left-foot shoe found beneath the floorboards at Croft has been considered by some a clue. If it *were* done, the damage to the self from such an unempathic rejection of the child as he is would have been devastating, as its accomplishment would most likely have involved punishments more than rewards as well as physical violation of body space and integrity.

Formal education began very early for the Dodgson children, conducted in the home for all of the girls, and until about age 11 for the boys, at which time they were sent off to public school. An undated letter from Mama to Charlie when he was still a young boy, which he treasured and warned others away from with the note that it was "covered with slimy pitch," [21] reflects that he was already studying Latin and Greek. Later writings reflect in retrospect the extent to which he viewed such heavy doses of lessons as a burdensome intrusion on childhood. Papa provided most of the tutoring, eventually expanding his teaching duties by taking in paid students to augment his income; Mama and the older children assisted in the teaching. The extent to which his father shared teaching duties with his wife by laying out lessons and having them supervised by her or one of the staff is not known. It certainly is possible, with firm discipline the ingredient which would prevent either parent from neglecting other essential duties. Before her death, Mrs. Dodgson did remark to her sister Mary that the taking in of additional students was her worst memory of the Daresbury days.

In an often quoted passage reflecting Charlie's early academic interests Collingwood writes:

> ... One day, when Charles was a very small boy, he came up to his father and showed him a book of logarithms, with the request, `Please explain.´ Mr. Dodgson told him that he was much too young to understand anything about such a difficult subject. The child listened to what his father said, and appeared to think it irrelevant, for he still insisted, `But, please, explain!´ [22]

It is interesting to note the details that children remember long into their adult lives, most likely from the impressions left by the experience; this is the one remembered by the Dodgson children for inclusion in the biography of their brother. This incident could easily represent the efforts of a youngster to engage his revered father's attention on a subject and time of *his* choosing, or just to engage him at all. Papa's response has all the characteristics of a dismissal of the boy, perhaps due to his being too busy with other things, perhaps a common experience with the other children, which helped keep it in their memories. This incident is reminiscent of the lines from "Poeta Fit. . .": "Then tell me how! Don't put me off / With your `another time´!" It would appear that Charlie found something else to occupy his mind when his interests were ignored.

The Mock Turtle's Story quoted below from *Alice's Adventures in Wonderland* provides insights into Charlie's deep feelings about his lessons, no doubt also parodying the common Victorian experience. Dodgson describes the Mock Turtle as being taught by the Tortoise ("because he taught us") such regular subjects as:

> . . . the different branches of Arithmetic — Ambition, Distraction, Uglification and Derision. . . Mystery, ancient and modern, with Seaography. . . then Drawling, Stretching, and Fainting in Coils. . . . [The Classical master] was an old crab. . . . He taught Laughing and Grief.

Clark provides insights into the kinds of books read by and to the children in the parents' efforts ". . . to foster such virtues as honesty, hard work, obedience, and contentment with small means." [23] Their themes were typically Victorian with good rewarded, evil punished, usually by the timely arrival of a powerful symbol of righteousness. One of them, *The Cheapside Apprentice*, is of particular interest. It reinforced the evils of the theatre as a place frequented by loose, wretched women. The young man in the story, so tempted, begets a child, loses all his money, and turns to robbery. Convicted and about to hang for his crimes he repents with these prayerful sentiments:

> `. . . Condemned to die by human laws,
> I own my sentence just,
> With mercy mild judge thou my cause,
> Who art my only trust.´ [24]

The moral here is clear, i. e., acceptance of a just human punishment following a crime committed, with a prayer for Divine forgiveness based on the individual circumstances involved. In the world of Wonderland, however, Dodgson reverses the sequence, with Alice challenging the Queen of Hearts, who insists on the "Sentence first — verdict afterwards!" The story ends with neither verdict nor sentence, indeed, not even the crime is clear, as Alice awakens and flings the playing-card characters in the final climactic scene. These themes re-emerge as Dodgson sought the reasons in justice for his suffering and again in his struggle with the concept of Eternal Punishment.

Collingwood provides several brief glimpses into Charlie's play life while at Daresbury. He frequently entertained his younger siblings dressed in a home-made magician's costume as he performed magic tricks, or played the puppeteer, complete with hand-made puppets, costumes, stage, and his own scripts. He carved a miniature tool kit about an inch long for one of his sisters. Of more significance are two other games. In one he made miniature instruments of battle for earthworms should they ever want them. While always presented as an idyllic fantasy game, I find it difficult to believe that rage was not being manifested quite early as, with little outlet for the expression of aggression, he most likely directed mock battles, where, in some way there were winners and losers, with all the accompanying injuries to the combatants from the battle instruments. The torturing of animals by children was always seen as a proof positive of their innate wickedness, with its view as a manifestation of frustration and powerlessness in the face of pressure from above never explored. [25]

A game in which even less speculation is required, again invariably described as idyllic in biographies, was the "train" Charlie operated around the garden after the family moved to Croft (at age 11) for the amusement of his brothers and sisters. Consisting of a wheelbarrow and other "vehicles" he called it the "Love" train, for which he had a complete set of schedules, fares, and rules for use. One of these rules directed any passengers feeling upset to lie down until they had been run over three times by the "Love" train, after which they would be entitled to medical assistance. [26] This seems as clear an indication as a precocious child could make that he viewed intrusively applied love to be as damaging to the spirit in its own forceful way as being run over by the train would be to the body.

Mr. Dodgson's transfer from Daresbury, where the family lived under severe financial constraints, to Croft provided significant benefits for the family, including a vastly improved stipend which significantly augmented the income derived from the production of livestock, gardens and from letting space on the glebe farm, also part of the Croft estate. With the parish church now next door, though well hidden in vegetation, the accommodations for the family were luxurious, including servants quarters, two living rooms, libraries and kitchens, and bedrooms for everyone, though most of the children chose to share the latter. While there was a school-room within the house and despite there being no need for extra income, Mr. Dodgson built a 15,000 square foot school building to provide school facilities for the community. He devoted the school to training children in

Christian principles under his direction and the primary subjects of reading, writing, and arithmetic, with needlework added for girls. Mrs. Dodgson's favorite activity was the cultivation of the flower gardens. She often sent flowers to her father and sisters, keeping records of what she sent "in order to avoid duplication." [27] As an adult Dodgson emulated his mother as he performed the same record-keeping for the same reasons regarding dinner invitations in his quarters at Oxford, both as to menu and seating arrangements.

While his mother lived only another eight years, dying when Dodgson was nineteen and just having entered Oxford, the remaining family would live there for twenty-five years, until their father's death in 1868. Life for Charles turned to formal schooling and began at the nearby boarding school at Richmond starting the next year. Family activities were now highlighted by the production of family literary "publications."

Before turning to a more detailed examination of his parents, it is worth turning to portions of his works to draw inferences on what this period of his life meant to him. The findings are clearly mixed. In *Useful and Instructive Poetry*, a collection of poems written at about age fourteen, we are provided a sense of how things were viewed and felt by the young adolescent. "My Fairy" (1845), as already noted, suggests an outside controlling force which discouraged all feeling — sleeping, weeping, laughing, biting, fighting. The writer pleads finally for what *can* be done, with the fairy responding that he should not ask. Dodgson's moral for the poem is "You mustn't." [28] "Punctuality" describes the need for promptness and strict scheduling of time, with the moral suggesting that the standard applies even to the cutting of a flower. As an adult Dodgson was a prodigious worker, even commenting in his diary on ways to save thirty minute periods that might otherwise be lost. Out of parental awareness, then presence, his rebellion occurred in the ways he spent those active times. "Charity" describes a boy losing his watch to the pick-pocketing of a poor, starving, young girl who stops him, begging for food; the moral suggests that one be always on the alert, an attitude which reflects an emerging cynical caution toward the poor. As an adult, Dodgson was able to respond to individuals in need as his father had, but, like many Victorians, was oblivious to the poor masses, if not in their existence, in terms of doing anything. "Rules and Regulations," with the moral "Behave," in addition to describing the various kinds of activities which will "avoid dejection," [29] lists instructions regarding all sorts of behavior, including stammering (two references), writing, singing, rising, smiling, eating and drinking, money management, closing doors, swimming (prohibited until learned!), care of buttons, closing doors, sitting at the table, and numerous others, many humorous to an adult, not so numerous to a child. While he may have been exaggerating his own experience, and even more so if he was, bitterness lies behind his fourteen-year-old parody. The attitude which produced this poem clearly reflects feelings toward over-involvement and intrusive external control, a sacrificing of self in favor of parental wishes.

By the age of twenty-one, his view of this childhood world had changed, and it was now becoming a world to which he longed to return. The idyllic view which Miller writes of as invariably accompanying the depleted self found in an adulthood "filled" with emptiness had emerged. Published after his death in *Three Sunsets and Other Poems*, is the poem:

Solitude

I love the stillness of the wood:
  I love the music of the rill:
I love to couch in pensive mood
  Upon some silent hill.

Scarce heard, beneath yon arching trees,
  The silver-crested ripples pass;
And, like a mimic brook, the breeze
  Whispers among the grass.

Here from the world I win release,
  Nor scorn of men, nor footstep rude,
Break in to mar the holy peace
  Of this great solitude.

Here may the silent tears I weep
  Lull the vexed spirit into rest,
As infants sob themselves to sleep
  Upon a mother's breast.

But when the bitter hour is gone,
  And the keen throbbing pangs are still,
Oh, sweetest then to couch alone
  Upon some silent hill!

To live in joys that once have been,
  To put the cold world out of sight,

And deck life's drear and barren scent
  With hues of rainbow-light.

For what to man the gift of breath,
  If sorrow be his lot below;
If all the day that ends in death
  Be dark with clouds of woe?

Shall the poor transport of an hour
  Repay long years of sore distress —
The fragrance of a lonely flower
Make glad the wilderness?

Ye golden hours of Life's young spring
  Of innocence, of love and truth!
Bright, beyond all imagining,
  Thou fairy-dream of youth!

I'd give all wealth that years have piled,
  The slow result of Life's decay,
To be once more a little child
  For one bright summer-day.

"Long years of sore distress" are the sentiments expressed at age twenty-one. At age twenty-eight, he wrote "Faces in the Fire", which was published among the serious poems in *Phantasmagoria. . . .* It reflects a young man longing for the past and filled with dread of the present:

Faces in the Fire

The night creeps onward, sad and slow:
In these red embers' dying glow
The forms of Fancy come and go.

An island-farm — broad seas of corn
Stirred by the wandering breath of morn —
The happy spot where I was born.

The picture fadeth in its place:
Amid the glow I seem to trace
The shifting semblance of a face.

'Tis now a little childish form—
Red lips for kisses pouted warm—
And elf-locks tangled in the storm.

'Tis now a grave and gentle maid,
At her own beauty half afraid,
Shrinking, and willing to be stayed.

Oh, Time was young, and Life was warm,
When first I saw that fairy-form,
Her dark hair tossing in the storm.

And fast and free these pulses played,
When last I met that gentle maid—
When last her hand in mine was laid.

Those locks of jet are turned to gray,
And she is strange and far away
That might have been mine own to-day—

That might have been mine own, my dear,
Through many and many a happy year—
That might have sat beside me here.

Ay, changeless through the changing scene,
The ghostly whisper rings between,
The dark refrain of "might have been."

The race is o'er I might have run:
The deeds are past I might have done;
And sere the wreath I might have won.

Sunk is the last faint flickering blaze:
The vision of departed days
Is vanished even as I gaze.

The pictures, with their ruddy light,
Are changed to dust and ashes white,
And I am left alone with night.

When originally written there was a different opening verse and an additional verse after the fifth above, both of which reflect a mixing of mother and, I believe, feminine self images:

> I watch the drowsy night expire,
> And Fancy paints at my desire
> Her magic pictures in the fire.

The sixth verse which was removed is as follows:

> 'Tis now a matron with her boys,
> Dear centre of domestic joys;
> I seem to hear the merry noise.

At twenty-eight, as a young adult longing for the past, Dodgson writes: "The race is o'er I might have run:/ The deeds are past I might have done;/ And sere the wreath I might have won." At thirty-one he completed and published *Phantasmagoria and Other Poems.* At thirty-four, buried in the gift he placed in the hands of Alice Liddell, *Alice's Adventures Under Ground*, is "The Marchioness of Mock Turtles."

Before attempting to determine what happened in the interim years that contributed to making the past appear so desirable and the present so dreadful for Dodgson, let us take a more detailed look at his father and mother and how he perceived them.

CHAPTER 7

FATHER AND MOTHER

It is always useful to look to the parents of a biographical figure in order to gain insights into the nature and character of the child-as-subject. If only the parental history were as well documented as that of the famous child! With the apparent inter-generational fusion so evident in this family, a large number of children, and an orientation toward publishing, it would seem that this might be a simple task. There are, though, relatively few sources for learning about the Dodgson parents. The Collingwood biography, although family produced, recorded little about either, but it does provide some photographs. Other biographers have produced a profile of Mr. Dodgson, who had been noticed for lifetime accomplishment in the Anglican Church. There is little or nothing on his mother, and most of what is available comes from Hudson and Clark. Since Dodgson wrote virtually nothing directly about his parents, one is left to examine his serious poems with their indirect allusions, the parent-like characters in his nonsense works which others have interpreted as "mother" or "father" figures (as I do with an even greater sense of certainty), and the anagrams, which clearly reinforce the notion that Dodgson used this vehicle as a means of such communication and that he felt he had issues to be communicated.

His Father

Mr. Dodgson was born in 1800, the first of two sons of a military officer who was killed in battle in Ireland in 1803. [1] Given the loss of his father at such an early age, the extent to which the elder Dodgson was able to draw on male as well as parental modeling and meet the need to idealize a parent figure who encourages selective emulation, not duplication, can only be inferred. A product of the Westminster (Abbey) School, he attended Oxford University, and achieved the uncommon distinction of gaining a double first in Mathematics and the Classics. There seems to be no question that he possessed the ingredients of genius, which could have been applied in a number of areas; but he chose a life of service to the Church as Archdeacon at Richmond, Rector at Croft, and Canon at Ripon Cathedral [2] where he was responsible for the examination of young Anglican priests. In addition he completed theological writings and translations in support of his friend and benefactor Dr. Edward Pusey, a leader of the Oxford Movement, during which significant changes in Church theology took place.

The order in which he prioritized his many interests is not known. It is clear, however, that he was an extremely busy man whose demands brought him well beyond the family circle. These included his primary parish in Daresbury, the ministry on the canal barge, the teaching he did in the in-home school he established at Daresbury to augment his income as well as provide education for his own growing brood, and the supervisory responsibilities associated with the farm, though there is no indication that he farmed directly. He maintained a social life with his own clerical friends among whom he was well known for his wit and ability as a raconteur. He also pursued cultural activities and his favorite hobby — mathematics.

Mr. Dodgson began publishing when Charles was six years old. His efforts include a translation of Tertullian, an early Church writer, which comprised 499 pages. This effort was undertaken at the request of Dr. Pusey who was attempting to link the teachings of the Anglican Church to its earlier roots in Roman Catholicism by providing sound translations of those early writers and thinkers for the benefit of the Anglican Church. In the next ten years, he established himself as a distinguished writer on a number of theological subjects. During the years prior to leaving Daresbury for Croft in 1843, he had published five books — one per year — a number which would grow to twenty-four by the time of his death in 1868. [3] Publishing had become a family tradition, one which began very early for the children, as they contributed to family-based publications which paralleled their father's efforts.

It is clear that the family lived on the edge of poverty while at Daresbury, a fact that reflects on the depth of the elder Dodgson's commitment, deep religious beliefs, and the strength of his family tradition of service. If ever considered, he rejected the pursuit of more lucrative activities in which he might have succeeded given his academic qualifications. Until the family rose quite suddenly to the upper middle class with the promotion to Croft, Mr. Dodgson was apparently quite willing to live the parsimonious life and provide an example of simple Christian living for his family and flock. He nevertheless struggled with additional income-generating activities, all of which must have drawn him away from his involvement with family. Whether the children who lived under these conditions observed and were affected by the apparent disparity between their perception of their father's potential and the sparse means made available to them can only be surmised. There are indications that these conditions were noticed in an early drawing by the son, a picture which depicts a scene of family members, all appearing to suffer from anorexia, gathered around the dinner table discussing meal portions measured in zillionths of an ounce.

Collingwood tells us little, but his comments are consistent with the anagram found describing Rev. Dodgson being a man of simple faith, as an examination of his published sermons reveals.

> He was a man of deep piety and of a somewhat reserved and grave disposition, which, however, was tempered by the most generous charity, so that he was universally loved by the poor. In moments of relaxation his wit and humour were the delight of his clerical friends, for he had the rare power of telling anecdotes effectively. His reverence for sacred things was so great that he was never known to relate a story which included a jest upon words from the Bible. [4]

Lennon writes that his grandniece was unable to recall much about him other than the fact that his thoughts on the development of children's character were very fixed. For a sensitive child, "a mere lifted eyebrow" could have a more coercive effect than the occasional physical beatings or punishment in a home that was less strict and controlled. [5] In the latter situation the child is able to recognize the punishment for what it is, rather than wonder in a state of anxiety the meaning and intensity of the signal, and then return to a more relaxed norm. In addition, having a father so strict, so close when he chose to be, and so altruistic in his daily work with the poor of the parish created an environment in which neither the son, nor any of the children would be able to do anything but submit. Efforts to grow through the idealization of a good but imperfect image, or the testing of limits, a necessary part of personal growth, were blunted.

Hudson describes Mr. Dodgson from a Collingwood photograph as "a solid and rather gloomy-looking divine," [6] while Greenacre describes him as:

> a man with large, sensitive, keen, startled-looking eyes in a face generally strong and massive with big, well-chiseled features. In a later picture [he] appears amiably stern in mien but relaxed in posture, and the face has lost any trace of the early apprehensive wistfulness. [7]

The seriousness and appearance of anxiety is totally consistent with the pressures of the early days. Hudson documents the reality of those pressures as he quotes from letters from Mr. Dodgson prior to the birth of their third child encouraging the College's efforts to pass a potato tithe which would provide £200 to augment his stipend [8] which was still less than £192. [9] At the time it required an income of about £500 to live comfortably with a small household staff. In closing his letter, he indicated he was doing the best he could under the circumstances, was seeing his domestic comforts diminish slowly but constantly; and he acknowledged feelings of anxiety regarding the situation as so precarious that the presence of two unfilled student desks were worthy of comment.

At Hudson's request, Dr. M. J. Mannheim performed a handwriting analysis of a letter from Mr. Dodgson as well as a number written by other family members, including Charles. He described Mr. Dodgson as being dignified, poised and capable of being irritable while hiding any such appearances behind a benign screen. Mannheim finds him "austere, puritanical, and fond of power" with a limited emotional range, most likely intolerant of failure by others to recognize and conform to his authority, while at the same time protective of those who do conform or are in need. [10] From all of the evidence he appears to be very much the Victorian prototype father: God-like, authoritarian, and self-controlled.

Papa's character as he dealt with his son is revealed in two letter sequences, both quite different. One written to his brother Hassard early in his Daresbury days as a young father reflects that he had very specific designs for his first son. It would be the second boy, Skeffington, who would fulfill the dream as he replicated the father's career, marriage, and large family. In the letter he was noting already the constitutional guidelines of the Chapter of Christ Church which would allow him at the appropriate time to gain an Oxford studentship for Charles through the influence of a member. [11] This was quite different from a letter written in 1853 in response to one from Charles who notified his father that Dr. Pusey had awarded him the

Studentship at Oxford. It is quoted in its entirety from Collingwood to display the style and also emphasize the extent to which his father devoted such a large portion of the letter to re-assuring Charles that he had gained acceptance on his own and *not* through his father's influence. What existed in the relationship that needed that extensive reassurance can only be inferred from the character of his father. Note the similarity in the use of italics (underlining in hand-written letters) with the style already seen in the works and letters of his son.

> MY DEAREST CHARLES, — The feelings of thankfulness and delight with which I have read your letter just received, I must leave to *your conception*; for they are, I assure you, beyond *my expression*; and your affectionate heart will derive no small addition of joy from thinking of the joy which you have occasioned to me, and to all the circle of your home. I say `you have occasioned,´ because, grateful as I am to my old friend Dr. Pusey for what he has done, I cannot desire stronger evidence than his own words of the fact that you have *won*, and well won, this honour for *yourself*, and that it is bestowed as a matter of *justice* to *you*, and not of *kindness* to *me*. You will be interested in reading extracts from his two letters to me — the first written three years ago in answer to one from me, in which I distinctly told him that I neither asked nor expected that he should serve me in this matter, unless my son should fairly reach the standard of merit by which these appointments were regulated. . . . [Mr. Dodgson quotes from two letters from Dr. Pusey regarding his unprejudiced selection criteria and his pleasure at selecting Charles].
>
> The last clause is a parallel to your own report, and I am glad that you should have had so soon an evidence so substantial of the truth of what I have so often inculcated, that it is the `steady, painstaking, likely-to-do-good´ man, who in the long run wins the race against those who now and then give a brilliant flash and, as Shakespeare says, `straight are cold again´. [12]

Another letter, written when Charlie was about eight is quite different. Apparently the youngster had written his father asking him to bring back from his trip to Leeds a screwdriver, a file, and a ring. Papa responded to the request with a letter assuring his son that he would do so. Cohen reproduces the entire letter, which includes an opening in which the father apologized to the son for the delay in his response, after which the elder Dodgson manifested his obvious ability to compose nonsense with much of the same inherent violence as the son did later. With rushing, flying, and screaming Papa would insist that the requested materials be presented to him in forty seconds or he would kill every cat in Leeds if he had the time to do so.

> ... Then what a bawling and a tearing of hair there will be! Pigs and babies, camels and butterflies, rolling in the gutter together — old women rushing up the chimneys and cows after them — ducks hiding themselves in coffee-cups, and fat geese trying to squeeze themselves into pencil cases. At last the Mayor of Leeds will be found in a soup plate covered up with custard, and stuck full of almonds to make him look like a sponge cake that he may escape the dreadful destruction of the Town. ... [13]

He finally spared the town when the things were brought, protected by an army of 10,000 men, ". . . as a present to Charles Lutwidge Dodgson from his affectionate Papa." [14]

This passage sounds strangely like segments from the Old Testament warning of the impending destruction of recalcitrant sinners against Yahweh. The God-like omnipotence of the father in the eyes of the son could only be re-confirmed, despite the fact that the boy was without a doubt well aware of its nonsensical qualities; Papa can and will do anything for Charlie. A little more subtle is the support of grandiosity within the child, whose simple wish for tools could generate such a response, and the extraordinary distance-creating grandiosity of the father, a figure not really allowing the child approach close enough, to merge with, in order to sustain confidence and confidence-maintaining techniques, all translatable into usable values and goals. Again, as happens when we draw on any isolated incident or document, we are left with the question: Was this a typical response and communication style, or a single occurrence? In any event, when we move on to the boy's experiences just three years later at the Richmond Grammar School, then Rugby, omnipotent Papa was either not available or not perceived by the boy as someone to whom he could turn.

Mr. Dodgson and his son maintained sparse communications until the father's death, the style of which appears to be very formal and which reflects a relationship based on an image of authority and distance, with his father seen as a source of advice on some matters. It would be much later in his father's life that Dodgson would record in his diary his surprise at his father's reaction to an off-color song/parody heard together as they attended a Masonic fete held annually on Commemoration Day. Reed describes Papa as "absolutely flabbergasted," though too "broad-minded" and "proud" not to be pleased with his son's public success he witnessed in the three years following publication of *Alice's Adventures in Wonderland.* [15] He most likely was more comfortable with the three publications in the field of Mathematics which his son produced during the same period.

Dodgson said little of his father's death during what was seen as a mild illness. The death occurred so unexpectedly at Croft that Charles was unable to get there in time. We know that he suspended entries in his diary for several weeks following the death, during which time he helped supervise the movement of the family to new quarters. In two letters written years later, the extent of his feelings are evident. The first is to someone also suffering the loss of a parent:

> We are sufficiently old friends, I feel sure, for me to have no fear that I shall seem intrusive in writing about your great sorrow. The greatest blow that has ever fallen on *my* life was the death, nearly thirty years ago, of my own dear father; so, in offering you my sincere sympathy, I write as a fellow-sufferer. And I rejoice to know that we are not only fellow-sufferers, but also fellow-believers in the blessed hope of the resurrection from the dead, which makes such a parting holy and beautiful, instead of being merely a blank despair.

The second is to his young friend Edith Rix.

> MY DEAR EDITH, — I can now tell you (what I wanted to do when you sent me that text-card, but felt I could not say it to *two* listeners, as it were) *why* that special card is one I like to have. That text is consecrated for me by the memory of one of the greatest sorrows I have known — the death of my dear father. In those solemn days, when we used to steal, one by one, into the darkened room, to take yet another look at the dear calm face, and to pray for strength, the one feature in the room that I remember was a framed text, illuminated by one of my sisters, `Then are they glad, because they are at rest; and so he bringeth them into the haven where they would be!´ That text will always have, for me, a sadness and a sweetness of its own. Thank you

again for sending it me. Please don't mention this when we meet. I can't *talk* about it.

Always affectionately yours,

C. L. DODGSON. [16]

This last quoted text was engraved on the parents' tombstone; it also hung in an illuminated frame in the bedroom kept for Dodgson in the family home. Nothing being simple with Charles Dodgson, we shall find the theme a recurring one when we explore his own attitude toward death, as its sentiments reflect a longing for death and the promised resurrection.

We are left with the nonsense works for any further insights regarding how Dodgson may have felt about his father, as he said nothing directly. In the two *Sylvie and Bruno* works, the elderly father of the pair is a God-like "presence," dearly loved by the children and protective of them, arriving at various times when necessary. In the meantime, Sylvie and Bruno move through the plot pretty much alone, with the story's narrator as their company. In the *Alice* works, the image of father figures is reversed from the typical Victorian model Mr. Dodgson appears to have presented, at least outside of the family. Both the King of Hearts and the Red King are well meaning, a little disorganized, and clearly dominated by the female figures. This could very well be the view a child had of the home situation, the actual or perceived "castrated" father, a perception which may have been reflective of reality or just of the most likely severe split in parental responsibilities as typically Victorian, as necessary given the family circumstances, or as parents who due to their own personalities, withdrew into compartmentalized roles.

Perhaps the most telling portrait comes from an excerpt from *Through the Looking-Glass*, where the central theme of life as a dream is pursued with a sequence involving the Red King. In Chapter IV — "Tweedledum and Tweedledee" — Alice observes the Red King as he sleeps, the only way he is presented in the story.

`He's dreaming now,´ said Tweedledee: `and what do you think he's dreaming about?´

Alice said `Nobody can guess that.´

`Why, about *you*!´ Tweedledee exclaimed, clapping his hands triumphantly.  `And if he left off dreaming about you, where do you suppose you'd be?´

`Where I am now, of course,´ said Alice.

`Not you!´ Tweedledee retorted contemptuously. `You'd be nowhere. Why, you're only a sort of thing in his dream!´

`If that there King was to wake,´ added Tweedledum, `you'd go out — bang! — just like a candle!´

`I shouldn't!´ Alice exclaimed indignantly. `Besides, if *I'm* only a sort of thing in his dream, what are *you*, I should like to know?´

`Ditto,´ said Tweedledum.

`Ditto, ditto!´ cried Tweedledee.

He shouted this so loud that Alice couldn't help saying `Hush! You'll be waking him, I'm afraid, if you make so much noise.´

`Well, it's no use *your* talking about waking him,´ said Tweedledum, `when you're only one of the things in his dream. You know very well you're not real.´

`I *am* real!´ said Alice, and began to cry.

`You wo'n't make yourself a bit realler by crying,´ Tweedledee remarked: `there's nothing to cry about.´

`If I wasn't real,´ Alice said — half-laughing through her tears, it all seemed so ridiculous — `I shouldn't be able to cry.´

`I hope you don't suppose those are *real* tears?´ Tweedledum interrupted in a tone of great contempt.

`I know they're talking nonsense,´ Alice thought to herself: `and it's foolish to cry about it.´ So she brushed away her tears, and went on, as cheerfully as she could. . . .

Alice can have no existence of her own except as she exists and conforms to the dream of the father-figure *for* her, his "thing creation," to the point where even her emotional response to the reality of that fact requires denial. For the response, too, can exist only if a part of the king's dream. She concludes that any emotional response to her predicament regarding the extent to which she can have a self outside his dream is foolish. This represents a complete denial of one half of her existence, her own uniqueness and emotional life. Dodgson leaves Alice and us with an existential dilemma in Chapter XII, for after fretting about whether Alice exists only in the king's dream, he asks if, in fact, the king exists only in Alice's dream. Much earlier than 1889 we see the questioning of life as a dream-only reality.

His Mother

In attempting to understand Mrs. Dodgson, we are confronted with a quite different problem than that surrounding the identification of his father. There is very little material available about her or the Lutwidge family, as she spent her adulthood very much within the confines of the large family she was raising. We depend very much on the works of Collingwood, Hudson, and Clark, find nothing in the letters or diaries from the son, and turn to inferences drawn from the serious poems, nonsense works, and anagrams to determine both her character and Dodgson's perception of her.

Hudson indicates that Mrs. Dodgson's great-great-grandparents, Charles Hoghton and his wife Mary (Skeffington), were descendents of the "second Viscount Massareene in the peerage of Ireland" on the Skeffington side and from Matilda, the illegitimate daughter of William the Conquerer (11th century), a descendency claimed by Sir Charles. [17] Their common grandfather was the Archbishop of Elphin; [18] her own father, Charles Lutwidge, was a public servant for forty-two years in the local community; her cousin Menella Bute Smedley would become well known as a Victorian poetess. [19] No photographs of Mrs. Dodgson have been published; but a silhouette profile cut out at the Warrington Exhibition in 1840 when Charles was eight years old (done for father and son also) reflects their consanguinity, with Mrs. Dodgson having a more prominent (Roman) nose than her husband. [20]

This background of status with what appears to have been a middle or upper middle class immediate family, presented motherhood was all that was available for Victorian women. Coming from a large family, trained, perhaps by a governess, to be a governess-like mother, claiming a titled heritage, combined with the already discussed elevation of Victorian women and her marriage to a man having achieved considerable recognition at Oxford presents all the opportunity for Mrs. Dodgson to have possessed a sense of entitlement, a life of material comfort, high expectations regarding achievement and status, and her own notions regarding child-rearing. There is no question that the eleven years at Daresbury represented a decline in status, which, despite her sincere wishes to support her marriage and family, must have created strains for her with consequent strains on those around her. Combined with a high level of achievement directed to the home, the potential for that home and family to become indispensable objects in efforts to maintain her own self identity and sense of self esteem and accomplishment is high.

Hudson provides some insight into this notion with a letter following her death from her Aunt Mary to Mr. Dodgson dated February 13, 1851. She describes her niece as "happy *happy*... sainted... highly favored" by all her family, untouched by "earthly stain or sorrow." She described a recent walk in which Mrs. Dodgson had discussed the extent of her happiness, including the life at Daresbury (with the exception of the taking in of students), but that the life at Croft was what she had always imagined as "the perfection of earthly happiness." She had spoken of those seven years as being so filled with happiness that she felt alarmed at times to feel that not a single wish had gone unmet, to which Aunt Mary added "nor a duty also" for the benefit of Mr. Dodgson. [21] It appears Mrs. Dodgson felt anxiety over at least some issues, despite finding great happiness, strains which must have produced behavioral responses in the day-to-day living, pregnancies, and financial worries. In examining her handwriting Hudson suggests that she was a practical and effective performer, "in a tearing hurry" or "at a gallop." [22] This analysis was most likely done from a very affectionate letter from Mama to Charlie when he was about five years old, a letter which reflects a powerfully demonstrative and affectionate relationship with Charles and the other children.

My Dearest Charlie,

I have used you rather ill in not having written to you sooner, but I know you will forgive me, as your Grandpapa has liked to have me with him so much, and I could not write and talk to him comfortably. All your notes have delighted me, my precious children, and show me that you have not quite forgotten me. I am always thinking of you, and longing to have you all round me again more than words can tell. . . . It delights me, my darling Charlie, to hear that you are getting on so well with your Latin and that you make so few mistakes in your Exercises. You will be happy to hear that your dearest Grandpapa is going on nicely. . . . He talks a great deal and most kindly about you all. I hope my sweetest Will says 'Mama´ sometimes, and that precious Tish has not forgotten. Give them and all my other treasures, including yourself, 1,000,000,000 kisses from me, with my most affectionate love. I am sending you a shabby note, but I cannot help it. Give my kindest love to Aunt Dar, and believe me, my own dearest Charlie, to be your sincerely affectionate

Mama [23]

Speaking for the children, Collingwood writes the most quoted description of Mrs. Dodgson, one which is totally consistent with the tone of that letter. ". . . In the words of one who had the best possible opportunities for observing her character, she was:

> one of the sweetest and gentlest women that ever lived, whom to know was to love. The earnestness of her simple faith and love shone forth in all she did and said; she seemed to live always in the conscious presence of God. It has been said by her children that they never in all their lives remember to have heard an impatient or harsh word from her lips. [24]

Collingwood does not identify the source of his quotation; perhaps he assumes that readers following his quite reverent style toward the gentle and loving son would identify the source as Charles himself. Langford Reed, who had considerable access to the Dodgson estate when preparing his biography, identifies the "one" as Charles. Hudson was not convinced that the description was real, concluding that it presented too idealized an image of her. [25]

Before commenting briefly on Dodgson's poems and entering into his world of Wonderland to find the kinds of mother figures he presented — figures that we will find totally different from the Victorian stereotype that otherwise presents itself — let us return to the world of anagrams. Drawing on the meager threads suggesting that the above quoted description was indeed from Charles, seemed "unreal" yet could be true for her as well as a description of a well-intentioned, loving, yet castrating mother, and already cognizant of the anagrammatic themes from his works, I hypothesized that this, too, could be an anagrammatic construct. Very sensitive to the risks involved attempting to work with 283 letters and remaining objective, yet challenged by the craftiness of Dodgson as game master, I offer the following anagram, using all the letters from the quotation. She was:

> . . . one of those sweet and gentle women that hobble blest, healthy, tempted children. As tenacious as a dog she never let them live their own lives. As her thin, mis-shapen, favorite charmed her, I came to resent every word from her lips. So, a horrid freak — a timid phony — sneered, revolted, wasted a talent, and showed how vile filth vanishes in foolish nonsense.

The word placement I question most is *tempted*; but placement seems proper, as it is consistent with children being children, and tempted to revolt, criticize, even (God forbid in the Dodgson household!) misbehave. Placed as it is, the word could have applied to all of the children. The word *So* in the last sentence, then means "therefore," reflecting his attribution of causality and justification with the prior statements. An alternative location for the word is in the last sentence before *So* — "Tempted so, a horrid..." — which would relate the temptation to the aforementioned relationship and be more personalized. Either way, the anagrammatic reconstruction becomes effectively the biographical summary of what Charles Dodgson saw as his source and target of rage expression. What we see in the reconstruction is evidence of compliance, the creation of the false self for the purpose of satisfying the needs of the parent for order and conformity. While such restrictive and controlled up-bringing creates a latent rage awaiting release, the extent of the release we have seen still seems to need something more than just parental strait-jacketing during childhood.

As we look at the mother-like figures in the nonsense works, we find the extremely controlling, castrating figures until we reach *Sylvie and Bruno*, when the more gentle women appear. We also find all these women titled — Duchess, Queen of Hearts, Red and White Queens, and Lady Muriel. Drawing on excerpts from *Alice's Adventures in Wonderland* — Chapter VI - "Pig and Pepper" — we meet the Duchess :

`If everybody minded their own business,´ the Duchess said, in a hoarse growl, `the world would go round a deal faster than it does.´

She interrupts every effort by Alice to converse, changing the subject on a word — *axis* to *axes*, finally ending with a `Oh, don't bother *me!*´ Singing her lullaby to her child (as Dodgson parodies a sweet Victorian lullaby), she sings:

> `*Speak roughly to your little boy,*
> *And beat him when he sneezes:*
> *He only does it to annoy,*
> *Because he knows it teases.´*

> `*I speak severely to my boy,*
> *I beat him when he sneezes;*
> *For he can thoroughly enjoy*
> *The pepper when he pleases!´*

The domestic scene involving the Duchess, Mock Turtle, Tortoise, and Alice appears in Chapter IX, "The Mock Turtle's Story. In the original version the Duchess was also the Marchioness of Mock Turtles. She makes several attempts to get physically close to Alice as she:

> . . . tucked her arm affectionately into Alice's. . . squeezed herself up closer to Alice's side as she spoke. . . digging her sharp little chin into Alice's shoulder. . . with another dig of her sharp little chin. . . .

All of these descriptions could represent an intrusively, perhaps seductively close mother supervising a child's struggles over lessons.

In the following quotation, I have inserted commentary within the brackets to reflect the underlying issues which would devastate a youngster and, if the norm, create strong and long-lasting feelings of frustration and powerlessness in the face of parental authority. Combined with religious proscriptions against disrespect or revolt, the parents appear to be aligned with the Deity against the child.

> `You're thinking about something, my dear, and that makes you forget to talk. I ca'n't tell you just now what the moral of that is, but I shall remember it in a bit´ [omniscient parent].

`Perhaps it hasn't one,´ Alice ventured to remark.

`Tut, tut, child!´ said the Duchess. `Every thing's got a moral, if only you can find it.´ And she squeezed herself up close to Alice's side as she spoke.

... `The game's going on rather better now,´ [Alice] said, by way of keeping up the conversation a little.

`'Tis so,´ said the Duchess; `and the moral of that is — "Oh, 'tis love, 'tis love, that makes the world go round!"

[Recalling the Duchess's comment on their first meeting Alice says] `Somebody said,´ Alice whispered, `that it's done by everybody minding their own business!´

[Ignoring her own earlier statement] `Ah, well! It means much the same thing,´ said the Duchess... `and the moral of *that* is — "Take care of the sense, and the sounds will take care of themselves."´

`How fond she is of finding morals in things! Alice thought to herself [a plot unfolding in the mind of Dodgson-as-Alice to turn the tide?].

`I dare say you're wondering why I don't put my arm round your waist,´ the Duchess said, after a pause [another attempt at omniscient mind reading, this time incorrectly]: `the reason is, that I'm doubtful about the temper of your flamingo. Shall I try the experiment?´

`He might bite,´ Alice cautiously replied, not feeling at all anxious to have the experiment tried.

`Very true,´ said the Duchess: `flamingoes and mustard both bite.´

Dodgson-as-Alice now introduces his anagram as an insult to this moral-quoting mother figure: *In fevered rut, I gamely masturbate both dons*. The Duchess responds: "And the moral of that is — `Birds of a feather flock together.´" This time, though totally unaware of it, she hits the mark with her morals. But she just proceeds on with more of them: "The more there is of mine, the less there is of yours," playing on the word *mines* in which the ingredients for mustard are found. When reminded that mustard is a vegetable, she adds:

`Be what you would seem to be´ — or if you'd like it put more simply — `never imagine yourself not to be otherwise than what it might appear to others that what you were or might have been was not otherwise than what you had been would have appeared to them to be otherwise.´

Dodgson has this mother figure totally confuse the child of any notion of how to maintain self-identity. Alice finally abandons her attempt to understand, and Dodgson changes scene by bringing in the Queen of Hearts, who follows with her own persistent "Off with his [her, their] head[s]," taking up the same theme that the Duchess had introduced.

What is evident in the exchange is a constantly interrupting mother figure who turns everything into a moral of questionable applicability to the child's statement, contradicts her own prior moral statement when it is in turn used by the child, and finally and intrusively achieving bodily closeness in the process, often done by a sweet and gentle mother, but seductive to a growing boy. The child, unable to attack openly, attacks in secret, out of the parents' awareness, just as Dodgson did with the anagrams and doublets.

In the final two chapters, the Queen of Hearts, who calls for the severest punishment for all who fail to comply with her wishes (but never follows up to see that the punishment is executed), seeks to punish her son, the Knave of Hearts, before any verdict is rendered. In the process she "allows" the King of Hearts to struggle in his ineffectual way to maintain a semblance of order in the trial process but he, too, eventually accedes to her commands. It is Alice who finally upsets the process and ends the sham trial as she upsets the deck of card-characters and awakens from her dream.

In *Through the Looking-Glass*, the domestic scene with the Black Kitten that occurs prior to Alice stepping through the looking-glass is a very telling reproduction of what was likely seen in the Dodgson household — unassailable coercive sweetness and goodness. I quote here only the relevant portions, with italics mine except as indicated. Their purpose is to emphasize the incongruity between feelings and words.

> `Oh you wicked wicked little thing!´ cried Alice, catching up the kitten, and *giving it a little kiss to make it understand that it was in disgrace.* . . .
>
> . . . `Do you know, I was so angry, Kitty,´ Alice went on,. . . `when I saw all the mischief you had been doing, I was very nearly opening the window, and putting you out into the snow! And you'd have deserved it, *you little mischievous darling!* What have you got to say for yourself? *Now don't interrupt me!´* she went on, holding up one finger. `*I'm going to tell you all your faults.* Number one: you squeaked twice while Dinah was washing your face this morning. *Now you ca'n't deny it, Kitty: I heard you!* What's that you say?´ (pretending that the kitten was speaking). `Her paw went

into your eye? *Well, that's* your *fault,* for keeping your eyes open — if you'd shut them tight up, it wouldn't have happened. *Now don't make any more excuses, but listen!* Number two: you pulled Snowdrop away by the tail just as I had put down the saucer of milk before her! What, you were thirsty, were you? How do you know she wasn't thirsty too?

[Later, after Number Three] `. . . Kitty. . . you've not been punished for any of them yet. *You know I'm saving up all your punishments* for Wednesday week — Suppose they had saved up all *my* punishments? [Dodgson's italics and hereafter] She went on, talking more to herself than the kitten. `What *would* they do at the end of a year? I should be sent to prison, I suppose, when the day came. . . .

In Chapter V — "Wool and Water" (the most nightmarish sequences I found in any of Dodgson's works) — the White Queen, attempts to clarify the schedule for eating jam:

[Alice says] `Well, I don't want any *to-day*, at any rate.´

`You couldn't have it if you *did* want it,´ the Queen said. `The rule is, jam to-morrow and jam yesterday — but never jam *to-day*.´

`It *must* come sometimes to "jam to-day,"´ Alice objected.

`No, it ca'n't,´ said the Queen. `It's jam every *other* day: to-day isn't any *other* day, you know.´

`I don't understand you,´ said Alice. `It's dreadfully confusing!´

Daniel Kirk notes the play on language: i. e., the issue might have been easily clarified linguistically by stating the rule that jam is available only on alternate days [26], which suggests a faulty communication style with children. But the sequence appears also to play on what a child would see as the arbitrariness of a powerful parent over a really trifling matter, although perhaps not trifling in the Dodgson family circumstances at Daresbury. We have already seen the extent of the behavioral rules and regulations in the household. In his Preface to *A Tangled Tale* Dodgson acknowledged that his mother used jam to conceal medicine, perhaps a very legitimate parental reason for alternating days but apparent arbitrariness to the children.

Immediately following that sequence, the White Queen talks of living backwards, pursuing the issue around the imprisonment of the King's Messenger:

`... He's in prison now, being punished: and the trial doesn't even begin till next Wednesday: and of course the crime comes last of all.´

`Suppose he never commits the crime?´ said Alice.

`That would be all the better, wouldn't it?´ the Queen said. . . .

Alice felt there was no denying *that*. `Of course it would be all the better,´ she said: `but it wouldn't be all the better his being punished.´

`You're wrong *there*, at any rate,´ said the Queen. `Were *you* ever punished?´

`Only for faults,´ said Alice.

`And you were all the better for it, I know!´ the Queen said triumphantly.

`Yes, but then I *had* done the things I was punished for,´ said Alice: `that makes all the difference.´

`But if you *hadn't* done them,´ the Queen said, `that would have been better still; better, and better, and better!. . .

Alice was just beginning to say `There's a mistake somewhere ____ ´ [and the subject changes].

Like the Queen of Hearts, who sought the punishment before the verdict, the White Queen advocates punishment for its own sake in anticipation of a crime being committed, as a preventative before the fact rather than a punishment after the fact. Carried to its logical conclusion, there need never be a specific transgression, just the possibility of one. This may be translated as punishment for simply being in the human condition.

In the same chapter the White Queen assumes that Alice must be happy in the wood.

`... You must be very happy, living in this wood, and being glad whenever you like!´

`Only it is so *very* lonely here!´ Alice said in a melancholy voice; and, at the thought of her loneliness, two large tears came rolling down her cheeks.

`Oh, don't go on like that!´ cried the poor Queen, wringing her hands in despair. `Consider what a great girl you are. Consider what a long way you've come to-day. Consider what o'clock it is. Consider anything, only don't cry!´

The Queen then goes on to convince Alice that she should consider and believe impossible things as a distraction.

> `... When I was your age, I always did it for half-an-hour a day. Why, sometimes I've believed as many as six impossible things before breakfast. ...´

The White Queen is unable to tolerate the presence and manifestation of sad feelings of loneliness. Her first piece of advice is to "consider what a great girl you are," an encouragement to deny her true feelings and re-confirm what may very well be a false self, a not feeling very "great" self; a self in need of fully experiencing her feelings as they occur. Moving on to the ridiculous, Dodgson tells us that *anything* done to distract one from bad feelings will suffice, even considering the time of day.

In "The Garden of Live Flowers", the Red Queen takes Alice by the hand and in the manner of a whirling dervish flies around the garden getting nowhere.

`Now! Now!´ cried the Queen. `Faster! Faster!´ And they went so fast that at last they seemed to skim through the air, hardly touching the ground with their feet, till suddenly, just as Alice was getting quite exhausted, they stopped, and she found herself sitting on the ground, breathless and giddy.

The Queen propped her up against a tree, and said kindly, `You may rest a little, now.´

Alice looked round her in great surprise. `Why, I do believe we've been under this tree the whole time! Everything's just as it was!´

`Of course it is,´ said the Queen. `What would you have it?´

`Well, in *our* country,´ said Alice, still panting a little, `you'd generally get to somewhere else — if you ran very fast for a long time as we've been doing.´

`A slow sort of country!´ said the Queen. `Now, *here*, you see, it takes all the running *you* can do, to keep in the same place. If you want to get somewhere else, you must run at least twice as fast as that!´

`I'd rather not try, please!´ said Alice. `I'm quite content to stay here — only I *am* hot and thirsty!´

`I know what *you'd* like!´ the Queen said good-naturedly, taking a little box out of her pocket. `Have a biscuit?´

Alice thought it would not be civil to say `No,´ though it wasn't at all what she wanted. So she took it, and ate it as well as she could: and it was *very* dry: and she thought she had never so nearly choked in all her life.

`. . . have another biscuit?´ [the Queen said].

`No, thank you,´ said Alice: `one's *quite* enough!´

`Thirst quenched, I hope?´ said the Queen.

Alice did not know what to say to this [but the Queen prepared to depart].

Here we have the hurrying mother figure, "at a gallop," with an agenda of getting ahead, wasting no time, yet in the eyes of the child Alice, just maintaining position. After the exhausting flight, the omniscient Queen "knows" what Alice wants for refreshment for her thirst and gives her a dry biscuit, totally oblivious to her real needs. Since it is offered to her good-naturedly, Alice feels coerced to accept so as not to offend and does so, despite nearly choking. When offered another, she can now, finally, defer. The Queen concludes by the deferral that she must have quenched her thirst — she "hopes" — again oblivious to any real interest in whether Alice has or not.

As Alice moves to the last [Chess] row thereby becoming Queen in "Queen Alice" she begins to inquire timidly if the game is over:

`Speak when you're spoken to!´ the Queen sharply interrupted her.

`But if everybody obeyed that rule,´ said Alice, who was always ready for an argument, `and if you only spoke when you were spoken to, and the other person always waited for

you to begin, you see nobody would ever say anything, so
that ____'

`Ridiculous!´ cried the Queen. . . .

[Later] `. . . Always speak the truth — think before you
speak — and write it down afterwards.´

`I'm sure I didn't mean ____´ Alice was beginning, but
the Red Queen interrupted her impatiently.

`That's just what I complain of! You *should* have
meant! What do you suppose is the use of a child without
any meaning? Even a joke should have some meaning — and
a child's more important than a joke, I hope. You couldn't
deny that, even if you tried with both hands.´

`I don't deny things with my *hands*,´ Alice objected.

`Nobody said you did,´ said the Red Queen. `I said you
couldn't if you tried.´

`She's in that state of mind,´ said the White Queen,
`that she wants to deny *something* — only she doesn't know
what to deny!´

`A nasty, vicious temper,´ the Red Queen remarked;
and then there was an uncomfortable silence for a minute or
two.

The Red Queen broke the silence by saying, to the
White Queen, `I invite you to Alice's dinner-party this
afternoon.´

The White Queen smiled feebly, and said `And I invite
you.´

`I didn't know I was to have a party at all,´ said Alice;
`but, if there *is* to be one, I think I ought to invite the
guests.´

`We gave you the opportunity of doing it,´ the Red
Queen remarked: `but I daresay you've not had many
lessons in manners yet?´

`Manners are not taught in lessons,´ said Alice.

Again we have the denial of the child, who verges on having no
more meaning than a joke. With constant interruptions, the meaning
of Alice's words are distorted to suit the needs of the adults, who,
needing to maintain their self image, deny their own anger, and accuse
the child of having the bad temper. And Dodgson reminds us that
manners, like love, are best taught by example, not lessons.

It would be easy to dismiss many of these descriptions of
child/parent interactions and relations as merely Victorian parody.
But the principles involved, denial of the child's selfhood occur across

cultural lines, with only the details and style varying between cultures. The modes of communication which Dodgson describes are, unfortunately, all too common more than a century later.

Dodgson's serious poems contain many references to a fairy-like girl or woman, and most biographers and critics relate them to his images of his mother and his love for her (cf. "Faces in the Fire" from the last chapter). While I think this is totally consistent with a love/hate relationship and his wish to return to a simpler time and relationship which he still saw as better than the pain of the existing condition, I feel they relate as well, perhaps more so, to the emergence of his own self-image as a wished-for little girl, an image which took on for him a persona fused with the loved/hated object. This image became increasingly real to him as time went on, with bitterness at the loss or "what might have been" for him only increasing.

This chapter closes with a domestic scene from *Sylvie and Bruno* and is the only example drawn from this work. In Chapter III — "Birthday-Presents" — we have one of the best examples of the denial of angry feelings by both children and adults, a possible scene re-enactment from the Dodgson household. In the story, having learned that it is Sylvie's birthday, Bruno, after a disappointed search of his pockets for money for a present, leaves the room while others give Sylvie their presents. The Professor gives Sylvie a pincushion with fifteen pins, one of which is bent.

`I'll make the bent one into a *hook*!´ said Sylvie. `To catch Bruno with, when he runs away from his lessons!´

`You ca'n't guess what *my* present is!´ said Uggug, who had taken the butter-dish from the table, and was standing behind her, with a wicked leer on his face.

`No, I ca'n't guess,´ Sylvie said without looking up. She was still examining the Professor's pincushion.

`It's *this*!´ cried the bad boy, exultingly, as he emptied the dish over her, and then, with a grin of delight at his own cleverness, looked round for applause.

Sylvie coloured crimson, as she shook off the butter from her frock: but she kept her lips tight shut, and walked away to the window, where she stood looking out and trying to recover her temper.

Uggug's triumph was a very short one: the Sub-Warden had returned, just in time to be a witness of his dear child's playfulness, and in another moment a skilfully-applied box on the ear had changed the grin of delight into a howl of pain.

`My darling!´ cried his mother, enfolding him in her fat arms. `Did they box his ears for nothing? A precious pet!´

`It's not for *nothing*!´ growled the angry father. `Are you aware, Madam, that I pay the house-bills, out of a fixed annual sum? The loss of all that wasted butter falls on *me*! Do you hear Madam!´

`Hold your tongue, Sir!´ My Lady spoke very quietly — almost in a whisper. But there was something in her *look* that silenced him. `Don't you see it was only a *joke*? And a very clever one, too! He only meant that he loved nobody *but* her! And instead of being pleased with the compliment, the spiteful little thing has gone away in a huff!´

The Sub-Warden was a very good hand at changing the subject. He walked across to the window. . . .

At this moment Bruno re-entered the room, and passing Uggug (who was blubbering his loudest, in the hope of attracting notice) as if he was quite used to that sort of thing, he ran up to Sylvie and threw his arms round her. `I went to my toy-cupboard,´ he said with a very sorrowful face, `to see if there were *somefin* fit for a present for oo! And there isn't *nuffin*! They's *all* broken, every one! And I haven't got *no* money left, to buy oo a birthday-present! And I ca'n't give oo nuffin but *this*!´ (`*This*´ was a very earnest hug and a kiss.)

`Oh, thank you, darling!´ cried Sylvie. `I like *your* present best of all!´ (But if so, why did she give it back so quickly?)

. . . Sylvie and Bruno went away hand in hand: but, on reaching the door, Sylvie came back again and went up to Uggug timidly. `I don't mind about the butter,´ she said, `and I — I'm sorry he hurt you!´ And she tried to shake hands with the little ruffian: but Uggug only blubbered louder, and wouldn't make friends. Sylvie left the room with a sigh.

The Sub-Warden then yelled at Uggug "as loud as he dared" but his wife ignored him.

Dodgson is clearly pointing to the "mother's favorite" position which Uggug possesses between his mother and father, whom she can silence with a "look." He is also pointing to Uggug as an example of the type of child which results from such a parenting and communication style. Sylvie, the offended child, not only must stifle her anger, but then must deny her even being offended, expressing her sympathy for the deserved punishment Uggug had received. The mother seeks any basis for Uggug's behavior that will deny any evil intent. The spoiled Uggug seeks sympathy from any quarter as the offended and injured party. Both parents stifle their own anger at one another by finding distractions which allow them to ignore one another and any further involvement in the incident. If this is truly a window to the domestic household of the Dodgson family, the sweetness and love which coated the surface of the parental relationships covered a bitterness over roles and responsibilities, and hostility which manifested itself in a distorted way. The model for interpersonal conflict resolution did not exist in the home.

Critics interpret these two characters as really representing the parents of Alice Liddell, as their "Vice" and "Sub" positions mirror the Oxford hierarchical structure in which Mr. Liddell held a position as Dean of the College. It is believed also that Dodgson had strong feelings about both, Dean Liddell on College disagreements, Mrs. Liddell on her sudden withdrawal of permission for Alice and the other children to associate with Dodgson and her burning of all the letters he wrote to Alice. While there may be some truth to this interpretation as part of a total composite character creation, I believe the financial concerns have more auto-biographical applicability and the scene is a screen for his discussion of his own family.

Conclusion

The analyses of Dodgson's parents lead us to conclude that while we are dealing with some typical Victorian characteristics including the strait-jacketing of children, Charles Dodgson emerged into puberty and his first venture away from home — school at Richmond — a very sensitive, precocious child, stammering, socially unprepared in terms of peer boy interaction, rigidly contained, already escaping into fantasy, with strong, as yet undifferentiated feelings toward his parents. These feelings were founded within an environment of total trust on the one hand and total control on the other. For what appears to have been a mother-dominated home from the perspective of the children, the greatest concentration of both his positive and negative feelings were directed toward her. The youngster had been for them all they could have wanted. While he may have been intellectually prepared for the school environment that was to come, he was totally unprepared emotionally for what might be seen as betrayal or abandonment or any attack on his precarious self.

CHAPTER 8

DEATH IN ADOLESCENCE

If there is a period during the life of Charles Dodgson which is conspicuously absent in biographies it is the emotional public school experience at Richmond Grammar School and Rugby, and finally at Oxford University. While more recent writers have suggested this period as being critical to an understanding of what was perceived as Dodgson's sexual repression, none have attempted to explore in detail the nature of the experiences to which he was surely exposed. The earlier writers, while acknowledging that as a sensitive boy he most likely had difficulties with the environment, there seems a virtual conspiracy aimed at protecting the reputation of an educational system which was filled with violence. Greenacre suggests that no full analysis of Dodgson can be done without knowledge of this missing period. John Pudney expressed surprise that this aspect of Dodgson's upbringing, specifically the sexually "deviant" behavior to which he was exposed, had not been properly covered. [1] My hope is that it will be here. For it was during these years that the spirit of Charles Dodgson, the special and perfect child, with an already damaged and depleted self, filled with latent rage, died. But he would survive, finally resurrecting himself, but now fueled with the venom of full-blown rage that would go unabated to his final death at age sixty-five. It was during this period in his life that the thwarted mischievous Bruno was transformed into the despicable Uggug.

This chapter reviews the nature and history of the English educational system and what made it so difficult for some to endure (despite the fact that thousands of students "prospered" under it) and what we know of Dodgson's experience and memories of it. We shall also examine the little that is known about his family life during this period. This family life was especially focused on continuing the production of family publications, his soon-to-be chosen outlet for rage expression. And we shall explore the nature of his psychological death, its meaning to him then and the remainder of his life.

The Richmond Grammar School, was a boarding school located about ten miles from Croft. Founded in the 14th Century it was in 1843 under the leadership of James Tate II, who had succeeded his brother, by then Canon of St. Paul's Cathedral in London. The facilities consisted of two buildings; the largest and oldest was about forty-five feet by twenty feet and contained a single room with lines of pew-like benches for the students who faced the single teacher at one end. Charles, one of the 120 enrolled, was among those who paid for his room and board. He was assigned to live with one of fifteen others in the large main house with the Tate family of eight, an arrangement considered preferred and, therefore, more costly. Having a first class reputation, the school focused on the teaching of Greek and Latin literature as well as grammar, instruction in Christian beliefs and practices as presented by the Anglican Church, with extra tuition for mathematics, French, and basic accounting. Some tuition-free positions were reserved for sons of local tradesmen, a practice which provided an educational focus that met local commercial needs as well as the broader and primary focus, the preparation for the University for which knowledge of the Classics was an entrance requirement. With 120 boys boarding together for the twenty week terms (separated by six-week holidays), boy-organized games, roughhousing, fighting, and smoking were commonly reported. Corporal punishment was the basis for keeping order. [2]

While Mr. Dodgson had attended Westminster, a school associated with the Abbey, in preparation for his own matriculation to Oxford, he chose Rugby, one of several public schools (Eton and Harrow being the most prominent of the group) for his son. While the reasons for this selection are not known, they may very well have been influenced by the presence of Dr. Thomas Arnold, a peer of Mr. Dodgson, five years his senior and fellow Westminster and Oxford alumnus who had played a significant role in beginning the reformation of the school system at Rugby from his appointment in 1828 until he died unexpectedly in 1842 at the age of forty-seven. Ronald Pearsall writes that "no horror could overtake the cruelties, humiliations and curious sexual practices that the boy came up against at Harrow, Eton, Winchester, Shewsbury, Rugby or wherever." [3] Whether this was true in the early 1800's when Mr. Dodgson and Arnold attended is not apparent but may have been a part of Dr. Arnold's motivation for reform. It would be naive to think that Dodgson's father was unaware of what Charles would be exposed to; but he may very well have sent his son to the school he trusted would most likely reflect the progress of a much needed reform. By this time, however, Westminster School had declined in reputation, and, shortly after Charles began studies at Rugby, was seriously affected by an outbreak of infection (blamed on defective sewers) from which several boys died.

In his 1918 biography entitled *Eminent Victorians*, Lytton Strachey describes the ascendancy and efforts of Dr. Arnold to reform the school as part of a general outcry from primarily the upper middle class in search of a "more liberal [reduced concentration on Latin and Greek] curriculum. . . [and] a demand for a higher moral tone." Describing Eton as a typical example of an English public school, Strachey uses such adjectival phrases as "virgin forests, untouched by the hand of reform," "a system of anarchy tempered by despotism," living arrangements at "whose name in after years aged statesmen and warriors would turn pale." [4] It was:

> . . . a life in which licensed barbarism was mingled with the daily and hourly study of the niceties of Ovidian verse. It was a life of freedom and terror, of prosody and rebellion, of interminable floggings and appalling practical jokes. [5]

The scene at chapel during a lengthy and boring sermon included the release of rats "to scurry among the legs of the exploding boys." [6] Pubertal and adolescent boys slept as many as five to a bed, a practice eliminated by Arnold at Rugby [7], no doubt in part due to activities taking place there. While the forgiveness of sin was promised in chapel, small academic errors would produce corporal punishment severe enough to draw blood. One contemporary described the public schools as "the very seats and nurseries of vice." [8]

Dr. Arnold's stated goals for reform were to focus on: "first, religious and moral principle; secondly, gentlemanly conduct; thirdly, intellectual ability." [9] In order to accomplish those goals, Arnold built on the existing hierarchical student structure which reflected six forms or levels, the Sixth Form being the highest. He gave these older students (as old as twenty-three with Dodgson himself reporting in a letter home a friend as young as seven [10]) a position reporting directly to him, leaving them "excused from chastisement. . . and given the right to chastise." [11] Under the belief that such a hierarchical structure of authority provided students with the learning experience of self government, the after-school-hours of the boys were in the total control of the older students, virtually without adult supervision or interference. Younger students, then were at risk of corporal punishment from Headmaster, teachers, Sixth Form elder students and anyone who could bully them. In addition there was the requirement that they write out of Latin and Greek "impositions" for infractions committed in and out of the classroom. A consummate preacher, Arnold considered the primary means for transforming the boys into Christian gentlemen to be the experience in chapel, not in the classroom or living quarters. A massive physical presence throughout all aspects of the Rugby setting, Arnold undertook a very personal effort at reforming a system that had evolved over many decades into one in bad need of reform.

The authority to punish given to the Sixth-Form students (Praeposters) by Arnold was reduced somewhat by Dr. Archibald Tait (later to become Archbishop of Canterbury), successor to Arnold as Headmaster when Dodgson arrived at Rugby on his fourteenth birthday in 1846. Tait himself had never attended public school as a student. If bullying had in fact been significantly reduced under Arnold, it still represented the only means for upper classmen to exercise authority, to coerce or punish under-classmen, and to regain some sense of power in an environment which made many powerless.

These experiences are described in Thomas Hughes' *Tom Brown's Schooldays*, written in 1850 by a father attempting to prepare his own son for public school at Rugby. He describes the much abused "fagging" activities, in which the younger boys were required to provide "services" for the older students for as long as they were unable to establish by physical prowess or the protection of group membership the ability to withstand the pressed service.

> True, the general system was rough and hard, and there was bullying in nooks and corners, *bad signs for the future*; but it never got further, or dared show itself openly, stalking about the passages and hall and bedrooms, and making the life of the *small* boys a continual fear [my italics]. [12]

> . . . In fact the unfortunate [small boys most susceptible to be made] fag had to submit in silence to any indignity inflicted by an older boy for if by chance a report of such doings came to the ears of the Head-Master or his associates, the talebearer was `sent to Coventry,´ in other words, he was shunned and left to himself by all his companions. [13]

Hughes describes the typical day and experience of the fags:

> From supper until nine o'clock, three fags taken in order stood in the passages, and answered any praepostor

who called Fag, racing to the door, the last comer having to do the work [which consisted of] going to the buttery for beer and bread and cheese. . . cleaning candlesticks, and putting in new candles, toasting cheese, bottling beer, and carrying messages around the house. [14]

At times fags would get together to attack the bullies:

. . . and the house was filled with constant chasings, and sieges, and lickings of all sorts; and in return, the bullies' beds were pulled to pieces, and drenched with water, and their names written up on the walls with every insulting epithet which the fag invention could furnish. [15]

From later anagrammatic material I suspect strongly that the beds were often drenched with urine as well as water, and that practical jokes included the use of urine, semen, and feces.

Boys were sometimes dragged to the fireplace, their bottoms bared and "roasted" against the fire, sometimes until medical aid was needed.

Each new boy. . . was mounted in turn upon a table, a candle in each hand, and told to sing a song. If he made a false note, a violent hiss followed, and during the performance pellets and crusts of bread were thrown at boy or candles, often knocking them out of his hands and covering him with tallow. The singing over, he descended and pledged the house. . . . [16]

Fags were ". . . always getting laughed at, and called Molly, or Jenny, or some derogatory feminine nickname." [17]

Hughes describes the attitude that other students had toward the fags who lived in the School House, the building which comprised the Headmaster's home as well as housing for about eighty boys who were perceived as being "special" by the other boys due to their proximity to the Headmaster. This was was similar to the house in which Dodgson lived on entering Richmond [18], but not at Rugby. The younger boys were

petted and pampered by some of the big fellows [who] taught them to drink and use bad language, and did all they could to spoil them for everything* in this world and the next. [19]

The asterisk is Hughes' and points to the only, albeit oblique, reference to sexual services being part of the fagging experience. He footnotes:

> A kind and wise critic, an old Rugbeian, notes here in the margin: The `small friend system was not so utterly bad from 1841-1847.´ Before that, too, there were many noble friendships between big and little boys, but I can't strike out the passage; many boys will know why it is left in. [20]

"Noble friendships" is a euphamism for the Classical Greek relationship between older and younger men, which in its purest Platonic form did not include sexual activities. Hughes can only be pointing to sexual activities, most likely youthful homosexual activities among boys of similar age or pederasty when younger boys were coerced or enticed into sexual activities by the older boys. In modern terms, many of the boys were raped. Yet, despite the purpose of his book, i. e., to prepare his son for the experience, Hughes could not be explicit, probably in deference to alumni or fearful of repercussions deriving from disclosure to parents who might have been unaware, if there were any.

While *Tom Brown's Schooldays* is a fictionalized account of life at Rugby during the later reform years, it was well read at the time and has been the primary source of material as biographers have attempted to piece together the "most likely" scenario for Dodgson's experience as a slight, effeminate boy, nearly deaf in his right ear, stammering, inexperienced, raised in a bevy of sisters, non-athletic, and coming from the protected isolation of Daresbury/Croft. It is clear that Pearsall considers the Hughes work a sanitized version of what went on, perhaps assuaging the fears of many parents but in its own way perpetuating the practices. H. Montgomery Hyde, in his history of homosexuality in Britain entitled *The Love That Dared Not Speak Its Name* references avowed Victorian homosexual John Addington Symonds (eight years Dodgson's junior and a Harrow/Oxford alumnus), who describes homosexuality as being:

> . . . rife in the English public schools of the period, which he attributed to compulsory classical studies and the lack of a co-educational system. . . [and to] idleness. . . wealth. . . and stupidity. . . [of the lower aristocratic students]. . . .
>   Every boy of good looks had a female nickname, and a boy who yielded his person to an older lover was known as the elder lad's `bitch´. . . . The talk in the

dormitories and studies was of the grossest character, with repulsive scenes of onanism, mutual masturbation, and obscene orgies of naked boys in bed together. There was no refinement, just animal lust, and it was little wonder that what he saw filled the young Symonds with disgust and loathing. [21]

Hyde goes further to describe how Symonds became aware that the headmaster, a "saintly" man, "a thorough hypocrite" as he preached against and punished the very behavior in others, pressured his classmate into a homosexual love affair, told his father, who, "horrified," threatened disclosure until the man resigned. The elder Symonds was later to thwart another visible promotional opportunity with the threat of disclosure. [22] I mention this passage only to point out how Symonds, who struggled with his own homosexuality, appears to have had a relationship with his father as an emotional resource upon which he was able to draw in his anxiety about his friend and his concerns that the school was being head-mastered by someone involved in such behavior with children. Symonds later turned his energies into pioneering early writings on the subject of homosexuality. Charles Dodgson does not appear to have had such a relationship with his father.

All aspects of the public school were difficult. The day ran from 7 a.m. to 10 p.m. every day except Sunday, which was marginally shorter and focused on religious subjects. With the stress from the academic requirements so high, combined with the schedule and lack of control students had over their environment, the potential for explosiveness of emotions and misuse of power for the brief periods in which it could be expressed were enormous. Dr. Tait allowed the boys to supplement the meals provided by cooking throughout the halls using open fires. The Sixth Form generally took their meals in their rooms. The amount of food allowed within the building attracted large numbers of rats, which the boys would capture by covering the rat holes with their socks. They trapped the victim and swung the sock against the furniture and walls, finally removing the dead animal so that socks could be worn the next day. One can only imagine what practical jokes were played with the carcass. The floorboards of the Sixth Form quarters were removed annually to collect the large quantities of bones from the remains of mutton chops which had been disposed of after eating meals in quarters. Dormitories were heated by centrally located fireplaces, so when the weaker boys had their blankets taken by the stronger they were left without protection from the cold. This repeated experience is believed to have comprised the origins of Dodgson's bronchial problems.

Dodgson's School Experience

On August 1, 1844, Charles arrived at Richmond to begin his public schooling. On the 5th, he wrote a long letter to his sisters Fanny and Memy. On the 10th, his parents arrived on a visit to check on his adjustment to the new environment. They returned home satisfied that he was doing well.

The letter to his sisters represents what I believe to be a key document in understanding these years and their aftermath, due in no small part to the work done by Derek Hudson and his handwriting analyst, Dr. M. J. Mannheim. The letter is produced from Collingwood, although the italics come from the version presented by Morton Cohen in his *Letters*. (I did this because I think the emphasis is real and an integral part of Charles' message.) I have omitted the opening greetings to the family and the identification of his new friends.

Richmond School, Yorkshire
August 5 [1844]

My dear Fanny and Memy,
... The boys have played two tricks upon me which were these — they first proposed to play at `King of the Cobblers´ and asked me if I would be king, to which I agreed. Then they made me sit down and sat (on the ground) in a circle round me, and told me to say `Go to work´ which I said, and they immediately began kicking me and knocking me on all sides. The next game they proposed was `Peter, the red lion,´ and they made a mark on a tombstone (for we were playing in the church-yard) and one of the boys walked with his eyes shut, holding out his finger, trying to touch the mark; then a little boy came forward to lead the rest and led a good many very near the mark; at last it was my turn; they told me to shut my eyes well, and the next minute I had my finger in the mouth of one of the boys, who had stood (I believe) *before* the tombstone with his mouth open. For 2 nights I slept alone, and for the rest of the time with Ned Swire. The boys play me no tricks now. The only *fault* (tell Mama) that there has been was coming in one day to dinner *just* after grace. On Sunday we went to church in the

morning, and sat in a large pew with Mr. Fielding, the church we went to is close by Mr. Tate's house, we did not go in the afternoon but Mr. Tate read a discourse to the boys on the 5th commandment. We went to church again in the evening. Papa wished me to tell him all the texts I had heard preached upon, please to tell him that I could not hear it in the morning nor hardly one sentence of the sermon, but the one in the evening was I Cor. i. 23. I believe it was a farewell sermon, but I'm not sure. Mrs. Tate has looked through my clothes and left in the trunk a great many that will not be wanted. I have had 3 misfortunes in my clothes, etc. 1st I cannot find my tooth-brush, so that I have not brushed my teeth for 3 or 4 days, 2nd I cannot find my blotting paper, and 3rd I have no shoe horn. The chief games are football, wrestling, leap frog, and fighting. Excuse bad writing.

Yr affect brother CHARLES.

To Skeff [*a younger brother, aged six*].

MY DEAR SKEFF, —
Roar not lest thou be abolished.
Yours, etc., —[23]

The analysis of this letter begins with the mysterious message to Skeffington. This greeting and sentence has been considered by all to be the earliest example of Dodgson's nonsense, laced with the recurring theme of violence and annihilation. I believe it is the earliest example of his communication in anagrammatic form, as it becomes: "*To Skeff: ask mother about the red lion; safer boys fled.*" I believe this represents at the age of twelve, on the fifth day of school, most likely confronting a traumatic event, the creation of a perfect anagram. For the sense of the original — being abolished if he roars like a lion — is matched by the lack of safety implied in playing the game of "Peter, the red lion." But his precocious sophistication doesn't end there; for in underlining "*To*" in the first greeting — the second greeting is redundant — he could produce another anagram: "*O, Skeff: ask mother about the red lion; faster boys fled.*" Perhaps he was not as fast in fleeing as the others. The word *peter* was Victorian slang for *penis*. The word *lion* would come to have a special dual meaning to Dodgson throughout his life, both in his comments about being "lionised" by worshippers of Lewis Carroll and his statement that he would never want to be referred to as a lion.

Examining that portion of the letter in more detail, we could truly ask the purpose of this finger pointing game, innocent enough for his sisters, perhaps. Was the boy holding out his finger to touch the mark on the tombstone or was it really "Peter," his "red lion?" Was "that something" really in the mouth of the boy standing before the tombstone or was the rectum involved? Is the italicized *before* a very precocious child's play on the word *behind*? Charlie "believed" the boy was standing "before" the tombstone; did he *ever* open his eyes? Or did he sub-consciously block out all memory of the traumatic moment. Was he the boy before the tombstone, in a looking-glass reversal of the story? Did he flee? Did the boys stop playing tricks on him because he accepted the initiation, capitulating to something very likely not in his prior experience, even if he had read of it in his Greek studies? If he were the last boy in line, observing all the others who went before him, did he know what was in store for him and prepare himself to "gut it out" in order to be accepted; or was he tricked? If so, why him among all the new boys?

Ironically, Mr. Tate's early discourse to the boys was on the 5th Commandment which prohibits violence and killing, perhaps not on the youngster's mind as he reviewed his earliest experience. This sermon was followed by one on *I Corinthians*, the only one he heard and remembered, whose theme is: "But we preach Christ crucified, a stumbling block to the Jews, and foolishness to the Greeks." Was Charlie suddenly introduced to the personal reality of "Greek foolishness" as he struggled to sort out the game behavior within a Christian school environment chosen by his parents for him? Was "Christ crucified" to become a stumbling block for him, too? Was the "bad handwriting" a sign of lingering anxiety? Was he hoping that his parents might recognize the nature of the game, especially his father, who had gone through the system, and provide relief? Why was this first letter home written to his older sisters, not to his parents? Unable to solve an anagram using *father*, I asked why he advised Skeff to "ask mother?" Was a pernicious cynicism already creeping in? Was Skeffington ever aware of the hidden message?

There may be no answers to these questions, although I doubt Skeffington ever understood the message; if he had, it is unlikely Collingwood would have been allowed to publish it. Perhaps some answers may come from the handwriting analysis performed for Derek Hudson by Dr. Mannheim, very fortunately done using this letter as representative of his youthful handwriting. Mannheim finds that the writing reflects an extremely high "maturity, tenderness and sensitivity," very demanding on the self, with signs of him being "overburdened" by stress. This causes him to wonder what brought

Dodgson to such a personality at such a young age. He finds no sign of the adolescent anxiety he says one would expect, finding him beyond that stage even at age 12, with an adult personality already formed; he views such precocity as having the principal undesirable effect of leaving Dodgson untouchable by "important influences." [24]

In her book, *The Drama of the Gifted Child* published in 1981, Alice Miller identifies the "gift" possessed by such abused children very much as extraordinary maturity, tenderness, and sensitivity. But this gift does not serve the self of the child and emerging adult. It represents the child's ability to respond to parental needs for the child to be what they want and need him to be to satisfy their own self-esteem needs. These children possess the innate gift of sensing that they must deny themselves in favor of the parent. This later becomes a unique sensitivity to the needs of others, especially parent-surrogates, with either learned constructive or pathological ways of responding.

Upon further examination of the letter, we find that after describing these two games, Charlie responded like the gifted child to what he perceived his parents' interests were in him. Mama is informed that he committed the *"fault"* of being late for dinner and grace, adding three insignificant details on what had been forgotten or lost, and that he brought more clothes than were needed; this saved Mama's reputation. Papa is told what the religious themes were at the various services, as best he could remember; Papa was assured his son was paying attention to the important things.

Collingwood follows the presentation of this letter with his description of the experience, in which he appears to reflect that the family believed Charles weathered the experience with the most positive effects on his emotional life.

> The discomforts which he, as a `new boy,´ had to put up with from his school-mates affected him as they do not, unfortunately, affect most boys, for in later school days he was famous as a champion of the weak and small, while every bully had good reason to fear him. Though it is hard for those who have only known him as the gentle and retiring don to believe it, it is nevertheless true that long after he left school his name was remembered as that of a boy who knew well how to use his fists in defence of a righteous cause. [25]

That description acknowledges their belief that most boys emerge from the experience callous to its effect on them and its victims. One could also wonder where they got their information. It seems safe to conclude that what was really happening to Charles and his response was kept pretty much from the awareness of his family. He would later describe the Rugby experience which followed that at Richmond only briefly in two oft-quoted passages. One is from his diary of 1855.

> During my stay I made I suppose some progress in learning of various kinds, but none of it was done *con amore*, and I spent an incalculable time in writing out impositions — this last I consider one of the chief faults of Rugby School. I made some friends there, the most intimate being Henry Leigh Bennett (as college acquaintances we find fewer common sympathies, and are consequently less intimate) — but I cannot say that I look back upon my life at a Public School with any sensations of pleasure, or that any earthly considerations would induce me to go through my three years again. [26]

There are two observations to be made with this entry. First is the generalization ". . . a Public School," which reflects that he was no doubt aware that things were no different elsewhere. Secondly, he refers to the experience as lasting "three years." Clark indicates that he entered Rugby on his fourteenth birthday (January 27, 1846), and completed his studies in December, 1849, which reflects a nearly four year duration unless holidays are excluded. [27] One could wonder if he blocked out a whole year of the experience.

In another brief diary entry made on March 18, 1857, he comments on the more favorable conditions at Radley School, which had private rooms for its students:

> . . . I can say that if I had been thus secure from annoyance at night, the hardships of the daily life would have been comparative trifles to bear. [28]

Nighttime would become a problem for Dodgson for the remainder of his life and is mentioned frequently in his serious poems.

No doubt due to his influence, his brothers would attend Twyford School, Hampshire, headed by his friend George Kitchin, a school of which he wholeheartedly approved both for its teaching quality and its being ruled by love. [29]

Charles lived up to his parents' expectations academically, a not unexpected achievement for bright children given to pleasing others. At Richmond, mathematics proved to be his best subject; he had more difficulty with the Classics since he took liberties with its grammar.

Nevertheless, he did exceptionally well. After the first term, the Headmaster, Dr. Tate (Tait was at Rugby), wrote the following letter to his parents:

> Sufficient opportunities having been allowed me to draw from actual observation an estimate of your son's character and abilities, I do not hesitate to express my opinion that he possesses, along with other and excellent natural endowments, a very uncommon share of genius. Gentle and cheerful in his intercourse with others, playful and ready in conversation, he is capable of acquirements and knowledge far beyond his years while his reason is so clear and so jealous of error, that he will not rest satisfied without a most exact solution of whatever appears to him obscure. He has passed an excellent examination just now in mathematics, exhibiting at times an illustration of that love of precise argument, which seems to him natural.
>
> [There are, however, two faults] . . . of which the removal as soon as possible is desirable, tho' I am prepared to find it a work of time. . . [Tate closes with] . . . You may fairly anticipate for him a bright career. Allow me, before I close, one suggestion which assumes for itself the wisdom of experience and the sincerity of the best intention. You must not entrust your son with a full knowledge of his superiority over other boys. Let him discover this as he proceeds. The love of excellence is far beyond the love of excelling; and if he should once be bewitched into a mere ambition to surpass others I need not urge that the very quality of his knowledge would be materially injured, and that his character would receive a stain of a more serious description still. . . . [30]

It would appear that Dr. Tate sensed something in Charles' way of approaching the learning process, enough to warrant the risk of commenting and thereby offending his parents. From what we have already seen, he may have noticed an overriding willingness in Charles to satisfy others, him as headmaster in particular, of whom in his later years, Dodgson spoke fondly. Perhaps he saw a goal of excelling already being chosen over the aim for excellence. This is a frequent learning response to the achiever already having spent his young life responding to externally defined concepts of "excellence" rather than the true self's desires and expectations: excellence as self-defined, based on self experiences which are necessarily different from those of the parents. It reflects a boy with distorted ideals and values striving to satisfy distorted goals and ambitions — the depleted self — continuing to focus all psychic energies on satisfying the needs and expectations of parents or parent-surrogates by excelling in order to receive parental acceptance, approval, and praise. When Dodgson finally embraced his own goals and values, however distorted they may be considered, he pursued excellence as he saw it, an excellence which included the technique of excelling over everyone else by fooling them.

As best can be determined, since very few letters were saved from the Rugby days, Charles never communicated with his family the problems that he would refer to later regarding these years. The letters reflect only polite inquiries into family matters and descriptions of non-controversial happenings at school.

A surviving notebook dated November 13, 1846, contains his name and school address on the cover with the words *is a muff* written in another hand next to his name. [31] OED defines the word as a milksop, a usage consistent with its appearance in *Tom Brown's Schooldays*, while the *1811 Dictionary of the Vulgar Tongue* identifies it as a word for *prostitute*. Fifteen at the time and on the second half of his public school stay, the word could very well have either meaning attached, particularly if he had succumbed at this stage to embrace the behavior either in rage or as a survival mechanism. A common defense against a total loss of control over one's environment when victimized is to join or identify with the aggressor by taking on the offending behavior. In this case, he would take on aggressive deviant behavior because he may not have been physically capable of bullying others. By the same token, it is entirely possible that Charles became a surrogate for other boys, possibly for a fee. Driven by the principles upon which he was raised, a simultaneous wish to turn the tables on the aggressor, a view of himself as dirty, which is a common response of those who have been sexually abused, the forces of a second defense against annihilation could have come into play. This is the repetition compulsion the compulsion to attempt to master the effects of a trauma by repeating it over and over again, rarely with success. The anagrams point uniformly to the passive position in sexual behavior, in this case as receiver of what may have been perceived originally as violence, then embraced as a full-fledged but perverse effort to restore the self.

In a letter written in this period, dated June 25 and attributed to 1847, to her sister Lucy, Mama reflected how proud she was at Charlie's successes in school, expressed concern about him appearing "*thinner*" (a concern of hers throughout his childhood), commented that he appeared well, reflecting the "*highest* spirits," and that he was "*delighted*" with his school achievements [Mrs. Dodgson's italics]. [32]

His academic achievements at Rugby were no less remarkable than those at Richmond. Rarely did he return home without prizes (usually books of his choosing). Often his receipt of awards was limited only by the rule of the school that no more than one prize could be received by a student per term, for he was more often at the top of his class of fifty classmates than the number of awards would indicate. He won eleven prizes while there, with eight being in Mathematics, three in the Classics. His mother kept meticulous records of all of them. In his last term his father received a letter from the Headmaster which recognized his son's achievements in Divinity. [33]

In December of 1849, Dodgson returned home, Rugby finally complete. In May of 1850 he visited Oxford, completed the matriculation requirements which consisted of examination by a tutor, was fitted for the academic cap and gown worn on the campus by all students, and participated in the formal induction ceremony by swearing on his knees to observe the Statutes of the school and the Thirty-Nine-Articles guiding the Anglican Church. There still not being living quarters available for him, he returned home and waited until he could begin studies, finally using temporary quarters provided by a friend of his father's, arriving for study just shy of his nineteenth birthday, on January 24, 1851.

This period at home is an important one because during it he published, with the assistance of his parents, works very much his own since his siblings did not contribute this time, *The Rectory Umbrella*, as a sequel to earlier publications (*Useful and Instructive Poetry*, *The Rectory Magazine*, *The Comet*, *The Rosebud*, *The Star*, and *The Will-o'the Wisp*) and all of which were distributed only within the family. It endured for only this short period, to be replaced later by *Mischmasch*, composed of works developed while at Oxford. [34]

The frontispiece to *The Rectory Umbrella* consists of a drawing by Dodgson which Phyllis Greenacre finds curious to the point of being "arresting." [35]   I believe it can now be interpreted with great certainty, as we recall the anagrammatic re-working of its title. The illustration depicts what appears to be a smiling bearded man with shoulder length hair dressed in a gown with feminine decoration, lying on his side supported by his elbow. He is holding an open umbrella over his head with the fabric between the umbrella's ribs containing the words *Jokes*, *Riddles*, *Fun*, *Poetry*, and *Tales*. Rushing in toward him from either side are seven female-looking, gowned, angelic or fairy-like creatures carrying small baskets, each with a name describing what she is ministering to him — *Cheerfulness*, *Content*, *Mirth*, *Good Humour*, *Taste*, *Liveliness*, and *Knowledge*. Above the umbrella are six fully formed (except for genitals) boy-like imps with angry looks and tousled hair hurling rocks toward his head but which strike the umbrella; each rock is labeled — *Gloom, Spite, Ennui, All-Overishness, Crossness,* and *Spite.*

Knowing that this publication contains Dodgson's first effort at narrative nonsense *The Walking-Stick of Destiny* in which he introduces Baron Slogdod and Signor Blowski, this frontispiece expresses his challenge to his family through publishing, a challenge in which he — depicted as of questionable gender — administered to by fairy-like figures to insure he maintains his smile, protected by the umbrella of his nonsense and poems, will ward off all of the bad feelings which continuously intrude to destroy him. The targets of his rage and weapons for its expression are chosen; and throughout it all, he will maintain the facade of a false, happy, and contented self.

I believe the basis for Dodgson's rage, now becoming acted out revenge, stems from the realization that he was betrayed by his parents as a child. Having responded to all their wishes for him as best he could, he felt thoroughly betrayed in their abandonment of him to the public school experience, for which he had been totally unprepared; an abandonment which raised intense feelings of annihilation of both his body and spirit. He came to see his parents and the adult-approved environment as totally hypocritical, in total contradiction to espoused principles. He saw them as contradicting in action virtually every word of the love that had been preached, and he finally concluded that the love shown was not for him as he was but for what he was and would be for them. This was well beyond the feelings of abandonment felt by many damaged children as they enter into and move beyond adolescence, created by feelings of alienation from the values taught and an awareness of lack of preparation or "fit" with the society they see themselves about to enter. For Charles, the loyalties created by family fusion were ripped apart with feelings of utter personal destruction. Just as absolute loyalty was the family tradition, his revolt would take the form of absolute family disloyalty.

On May 21, 1856, having just read Emily Bronte's *Wuthering Heights*, Dodgson commented in his diary (one wonders if it were for future biographers) that he could not fathom any personalities more despicable than Catherine and Heathcliff. In that story Catherine, madly in love with Heathcliff, married another who could provide the life of material comfort she longed for and she never lived to be her true self. Heathcliff is considered a nearly satanic figure by critics because he lived a life of rage-fueled revenge directed towards every family member, whom he destroyed economically, emotionally and physically in retaliation for his own abuse and rejection by his step-siblings and his beloved step-sister Catherine whom he loved obsessively. He finally becomes haunted by the ghost of Catherine which appears to him periodically after her premature death.

Perhaps Dodgson was angered anew by the wretchedness so obvious in the characters involved in what could be perceived as a somewhat incestuous relationship, and the fact that it reminded him of his own parents' kinship. Perhaps he saw himself as both Heathcliff and Catherine incarnate since he made a very close emotional connection to a passage in Bronte's in Chapter XII, in which Catherine's mad delirium is described. I have shown in brackets and italics the words that would have made the passage his own:

My late anguish was swallowed in a proxysm of despair. I cannot say why I felt so wildly wretched: it must have been temporary derangement; for there is scarcely cause. But, supposing at twelve years old I had been wrenched from the Heights *[Daresbury/Croft garden]* and every early association, and my all in all, as Heathcliff *[my mother]* was at the time, and been converted at a stroke into Mrs. Linton, the lady of Thrushcross Grange, and the wife of a stranger *[a fag student at public school]*: an exile, an outcast, thenceforth, from what had been my world. You may fancy a glimpse of the abyss where I grovelled! [36]

His Mother's Death

Two days after finally arriving at Oxford, and one day before his nineteenth birthday, his forty-seven year old mother died very unexpectedly. There was not time for him to be in attendance during her last hours. Upon learning of her death he went home immediately, and stayed for a short time before returning to Oxford. We know nothing about the reactions of individual family members to her death. He says nothing about it and family reports state that there was a note of melancholy about him for several months thereafter. This melancholy no doubt had several complex sources, given what appears to be the love/hate relationship he had toward her. But it would seem that with the memories of love being past-related and hate as the current operative emotion, that the melancholy may have been associated with the thought that she would escape the full fury of his revenge. Alternatively, and perhaps more likely, it is very possible that the loss he was suffering was the realization that he would be frustrated in his efforts to attack his mother in secret right under her nose while he continued to play the role of the loyal and devoted son.

With the absence of a mother in the still large family of young children, Edwin the youngest just five years old, they were fortunate in the response provided by Aunt Lucy Lutwidge, Mrs. Dodgson's sister. A spinster, she was probably as well trained as her sister had been in household management and child rearing. There had been nothing to fill her life since the death of her sickly father three years earlier and she assented to move into the household and fulfill a mother's duties. She stayed there for the rest of her life and biographers report that her outgoing personality and ways were much welcomed by the children [37], most likely in acknowledgment of the contrast to their mother.

Oxford

In this text, only a cursory focus is given to Dodgson's years as an Oxford student where studies occupied nearly all of his time. He did exceptionally well in mathematics, became a teaching Fellow in 1852, and received his B.A. with First Class Honors in Mathematics and Second Class Honors in Classics in 1854. He began his full time teaching duties in 1855, having been awarded the Studentship by Dr. Pusey. This provided him with an income of £25 per year, a residence, and assurance that he could remain at Oxford for life, with assigned duties that were modest in their demands, and without any requirement to test his qualifications. [38] He was to remain at Oxford the rest of his life as a lecturer until 1881, and served as Sub-Librarian until 1857 when he replaced his close friend Vere Bayne. He would receive his M.A. in 1857 and be ordained Deacon in 1861. There was the requirement that dons take orders as priests in the Church and, until shortly after he was awarded the Studentship, there was also the requirement that dons remain celibate. However Dodgson never went on to full priesthood, the circumstances of which will be reviewed as we discuss the place of religion in his adult life in Chapter 12.

During these years he began keeping a daily diary, but these earliest volumes, the first of which contained fifteen months material, were among the four missing and presumed lost between 1898, when Collingwood used them, and 1932, when the remainder were found in the basement of the family home. Dodgson had just a few close friends, including a Richard Colley, whom he also accompanied on long walks, until Colley left Oxford in 1859.

Clark suggests that the community of celibate men was hardly a healthy atmosphere, with the defects "obvious." [39] Hyde is more specific, and quotes a letter written to the *Daily Cronicle* in 1895, the unidentified writer responding to the trial of Oscar Wilde, who "got caught" in a practice more common than was admitted:

> ... Why does not the Crown prosecute every boy at a public or private school or half the men in the Universities?
> In the latter places `poederism´ is as common as fornication, and everybody knows it. ... [40]

If the activities which it appears were very much a part of Dodgsons public school experience had become a way of life for him, the opportunities for them, perhaps with internal, self-soothing, feeling-generating compulsions replacing external coercion, were there at Oxford. In the meantime, well before he was to meet the Liddell children, he was already gaining a reputation as a storyteller at the seashore, usually surrounded by a crowd of delighted children. [41]

Dr. Mannheim studied the handwriting of a letter written by Dodgson (pictured on page 65 of Hudson's work) in 1852 at age twenty. He found him more than before "rigidly set in his ways," less sensitive and less open to both people and events, "decidedly introverted" with nearly all stimulation coming from "within," considerably more egotistical with impulses fixated in the past. "... There is a facade of social adjustment" covering a "*very* rebellious mind" [Hudson's (Mannheim's) italics]. He saw Dodgson's interests as in things systematic which do not touch the emotions. [42]   The extraordinary sensitivity directed outward in puberty (recalling Mannheim's analysis of the "Dear Skeff..." letter) had been turned totally inward, with all energies now directed toward rebellion and the maintenance of self-cohesion.

Dodgson's psychological condition upon completing this experience might be best described by a segment from J. A. Symonds' work on sexual inversion which depicts the situation a young boy might find himself in with no ability to disclose or express what is to him a natural orientation or experience:

> In some cases the nerves give way altogether: mental alienation sets in; at last the wretch finds in a madhouse that repose which life would not afford him.   Others terminate their unendurable situation by the desperate act of suicide. . . . [43]

In a letter to one of his sisters written in 1896, two years before his death, Dodgson responded to the passing of a family member and wrote of his own feelings toward death:

> It is getting increasingly difficult now to remember *which* of one's friends remain alive, and *which* have gone `into the land of the great departed, into the silent land.´ Also, such news comes less and less as a shock, and more and more one realises that it is an experience each of *us* has to face before long. That fact is getting *less* dreamlike to me now, and I sometimes think what a grand thing it will be to be able to say to oneself, `Death is *over* now; there is not *that* experience to be faced again. . . .´ [44]

He then goes on to describe some of the writing work he still hopes to accomplish before his death.

I interpret that final statement differently than others, seeing it not as an acknowledgement of his own mortality looking forward, but as a statement of relief; that his death-like experience begun long ago, which has been reoccurring daily, will finally be over, never to be endured again as the final rest of *real* death occurs.

A poem written in 1868, thirty years before his death and published posthumously in *Three Sunsets* closes this Chapter. From an objective literary standpoint it may well be the worst poem in the book, as Lennon described it. [45] But believing that it was and is misunderstood, I invite readers to view it from the perspective of the psychological and emotional state of Charles Dodgson at the time and thus disregard its "objective" merit. I suggest it be viewed as the effort of a man with all wholesome emotions totally destroyed. This attempt to write about his deepest feelings, incorporates all the character images except the "listener" aspects of himself. He portrays himself as an adult of forty-four recalling two childhood images of himself, a girl, and a boy — "twin spirits," and refers to a trauma that occurred "half a life behind," and the period in his life when the nighttime became a constant dread. The poem even contains hints of suicidal ideation.

The Valley of the Shadow of Death

Hark, *said the dying man, and sighed,*
  To that complaining tone —
Like sprite condemned, each eventide,
  To walk the world alone.
At sunset, when the air is still,
I hear it creep from yonder hill:
It breathes upon me, dead and chill,
  A moment, and is gone.

My son, it minds me of a day
  Left half a life behind,
That I have prayed to put away
  For ever from my mind.
But bitter memory will not die:
It haunts my soul when none is nigh:
I hear its whisper in the sigh
  Of that complaining wind.

And now in death my soul is fain
  To tell the tale of fear
That hidden in my breast hath lain
  Through many a weary year:
Yet time would fail to utter all —
The evil spells that held me thrall,
And thrust my life from fall to fall,
  Thou needest not to hear.

The spells that bound me with a chain,
  Sin's stern behests to do,
Till Pleasure's self, invoked in vain,

A heavy burden grew —
Till from my spirit's fevered eye,
A hunted thing, I seemed to fly
Through the dark woods that underlie
  Yon mountain-range of blue.

Deep in those woods I found a vale
  No sunlight visiteth,
Nor star, nor wandering moonbeam pale;
  Where never comes the breath
Of summer-breeze — there in mine ear,
Even as I lingered half in fear,
I heard a whisper, cold and clear,
  "That is the gate of Death.

"O bitter is it to abide
  In weariness alway:
At dawn to sigh for eventide,
  At eventide for day.
Thy noon hath fled: thy sun hath shone:
The brightness of thy day is gone:
What need to lag and linger on
  Till life be cold and gray?

"Oh well," it said, "beneath yon pool,
  In some still cavern deep,
The fevered brain might slumber cool,
  The eyes forget to weep:
Within that goblet's mystic rim
Are draughts of healing, stored for him
Whose heart is sick, whose sight is dim,
  Who prayeth but to sleep!"

The evening-breeze went moaning by,
  Like mourner for the dead,
And stirred, with shrill complaining sigh,
  The tree-tops overhead:
My guardian-angel seemed to stand
And mutely wave a warning hand —
With sudden terror all unmanned,
  I turned myself and fled!

A cottage-gate stood open wide:
  Soft fell the dying ray
On two fair children, side by side,
  That rested from their play —
Together bent the earnest head,
As ever and anon they read
From one dear Book: the words they said
  Come back to me to-day.

Like twin cascades on mountain-stair
  Together wandered down
The ripples of the golden hair,
  The ripples of the brown:
While, through the tangled silken haze,
Blue eyes looked forth in eager gaze,
More starlike than the gems that blaze
  About a monarch's crown.

My son, there comes to each an hour
  When sinks the spirit's pride —
When weary hands forget their power
  The strokes of death to guide:
In such a moment, warriors say,
A word the panic-rout may stay,
A sudden charge redeem the day
  And turn the living tide.

I could not see, for blinding tears,
  The glories of the west:
A heavenly music filled mine ears,
  A heavenly peace my breast.
"Come unto Me, come unto Me —
All ye that labour, unto Me —
Ye heavy-laden, come to Me —
  And I will give you rest."

The night drew onwards: thin and blue
  The evening mists arise
To bathe the thirsty land in dew,
  As erst in Paradise —
While, over silent field and town,
The deep blue vault of heaven looked down;

Not, as of old, in angry frown,
    But bright with angels' eyes.

Blest day! Then first I heard the voice
    That since hath oft beguiled
These eyes from tears, and bid rejoice
    This heart with anguish wild —
Thy mother, boy, thou has not known;
So soon she left me here to moan —
Left me to weep and watch, alone,
    Our one beloved child.

Thou, parted from my aching sight,
    Like homeward-speeding dove,
She passed into the perfect light
    That floods the world above;
Yet our twin spirits, well I know —
Though one abide in pain below —
Love, as in summers long ago,
    And evermore shall love.

So with a glad and patient heart
    I move toward mine end:
The streams that flow awhile apart,
    Shall both in ocean blend.
I dare not weep: I can but bless
The Love that pitied my distress,
And lent me, in Life's wilderness,
    So sweet and true a friend.

But if there be — O if there be
    A truth in what they say,
That angel-forms we cannot see
    Go with us on our way;
Then surely she is with me here,
I dimly feel her spirit near —
The morning-mists grow thin and clear,
    And Death brings in the Day.

Dodgson's italicized segment in the first line, "[Hark,] *said the dying man, and sighed*," is an anagram for "*Gay men hid as things. . . and died*," and defines along with the poem his life for him as a living death.

CHAPTER 9

RESURRECTION: A NEW IDENTITY

Thus far the published psychological analyses of Charles Dodgson have followed the Freudian model based on the story of Oedipus' conflict between father and son over the son's affection for his mother. The work most cited is Phyllis Greenacre's 1955 work *Swift and Carroll: A Psychoanalytic Study of Two Lives* which is still considered the most complete and authoritative text in the field. In 1977 Jean Gattegno explored the issues in his chapter "Papa and Mama" in *Fragments of a Looking-Glass*. He finds a problem with the Oedipal interpretation, and suggests that Dodgson's life seemed to lack an Oedipal struggle. In a footnote he reflects that things would be far more explainable, except for Dodgson's fixation with pre-pubertal girls, if he were a girl instead of a boy. Finally, he posits an *anti* or *an*-Oedipal situation. Drawing on Freud's thinking prior his development of the notion of an Oedipal complex, Gattegno suggests that Dodgson neither wished his father dead nor considered his mother castrating, but instead accomplished the development task of revolt from parents in a passive way, by escape into fantasy. This is the world of imagination embraced over the real world of conflict and the special world of gifted people and neurotics. While Gattegno's thinking is better than the suggestion that Dodgson suffered only from neuroses deriving from Oedipal issues, we know today that the existence, quality, and intensity of Oedipal conflict and resolution are conditioned by the quality of earlier parental relationships in the development of the child's sense of self. Any passivity that Dodgson possessed was not a healthy passivity, but reflected the blunting of healthy aggression. Such blunting by parental aggression (manifested by outright abuse or subtle coercion) directed toward the child occurs far earlier than the Oedipal stage, continues through it, and forms the seeds for rage. This chapter explores the notion that Dodgson was such a blunted child, who, rather than not revolting at all, engineered his parental revolt well after the Oedipal stage, during adolescence. This is a time when a revolt is often quite obvious and its quality and character is very much conditioned by the way separation has proceeded thus far. I suggest that this revolt was triggered by the total betrayal by his parents that he felt during the Public School experience. The foundations for the revolt were laid in the early years during which he, though in fact coerced, felt he had devoted himself to being all his parents wanted of their child. Sacrificing his real self to satisfy them, he created a false self which conformed to their wishes and which they would love. When betrayed, he in turn betrayed them by living the Jekyll/Hyde existence right in their presence, then right through his life. During this time, not consciously but totally consistent with his store of learned knowledge, he assumed a new identity, that of another childhood victim from Greek mythology. He incorporated into his life all of the themes from the mythical story of Orestes, and in his life updated the ancient story for modern man. Some of the themes are reflected in his works, thus making them even further autobiographical. Dodgson most likely possessed the insights to know in Greek terms who he was and who he was not; and in the example of his life we learn the intensity rage takes when created by the destruction of the early self.

The story of Orestes has been written many times, most likely because it has resonated with thinkers and audiences as a basic and precious story of man's struggle to achieve psychological survival. It was first written by Aeschylus around 400 B.C., with later versions produced by Sophocles, Euripides, and in more modern versions by Robinson Jeffers in his "Tower Beyond Tragedy" and Eugene O'Neil in his "Mourning Becomes Electra". My analysis draws on the trilogy written by Aeschylus: *The Agamemnon*, *The Libation Bearers*, and *The Eumenides* (Furies), as translated by Paul Roche in 1962.

To summarize briefly, the story of Orestes concerns intergenerational family deception and violence which reaches its climax when Orestes avenges the murder of his father by his mother by in turn murdering her. In retribution for that act of matricide, he must endure sleepless nights in which he is hounded by the Furies, protectors of parents. In desperation he finally entreats the god Apollo that he be granted a trial, to finally resolve the justice of his act. Orestes is acquitted by Pallas Athena, the goddess of Wisdom, who breaks the tied vote of the jury. Orestes is vindicated of the crime of matricide on the basis that he was commanded to do so by the god Apollo but also on the broader principle that revenge and retribution — even matricide — is justified for some crimes.

For at the beginning it was matricide that became the young Charles' obsession, matricide committed silently by incorporating into his works everything that would have been rejected most by his mother, would have killed her if she had known. It is most likely that he incorporated into his own life some of the themes about which he wrote and described so obsessively until his death. The Orestes story is not, however, a perfect parallel to Dodgson's experience. For reasons we shall see below, he also came to hold his father responsible for his betrayal and abandonment. It appears that he slowly devised the means to attack him directly when he incorporated into his explicit sexual imagery and disclosure segments of the Christian Bible, the text that his father held most sacred. For while it appears to have begun as metaphorical matricide only, it very quickly broadened to include his father and siblings, indeed the entire Dodgson family and name. Totally lacking in any reasoned control, he risked and challenged disclosure constantly, and left for future generations the total burden of the suffering that disclosure during his lifetime would have created for himself.

Lest readers raise the question, there is certainty that Charles was familiar with the plays in question as he quoted from The *Agamemnon* in a mock epic he wrote in 1853 at age 21 entitled "The Ligniad" in which he played on *The Iliad* by Homer as well as the Latin derivative (Lignum -wood) for the last name of a friend by the name of Woodhouse for whom it was written. The work is not published in collected works, so I cannot place into context the line quoted by Clark "`Ah, me, I am smitten´." While the second Book of "The Ligniad" focuses on the game of cricket, in the first he writes of his own "precocity in the classics as an infant, his resolve to read no Greek till he found the lost plays of Euripides, and his stoicism in adversity." [1]

The Orestes Story

There are many passages in the Orestes story which could only have resonated with the young man based on what we already have seen and inferred about his life through adolescence. In order to identify the pertinent similarities and differences as the story applies to Dodgson's life, I shall review it in more detail. Agamemnon, husband of Clytemnestra, has been away for ten years leading the fight against Troy over the kidnap and rape of Clytemnestra's sister, Helen, by Paris. While away, he sacrificed their oldest daughter as an offering to the gods for success in battle, an act that his wife felt was a

terrible betrayal of her.   During her husband's long absence
Clytemnestra took Agamemnon's first cousin Aegisthus as a lover and
they lived together in Agamemnon's house with her youngest daughter
Electra. Orestes, ostensibly due to his mother's wish to protect him as
he was growing up, had been sent away at an early age to be raised "in
a safe place." When Agamemnon returns from battle victorious with
his own slave-lover Cassandra in tow, Clytemnestra and Aegisthus
murder them both that very day. Mother and lover continue their rule
of the city of Argos, an activity had assumed in Agamemnon's absence.
Before Cassandra dies, she predicts:

> One day a young avenger shall arrive,
>   A shoot of the stock:
> Both matricide and patri-punisher.
> Exile, outlaw, ostracized from here,
>   He shall come back
>   To fit the copingstone of sin
>   Upon the perfect disenchantment of this house. [2]

In the second of the three plays, Orestes returns home.

> ... in his whole person shines out the symmetry and the
> brilliance of white skin and lustrous hair which is seen in the
> young Greeks in the wrestling-schools of Athens. [3]

Orestes offers a lock of hair as a sign of love and mourning and
prays over the grave for support from Zeus in avenging his father's
death, a commitment he has already made. Electra joins Orestes and
they remain near the grave and provide mutual encouragement as
they decide to avenge the murder of their father. Orestes now claims
that he had received a command from the gods to avenge the death
— an oracle from Apollo received while at Delphi. This command from
the god Apollo carried with it not only encouragement which fueled the
hate required to perform the heinous acts necessary to avenge his
father's death but "dire predictions" regarding his own well being if he
failed to do so. [4]
         Orestes fears that failure to respond to this command will result
in his being hounded by the avenging Furies, those repugnant
creatures from the Underground who are bound by divine command to
avenge parents, especially mothers, against neglectful children. (It is
interesting to note that they also worked on behalf of older children
against younger ones. [5]) The Furies were "spirits of the night," with

hair "entwined with knotted snakes" who brought onto their targets all of the psychological torment wreaked by guilt.

In the meantime, Clytemnestra has had a dream which greatly disturbs her, and which causes her to send offerings to the tomb of Agamemnon to assuage her emerging fear and guilt. Orestes learns of the dream in which:

> . . . she gave birth to a dragon, who fed with his savage jaws at her own breast. She sprang up in terror, and could not rest till these libations had been sent to her husband's tomb. Even to Clytemnestra remorse has come at last, and conscience makes her connect every terror with her crime [chased herself by the Furies who protect her husband]. She could not know what this dragon meant, but Orestes accepts it as a type of himself: [6]

> By the earth, and by my father's tomb,
> I pray this dream comes true in *me*.
> Yes, I think it tallies all along.
> If this snake emerges from the place where I came from,
>   was snuggled in my baby clothes:
>   if it mouthed the breast that suckled me,
>   blent the sweet milk with clotted blood,
>   and if she shouted out with pain and shock —
>   then this hideous freak she nursed
>   means she surely dies: dies viciously.
> I turn snake to murder her.
> That is what this dream forebodes. [7]

After murdering her lover Aegisthus, Orestes confronts his mother even as she takes up an axe to defend herself from him. First she tries to call on her relationship as loving mother, then expresses a wish to share a home with him, and finally she threatens Orestes with the curse of a lifetime of torment at the hands of the Furies. Seeing Orestes' resolve as he turns toward her after killing her lover, Clytemnestra begins to plead for her life by reminding him that he once nursed at her breast:

> CL: Wait, son, wait. My baby, soften
>   towards this bosom where so many times
>   you went to sleep, with little gums
>   fumbling at the milk which sweetly made you
>   grow.

Orestes weakens momentarily but is reminded by his friend that he must respond to the god Apollo's command, that the risk of making enemies of the gods is far greater than making enemies among men.

> CL: I reared you up from babyhood. Oh, let me then
> grow old with you.
> OR: What! Slay my father ___ then come sharing homes with
> me?
> CL: Fate, my son, is half to blame for that.
> OR: Then Fate arranges for your dying now.
> CL: Son, does a parent's curse mean nothing to you?
> OR: Not a thing. You gave me birth, then flung me out
> ___to misery.
> CL: No, no ___ into a friend's house. Is that to fling?
> OR: Shamefully sold. A freeborn father's son.
> CL: Oh? Then where is the price I got for you?
> OR: *That*, in public, I should blush to say.
> CL: Then blush as well for those senseless things your
> father did.
> OR: Do not taunt him. *You* sat at home. *He* toiled.

Clytemnestra protests that a mother also suffers when left alone by her husband, but finally realizes that Orestes will hear nothing of it. She finally threatens him with the "mother's curse" of a lifetime of torment at the hands of the Furies; but Orestes indicates that he prefers her curse to that of the unavenged murder of his father. Clytemnestra then recalls her dream.

> CL: So *you* are the snake I bore and gave my breast to?

> ORESTES: Yes. Your nightmare saw things straight. [8]

Orestes murders his mother, again invoking the command of Apollo as his defense before the crowd that has gathered. He had assumed that this command would free him from the torment normally inflicted by the Furies for such a crime but as the scene ends he sees them rising from the Underground to begin their work.

In the last of the three plays, "The Eumenides," Orestes, nearly insane now from the unceasing pursuit by the Furies which have hounded him from land to land, finds refuge in the temple of Apollo. The god pledges he will defend him, but in fairness to the Furies, whose function of providing retribution for acts not specifically covered in the law was divinely sanctioned [9], Apollo calls for a trial. He designates Pallas Athena, the Greek goddess of Wisdom, who was generated out of the forehead of Zeus and, therefore, not born of woman, to preside. Apollo reassures Orestes that he will find a way to gain him an "absolute release" from the unending torment, indicating that Orestes was only responding to his command and should hardly be subjected to divine retribution. [10]

The Furies charge Orestes with matricide, for which they claim there can be no forgiveness. Orestes acknowledges the act and defends himself as a true and loyal son avenging the murder of his father, but expresses willingness to accept the judgement of Pallas Athena. Apollo defends Orestes by pointing out the primacy of father-hood over motherhood; he argues that the blood relationship of father to son is more important than that of husband and wife.

> The mother is not parent of her so-called child
> but only nurse of the new-sown seed.
> The man who puts it there is parent;
> she merely cultivates the shoot —
> host for a guest — if no god blights. [11]

After all arguments are completed, Athena turns the verdict over to the jury of twelve gods from Olympus. She charges them to support respect for authority and appropriate reverence and fear, and to consider a level of freedom that balances the issues of anarchy and excessive control. When the votes are counted, the jury is tied six to six. Athena casts the deciding vote in favor of Orestes as she acknowledges that she cannot side with a wife over a husband, or a mother over a son. Orestes is exonerated and freed from the grip the Furies, who in turn become convinced by Athena to turn from their life of creating torment to become spirits of goodness.

> Underneath this [story] lies a terrifying struggle of human passions, a conflict as profound and basic as any in human experience. [12]

While the story of Oedipus tells of the son's struggle with the powerful father, the Orestes story, in its most narrow interpretation tells of the fight for independence from the mother. But in a broader sense, as Rollo May points out in his 1953 work *Man's Search for Himself*, the story tells of the fight for independent existence, not only from the powerful mother, but from both parents and the effects of the struggle between them. [13] For in the story, although accepted by Greek culture based on role assignment, there was really a struggle between the parents which had already affected Orestes. Agamemnon did betray his wife by sacrificing their firstborn daughter to support his own cause and also by taking a lover for himself. He betrayed Orestes by being absent during important years and by remaining unaware of his son's shameful experiences undergone as a young boy. Orestes was abandoned by both parents, although Aeschylus suggests the ancient Greek tradition in having him abandoned only by his mother. Orestes' struggle is seen as a particularly difficult one when compared to the Oedipal conflict because it reflects an attack against the earliest caregiver, the mother, the one who has created the earliest imprints that influence behavior and feelings and against the earliest model for a young boy. But Aeschylus really goes beyond conflict with mother; for in fact, Orestes felt he would have been pursued by the Furies whichever side he took, that of mother or father. [14]

In truth, it was only the (external) command from Apollo to avenge the father's death and the implied protection which accompanied that newly defined relationship with the god that spurred him on. The promise of justification was an essential preface to his action. Aeschylus leaves us today with the dilemma unresolved just as the gods sitting in judgement were unable to reach a consensus, though for different reasons. It is only the same historical understanding we saw regarding the relative position of men and women in child generation which moved the decision in favor of Orestes. The existential issue becomes a striving for independence from both parents, who are individuals in a parental relationship with the child as well as a married couple with their own conflicts. The cry of Orestes is for independence from the need to be forever required to serve his parents' needs and forever subject to being abandoned despite his efforts.

Abandonment and betrayal are less dominant themes in the story as written but are the themes which would have resonated with Dodgson, for Orestes experienced and attributed his abandonment to his mother, not his father, who was unavailable to him for reasons justifiable in the Greek culture. A fact not acknowledged by Aeschylus is that Agamemnon had supported the decision which caused his son to be raised outside the home while the daughter Electra remained with her mother. Aeschylus presents Clytemnestra as "an incarnation of consummate wickedness, triumphant and unashamed. . ." [15] without showing her any real sympathy for the circumstances which brought her to murder her husband. In more modern terms, Aeschylus places Orestes in the position of those subject to blind rage, driven by their inner god-like commands and who act without regard to the motives and actions, and human limitations of others.

Roche points out in his Introduction that Aeschylus' message is that each person is responsible for his and her own behavior despite the influences of the past. He interprets Aeschylus as describing for us the dilemma of choosing between absolute and relative values, between "good and good" rather than good and evil; in any case the choice being made reflects a willingness to make a commitment to action when called for despite the risks. [16] In a very real sense it is the dilemma of "doing as best as one can" given the state of self, with the consequences of the choice not always providing effective self-restoration or seen favorably by others involved or by society. These choices may not be in any really objective sense best for the self because they provide only momentary relief, not resolution, as in Dodgson's case. But for the moment, given the tools developed, they were all he could do.

The Dodgson/Orestes Connection

In attempting to relate this to Charles Dodgson, there are several details which appear and reappear throughout his life. Dodgson had a preoccupation with locks of hair which he collected from his child friends and also exchanged them in his early years, a behavior no doubt also influenced by family behavior in childhood. He kept his hair longer than the style for the day, perhaps as long as he thought Oxford would tolerate. He suffered from insomnia, as we have already discussed and used various devices to keep tormenting thoughts at bay. His father presented himself or was perceived by the child as god-like, yet distant, certainly "away," busy providing support, "fighting the wars," as he supported Pusey in several areas of theological change as part of the Oxford Movement. In the Victorian tradition his mother stayed at home and she attempted to retain and provide the conditions to which she had been accustomed and hoped in turn for her family. The son was sent away to Public School, presumably to friends as there can be no question that his father knew both of the headmasters and what his son would likely be exposed to there. His mother would no doubt have been shocked and ashamed to hear the "price that was paid" in sending Charles into what he perceived to be "bondage." Inferences drawn from the last chapter support the notion that he would have perceived his father, not as murdered, but as castrated in the wife-mother dominated Victorian household in which he appears to have lived. So, there may have been at first an avenging aspect regarding ills done his father: the son attempting to diminish the mother-image in order to enhance the status of the powerless father by humiliating her in secret for what she had done openly in the home. This may have been the primary conscious motive for purposes of self-justification rather than the felt motive of his own betrayal and abandonment.   But, as there may have been some early sympathy toward his father, that would also be lost in rage. As we shall explore in detail later, much of his Christian religious troubles involved the question of "Eternal Punishment" which arose in the form of Fury-like torments about justification, the curse of feelings of guilt.

Orestes in *Alice's Adventures in Wonderland*

Beyond interpreting these incidents from his life, however, we can turn to his own writings.   *Alice's Adventures in Wonderland* represents one of the many "lands" to which he fled. These places of escape also include the land behind the looking-glass, and Outland, Fairyland, and Elveston in the *Sylvie* books. *Alice* itself contains strains of the Orestes story throughout.

The mouse's tale in Chapter III offers the first such thematic reference. A modification from the original work, the mouse tells Alice his long and sad tale, which Dodgson produced with words written in a long and winding figure of a mouse's tail but which I quote here in poetic form:

> Fury said to a mouse,
> That he met in the house,
> `Let us both go to law:
> I will prosecute *you* —
> Come, I'll take no denial;
> We must have a trial:
> For really this morning I've got nothing to do.´
> Said the mouse to the cur,
> `Such a trial, dear sir,
> With no jury or judge, would be wasting our breath.´
> `I'll be judge, I'll be jury.´
> Said cunning old Fury:
> `I'll try the whole cause, and condemn you to death.´

Alice and the mouse then get into an argument over whether or "not" she is paying attention to his tale. Alice, playing with the word *knot*, offers to help undo it. We have a vague allusion to the knotted hair of the Furies and the "knotty" logic of the trial itself with its questionable crime.

At the end of the story, of course, we have the trial of the Knave of Hearts, tried before the twelve animal jurors for the crime of stealing tarts. The major task becomes that of establishing self-identity in the presence of the mother and father figures using the mysterious note written in an unknown hand as evidence. With all of the evidence nonsense and the jurors found in total disarray, Dodgson establishes a sense of chaos which prevents them from reaching a verdict. He produces the same effect in nonsense as was produced in the Orestes dilemma, a tied vote.

When the Queen of Hearts calls for "Sentence first — verdict afterwards," Alice steps forward and with an orgastic climax ends the trial before either a sentence or a verdict is handed down. Perhaps "Pallas"/Dodgson was unwilling and unable at this time to satisfy his own questions regarding justification for the Knave/Dodgson crime against his mother, and thus causes Alice to awaken from the dream before a judgement is rendered. On a totally different level, he terminates the dream/nightmare on the note that he *has* been sentenced first as he refers to the fact that he must live in his "condition." It appears that he blames his mother for this and believes he emerged mother/damaged from the innocence of childhood on the basis that he has done nothing to contribute to his predicament. On another note and even more broadly, the establishment of self-identity becomes, not the evidence, but the crime itself. To the over-controlling mother, establishing self-identity *is* the crime; but the son turned the *means* for establishing self-identity into what a hypocritical society, selective in the obscenity it tolerated, would label a crime.

Quoting from Stuart Collingwood's *The Lewis Carroll Picture Book*, Lennon writes that Dodgson described the three major women figures from the *Alice* works as Furies just as there were three Furies in Greek myth. The Queen of Hearts was "`a sort of embodiment of ungovernable passion, a blind and aimless Fury.´" The Red Queen was a Fury of a different type:

> `*Her* passion must be cold and calm; she must be formal and strict, yet not unkindly; pedantic to the tenth degree, the concentrated essence of all governesses.´

The White Queen was:

> `gentle, stupid, fat, and pale; helpless as an infant. . . just suggesting imbecility but never quite passing into it.´ [17]

In all cases, Dodgson saw these mother figure "types" as ones who inflicted perverse suffering on all with whom they came in contact, especially their own children.

In his version of the Orestes story, Robinson Jeffers extends the conversation between Clytemnestra and Orestes prior to his killing her with a scene in which she attempts to seduce her son. This is a very appropriate interpretation of Clytemnestra's plea that she and Orestes share a home together, something she could in fact do now that both her husband and lover were dead. Such an interpretation fits well with Aeschylus' characterization of her as scheming and ruthless, offering herself in an incestuous relationship with Orestes in a final effort to save her life. It seems clear from the anagrams and Dodgson's depiction of the Duchess and Marchioness of Mock Turtles that physical closeness to the point of intrusiveness involving his mother was very much on his mind. It is very possible that in his psychological condition, where he perceived himself as her favorite, as most writers concur, he could have made interpretations with incestuous connotations. These would have only further fueled the fire of hate as incestuous closeness was linked with the feelings of abandonment.

Perhaps the most important aspect of the Orestes story is the importance of the claim of divine command. Because of this command Orestes virtually becomes an extension of the gods and an instrument of Apollo's own moral pre-judgement regarding the murder of Agamemnon. It is due to an acceptance of Orestes' claim of having received a divine command that justification finally comes. This justification is impossible for Dodgson within his Christian upbringing and the guilt from his acts creates a lifelong psychological disturbance for which the Furies are metaphors.

Jabberwocky

The best and most involved thematic reference to the Orestes story comes from *Through the Looking-Glass* in the material which involves "Jabberwocky." The opening verse that is repeated as the closing verse has already been reviewed and the anagrams found therein contain a theme whereby masturbation will take place until the "evil gender" is slain. A further analysis of the poem with its accompanying illustration becomes the focus now. This picture depicts the Jabberwock, a snake-like dragon, attacking a small long-haired boy who stands with raised sword and is obviously intent on standing his ground against the monster. The illustration was originally intended to be the frontispiece of the work; but Dodgson replaced it with a picture of the bumbling White Knight after he surveyed some parents to determine if his first selection might be too frightening for children. In the story Alice discovers the poem just after the White King faints, having been rebuked by the White Queen (metaphoric castration) for writing what turns out to be the anagram which points to the illustration of the kissing, masturbating courtiers from *Alice's Adventures Under Ground*. The poem is reproduced again for ease of reference and the full Tenniel illustration, the lower corner of which was used on the cover of this book, follows.

Jabberwocky

'Twas brillig, and the slithy toves
  Did gyre and gimble in the wabe:
All mimsy were the borogoves,
  And the mome raths outgrabe.

"Beware the Jabberwock, my son!
  The jaws that bite, the claws that catch!
Beware the Jubjub bird, and shun
  The frumious Bandersnatch!"

He took his vorpal sword in hand:
  Long time the manxome foe he sought —
So rested he by the Tumtum tree,
  And stood awhile in thought.

And, as in uffish thought he stood,
  the Jabberwock, with eyes of flame,
Came whiffling through the tulgey wood,
  And burbled as it came!

One, two! One, two! And through and through
  The vorpal blade went snicker-snack!
He left it dead, and with its head
  He went galumphing back.

"And hast thou slain the Jabberwock?
  Come to my arms, my beamish boy!
O frabjous day! Callooh! Callay!"
  He chortled in his joy. . . .

> 'Twas brillig, and the slithy toves
> Did gyre and gimble in the wabe:
> All mimsy were the borogoves,
> And the mome raths outgrabe.

This Jabberwock monster has all the characteristics of the serpent described in Clytemnestra's dream, but roles have been reversed. While in her dream she gave birth to a serpent, whom Orestes recognizes as himself, Dodgson causes the mother herself to be the serpent. The boy, soon to be freed by slaying the serpent-mother, is depicted, not as the serpent son, but as the human son. This conforms perfectly with Looking-glass logic, for if a mother can give birth to a serpent, it follows that a serpent can give birth to a man. And who is happy with the death of the monster, which at this stage in Dodgson's writing implies that the act is an avenging one? It is none other than the proud father who shouts "my beamish boy. . . Callooh! Callay!"

Sidney Halpern, in his very brief article "The Mother-Killer" which focuses on the Jabberwock, identifies the serpent monster as a persistent mother figure in literature, from the time of the Sumerians to the Egyptians. Halpern writes:

> As with Persus, or the legend of Horus, the monster is slain and her head brought back as proof of victory to a waiting father. The filiarchs have triumphed through the bravery of the young, innocent male in shouldering the guilt for killing the mother. The males then are free to rejoice because they had been liberated from the bondage in which they had served the female (72). . . .
> . . . For the imagined combat, the male substitutes sexual intercourse, to preserve his life and his sanity. . . (74). [18]

If we combine the theme of matricide from the Orestes story with Dodgson's explicit anagrammatic theme in the opening verse and more vaguely in the body of the poem, and identify the "vorpal sword" as the weapon of slaughter, we have the use of sexual activities abhorrent to the mother as the way in which Dodgson is telling us he will gain revenge as his mode of expression. He would later deny remembering what he had meant by *vorpal* sword when asked by an inquiring child. The notion of perversions as gross distortions of normal appetites such as sexual activities undertaken as efforts to restore the self and as expressions of rage in retaliation for the destruction of the self [19] is taught to us by someone quite conscious of both his rage-based actions, targets, and intent.

By re-reading the poem and substituting *penis* for *Jabberwock* (a Doublet *Jabbercock*?) we have the masturbatory fantasy of the boy attempting to control his compulsion. Rising from the "tulgey wood" (pubic hair) in response to erotic thought/images, it "burbled as it came." Dodgson defined *burbled* as his portmanteau word combining *boiled* and *bubbled* (the same words as used to describe the outcome of Bruno's rubbing). *Came* was a valid Victorian word for the experience of orgasm. Combining now the symbolic mother/Jabberwock/penis with the masturbatory activity of loving and loathing, cuddling and abusing, Dodgson points us clearly to the notion thoroughly explored by Khan of the penis serving the function of a transitional object in perversions as it is loved and loathed, cuddled and abused and abandoned when it has served its momentary function of soothing the self (see Appendix 2). [20]

The Dodgson Split

Some writers and biographers have discussed a perceived "split" in the Dodgson personality. Langford Reed takes the strongest position when he contrasts the pedantic, stammering, shy Oxford don with the humorous, childlike Lewis Carroll. There is generally a rejection of that notion. I reject it too as a clear split between Dodgson and Carroll; for as we shall see, both sides of Charles Dodgson appeared under both identities. But there most certainly was a split within the fragile Dodgson character. There was firstly the split that occurs when the damaged self unconsciously creates a false self and hides the true self within the one person. In Dodgson's case, we have a much more serious split, that much like Dr. Jekyll and Mr. Hyde, a story written and published in the mid 1880's. In this case, the split was very much under Dodgson's conscious control as he managed totally what he presented to the public. While the split seems to have occurred at this time, and the diaries indicate he struggled with it and its potential consequences; in his later years he seems to have been more reconciled if not comfortable with the constant presence of a manageable Hyde.

I feel certain that Dodgson came very close to or experienced for a time early in these school years a psychotic break with schizophrenic-type symptoms. I suspect that through some delusionary process he experienced the only thing that could restore the terrible narcissistic damage to his self, i.e., a divine command or permission to strike back, perhaps even to embrace in action the activities he found so destructive and abhorrent — as the only path to self-restoration. It is this kind of a command to which he would perceive himself duty-bound to follow, one that would both sustain him for a lifetime and involve him in the lifetime of torment regarding justification in the Christian sense. Out of this experience emerged the Orestes persona as he was even able to incorporate his parents' teaching of Greek literature into his new destructive role.

Interestingly, after denying her qualifications for attempting a psychological analysis of Dodgson, Elizabeth Sewell, in her seminal work *The Field of Nonsense*, comes closer than anyone in exploring this aspect of his personality. [21] She describes that one of the ways to interpret nonsense is to see it as reflecting "an annihilation of relations, either of language or experience"(4), with the sense of anarchy which results to be enjoyed as everyone's secret, if occasional, wish. While this destruction of relations could occur with peers and sub-ordinates, it could also occur with super-ordinates and even bridge the gap between man and the gods by means of usurpation or by response to a permission or a command. It is only the latter two proposals which would really bridge the gap in the real world (not the nonsense world), as in the god/man relationship that the gods define. In our example, Orestes clearly thought that his response to Apollo's command would render him immune to the revenge of the Furies, and therefore make his own human wish for revenge, otherwise legitimately subject to the Furies, moot. Fear and guilt were replaced momentarily by justification.

In her Chapter XIII entitled "Dodgefather, Dodgson & Coo," Sewell draws on a phrase from James Joyce's *Finnegan's Wake* which she finds remarkable in that Joyce ". . . unites the notions of the Holy Trinity, Carroll, dodging, and a limited liability company." [22] The phrase also connects the son to divinity as the means of limiting his own culpability and liability. Sewell suggests that Dodgson became a god within the self-contained structure of his nonsense works, and emerged as master of words, their meanings, and the relationships of characters. We can add to that list a master of spelling, of letters and a most God-like activity, that of the projection of himself into all of his creations. Sewell finds that when Dodgson moved out of the world of the early works into the world of the *Snark* and *Sylvie*, and let humanity in as is represented by "dreams, delirium, madness, the infinity of nothingness, [and] emotions," he lost God-like control over his environment and produced inferior nonsense . [23] His efforts to bridge the gap between the world of Nonsense in which he could be

God and the world of more reality-based human interaction created in his nonsense works reflected a deterioration in quality and clarity. This is a result similar to that which occurred in his efforts to bridge the gap between the Greek moral world of god-commanded/human-executed retribution and the Victorian Christian world that preached of Original Sin and Eternal Punishment. Throughout his adult life, Dodgson urged and insisted that religious subjects and fun-and-nonsense be kept separate in his presence. The reason seems clearly to be that they represented not just two different worlds for him, but more specifically, two very different worlds of morality, the world of Orestes and the Christian world which he feared giving up totally.

For a precocious adolescent who escaped into fantasy early and often, by his own admission exposed too early to some very sophisticated moral questions and concepts of behavior in his Greek and Latin readings long before he had the maturity to comprehend and integrate them, the stage was set for a traumatic event or sequence of events to cause him to search anywhere in his experience for relief. The world of Orestes provided both that escape and a place of solace and refuge as Dodgson attempted to rebuild a self, to redefine his own existence, "as best he could" by finding a youthful mythical hero he could emulate. As Charles/Orestes matured and his youthful mother-directed hate widened to incorporate his father, he teaches us, by going so far as to challenge the God in whom he was raised, that fathers also have responsibility for what happens to their children.

CHAPTER 10

CHARACTER AND PERSONALITY

Having established the nature and turmoil of Dodgson's inner world as an emerging adult that was buffeted by conflict in the areas of both sexual and moral identity but assuaged in part by his assumption of a reconciling persona, we can now examine how he presented himself physically to the world during his adult life. Despite his attempts to hide this inner world from public view, much of the character and behavior which was visible to the public reflected high levels of anxiety and the presence of an unhealthy self.

Anxiety can make its existence known in many ways. It can reflect inner conflict directly, as is manifested in delinquent or violent acts which place the individual in direct confrontation with societal norms. At such times all defenses become lowered in order to release built-up rage aggressively. Or, the behavior may represent a veiled plea for external intervention to take control of the self until it can regain its own control. Alternatively, behavior can represent a conscious or unconscious effort to present to observers the opposite of the inner reality as a defense against feelings of shame or guilt. This defense in turn causes further degradation in self-esteem and fears of what would happen if the real self became known to outsiders. Finally, with no psychically or physically controlled behavioral release available for the discharge of extreme inner conflict and stress, the body takes upon itself the suffering by the development of any of a variety of stress-related somatic conditions. Therefore, as we explore the character and personality of Charles Dodgson, we have four sources of information: the testimony of those who observed him; his own statements made in diaries and letters (though it is important to remember that some of such statements may represent the defensive building of a facade); later analytical interpretations of his reported behavior based on the state of knowledge regarding human behavior;

and an examination and analysis of the somatic conditions from which he is known to have suffered, especially his stammering and migraine.

There is a twofold purpose in this chapter. Firstly, I wish to complete the biographical picture of the man. Secondly, I hope to demonstrate how closely the picture which emerges fits into the knowledge bases that have been built over the years regarding the etiology of the described behavior and physical conditions. Perhaps unfairly, but consistent with a goal of this work, a complete, detailed biographical chronology is omitted. However, this chapter does explore nearly all aspects of Dodgson's adult life as they reflect his personhood with the exception of the quality of his adult and child-friend relationships and religious beliefs, both of which are allotted separate chapters. I have incorporated into this chapter bits of material from his letters and reported spoken words to refute the hypothesized "split" between Dodgson and Carroll. On very many occasions, Dodgson as Dodgson, not as Carroll appears to have amused himself or reflected anger with friends and family by using the same words and images we have seen in the "Carroll" works, words and images whose double or private meaning he kept from their awareness.

The descriptions of Dodgson's physical characteristics draw very much on Anne Clark's work [1] as well as that of Phyllis Greenacre. [2] Even as a young man, Dodgson presented a 5 ft. 9 in. very slim frame with somewhat rounded shoulders. He nevertheless appeared somewhat taller than he was due to the erectness of his posture. Some contemporaries, including Alice Liddell, said he looked as if he had swallowed a poker. [3] This is an interesting and unconsciously insightful allusion to the word in its slang meaning as Dodgson used it privately; he once chastised one of his child friends severely for describing her own hair as standing up like a poker, directing her to a more appropriate word, *wires*. His thinness had always been a preoccupation with his mother and remained so with his sibling family, who often referred to his "painful thinness." With a left shoulder lower than his right, he stood with a slight tilt and walked with a jerky gait. Skinner described it as a limp. [4] Since there is no indication that Dodgson indeed suffered from any physical deformity or injury to cause such posture or manner of walking, it is safe to conclude that the physical body distortion was at least partly a result of the self being so fragmented. An individual in this disturbed psychic condition, faced with such doubts regarding identity and body integrity, creates distortions in posture as an unconscious effort to "present" the self in a way more acceptable than what he feels is being presented. The natural, more relaxed body position of those feeling self-cohesion is replaced by a created posture. Usually, such a condition is temporary and the body returns to normal once the stress is relieved; but if the stress is never relieved, it can cause a permanently distorted body that reflects the permanently distorted self. Returning to Alice Liddell's allusion, Dodgson took on the appearance of someone whose preoccupation at least in imagery reflected oral/penile sexual behavior.

His face, highlighted by soft, gentle, blue eyes, had an effeminate cast which became increasingly evident as he aged. Despite this appearance, most likely further accentuated by extreme shyness, a high-pitched voice, and a full head of curly, brown hair, which Collingwood indicated always appeared in need of cutting, Dodgson presented a strong and firm handshake. The apparent effeminacy and his students' critical view of him as eccentric was so obvious that they wrote and distributed a parody of one of his own parodies under the name "Louisa Caroline." With his eyes slightly out of level, his frontal appearance was asymmetrical, which gave him a quizzical look. This in turn was accentuated by a slight smile that would move in and out around his lips. Such activity can be a sign of internal versus external emotional stimulation, where amusement is derived from thoughts and feelings which may be independent of or incongruous with what is happening at the moment in interactions. The real meaning to the person so stimulated is kept out of awareness of other parties present. With Dodgson's obvious facility for creating anagrams, he may very well have been collecting unintentional "litter" derived from the speech of others in normal conversation. Although he was rarely known to laugh aloud, there are several reports of incidents in which he laughed nearly convulsively at the behavior of others and of his efforts to suppress these responses.

Dodgson suffered from his stammer throughout his life. He struggled with P's and D's, and even played on his own difficulties and efforts to pronounce "Do-do-dodgson" with the introduction of the "Dodo" among the animals in *Alice's Adventures in Wonderland*. It was this character who suggested to a skeptical group of animals that some physical heat-generating activity be undertaken to dry themselves when they emerged from the pool created by Alice's tears. Skeptical of what he might suggest, they eventually turned to the Caucus Race. Dodgson also drew for his family's amusement a caricature of himself with his hand covering his mouth as he described his speaking style in his early teaching years. He did not find it really quite so humorous, however, and over a three day period in February, 1856, he became terribly discouraged over his inability to control his small class and dismayed at their lack of interest. He expressed wishes to give up teaching all together, but did not, though it did remain a struggle for him. For reasons that will be explored later, his stammer disappeared in the presence of his child-friends. He was deaf in his right ear from an unspecified childhood disease (suggested to be mumps by Selwyn Goodacre [5]). His upper lip trembled as he spoke. This caused him to speak in a very slow deliberate manner. [6] In his later years he finally mastered his affliction to a great extent by using stammer-reducing techniques taught him by the best speech doctors. These methods eventually allowed him to preach with some level of confidence that he would not lose control before the congregation.

Except for the somewhat less formal white trousers and straw hat worn while boating, Dodgson was always attired conservatively and groomed meticulously. He wore black — suits, boots, top hat and gloves — but he occasionally varied the attire when he chose gray gloves. When questioned by his child-friends about why he always wore them, even in summertime, he indicated it was because there was "love" inside them. This response may very well contain masturbatory sexual allusions as well as more obvious efforts to maintain more than appropriate appearances and amuse the children with his play with words and letters. He never wore an overcoat, even when out in winter storms; and he always suffered from colds during the winter. This susceptibility was no doubt exacerbated by a bronchial weakness which derived from a lengthy bout with whooping cough while at Rugby [7] during which time his blankets were either "borrowed" or "forfeited" as part of the fagging experience. This habit of going about under-dressed could have represented a continuation of a psychological denial that he was cold, forced on him during the Rugby years, combined with an unconscious effort to master what was to him a human weakness.

Dodgson ate sparsely, frequently choosing a dry biscuit with sherry (accompanied by restless pacing) instead of the more substantial lunches taken by friends. He ate sound evening meals usually followed by some port. While there has been no suggestion that Dodgson was alcoholic, at the time of its disposal his library revealed five books on the effects of alcohol and alcoholism. One book included notes in his hand, and another explored alcoholism as a mental disease. [8] Such a routine and daily intake can be interpreted today as the presence of non-abusive alcohol dependence. In light of the stress he was under and the fact that he was dominated by his rigid public self-control this intake most certainly functioned for him as a socially acceptable form of partial anesthetization for his distressed self even if he never lost control with it.

As already mentioned, Dodgson was a prodigious walker, even into his sixties. And his estate sale reflected the presence of dumb bells for upper body exercise. In his later years he also kept an exercising cycle. These activities provided both sound exercise and stamina for the long stints standing at his writing-desk, which was the way he did most of his writing. They also provided a release for the nervous energy reflected in his inability to sit for lengthy periods without getting up and pacing. While Dodgson often walked alone, Vere Bayne's diary reflects that he did accompany Dodgson on numerous occasions while the impressions of his child friends were that he and Bayne walked together daily. His own diaries mention them occasionally, especially when there were events he felt significant enough to record or if he found his distance traveled or calculated pace extraordinary.

Dodgson suffered from insomnia most of his adult life. He sometimes worked as late as 4 a.m., busying his mind with the mathematical "Pillow Problems" he acknowledged as his way of avoiding unholy thoughts. It is most likely, however, that he was also developing anagrammatic litter for his "litterature." He reports that he often wrote down his thoughts and discoveries during the night, and even invented a device (Nyctograph) for writing in code in the dark. While he claimed to be in good health most of his life, a claim that is supported by biographers, in his later years he suffered from severe migraine attacks, synovitis (most likely osteo-arthrosis [9]) ague, eczema, boils, and cystitis, all of which he reported in his diary from age fifty-three until his death. [10] It is clear from the 1982 work on migraine by Dr. Dominick Barbara [11] that Dodgson suffered from forms of migraine in his early adult years as well, as he experienced occasional black-outs, perceived and felt body expansions and contractions (as depicted in the *Alice* works, although we have seen they have other meanings, as well), visual distortions, and the occasional integration of and inability to distinguish between dream and reality states, all of which are manifestations of migraine. Using the knowledge of the day he feared these experiences represented epileptic fits derived from hereditary factors that he blamed on the consanguineous relationship of his parents. Most likely he blamed his mother for all his physical limitations, she being the nurturer of the body while his father was the nurturer of the soul in the human creation process as it was understood until later in the century. Although due partly to a lifetime filled with stress, it is relevant that these health problems peaked as he neared completion of the *Sylvie and Bruno* works and subsided thereafter. For they were filled with self-disclosure and involved mental exercises to build and maintain their structure.

Dodgson claimed to suffer from a weak heart, which was a Victorian pre-occupation and usually exaggerated. [12] But I think he was referring to or somatizing his emotional and sexual problems as referenced in *Sylvie and Bruno* with the book "*Diseases of the Heart*" (or did he mean *Hater?*). Reflective of his preoccupation with his health, there were over one hundred twenty books on medical subjects in his library at the time of his death, as listed on the auction sheets. [13]

Dodgson's own mental health seems to have been his prime concern, a theme which recurred in many ways, including a confrontation with a mother and daughter on a train trip. He had not revealed his identity to the mother and in the course of her discussion of the *Alice* books she commented that she had heard that Lewis Carroll had gone quite mad. Dodgson listened attentively and indicated he had not heard the story. The mother responded that she had heard it on good authority and was quite sure it was true. The conversation ended; Dodgson sent the daughter copies of the *Alice* books on his return home though he still did not identify himself as the participant in their conversation. He signed them "For So and So From the Author." Later, when the girl's mother met Dodgson-as-Carroll, she was mortified and promised never to gossip again, to which he cheerfully replied: "`Oh yes Mrs. ____you will.´" [14]

Since one of the books in his library was William Acton's book on prostitution [15] it is an appropriate time to review comments on the works of Acton by Steven Marcus in his 1964 work *The Other Victorians: A Study of Sexuality and Pornography in Mid-Nineteenth-Century England.* [16] This work describes the prevailing Victorian attitudes regarding sexual activities and their relationship to diseases, which may have been the subjects of Dodgson's concerns. A well known doctor specializing on diseases of the urinary and generative organs, Acton was a prime mover in obtaining passage of the Contagious Diseases Act (1866), which mandated that prostitutes located near military facilities be subject to periodic medical examinations and provided treatment for any of the sexually transmitted diseases discovered as part of the examination. [17] He was also author of the less sympathetic work *The Functions and Disorders of the Reproductive Organs, in Childhood, Youth, Adult Age, and Advanced Life, Considered in their Physiological, Social and Moral Relations.* This is a less sympathetic text because he excludes virtually all discussion of women by summarily typifying them as lacking in sexual interest except in a distorted way in prostitution. Marcus quotes Acton:

`The best mothers, wives, and managers of households, know little or nothing of sexual indulgences. Love of home, children, and domestic duties, are the only passions they feel.´ [18]

That position notwithstanding, Acton's attitudes toward male sexuality were equally contemporary even if at times just as poorly founded. Among the things he discussed was the notion that precocity leads to sexual excess because it encourages the development of intellectual faculties at the expense of the physical and emotional. This child development practice would be exacerbated by the reading of the classics where the emotionally immature child learns of the pleasures of self-indulgence as represented by "`abnormal substitutes for sexual intercourse. . .´" [19]; but they would know nothing about (nature's) punishments which can include death and self-destruction. Acton also characterized the public school system as a hotbed of vice badly in need of reform and the sharing of beds by pubertal and adolescent boys was a special target he marked for elimination.

To Acton, the worst of the male adolescent habits to be broken was masturbation. He described this practice as one concentrated among effeminate boys and which would lead to a stunted frame, sallowness, acne, cold damp hands, isolation, poor eye contact, and eventually idiocy, just as is found in the lunatic asylums:

`Apathy, loss of memory, abeyance of concentrative power. . ., loss of self-reliance. . ., [lethargy or impulsiveness], irritability of temper, and incoherence of language, are the most characteristic mental phenomena of chronic dementia resulting from masturbation in young men´. [20]

Acton posited a direct connection between masturbation and strict religious training. Insanity resulted from the large loss of semen — the vital force — and the diversion of energies needed to develop and maintain essential bodily functions. Concentration on right things during the day would prevent erotic dreams and the nocturnal emissions which resulted. He considered this phenomenon just as controllable as masturbation, i.e., a habit to be broken with the same resolve as the training in sphincter control.

The extent to which Dodgson practiced as an adult the activities of whose imagery he wrote so compulsively cannot be known conclusively. But combining his well known concerns about health, including mental health, with the state of knowledge and his search for information regarding those practices and their effects, there is strong inferential evidence that he struggled to become aware of and avoid the results if not the practices. It would not be inconceivable that he even modified his behavior so as not to appear the stereotype as part of his overall effort to avoid detection. The creation of a firm handshake could represent such a behavior modification, given the Victorian meaning given to a weak one. This kind of knowledge which he possessed regarding the etiology of sexual "perversions" was a knowledge which pointed clearly to adolescence as the formative period during which masturbatory practices developed and conflicted with the type of strict religious upbringing which was part of his experience. This offered Dodgson the opportunity to place the blame and justify the adult self as "already damaged" if he so chose.

Dodgson's memory was prodigious in his areas of interest, particularly strategy games such as chess, backgammon, and for anagrammatic construction. Nevertheless, he even developed techniques to improve it. On the other hand he is known to have had no memory at all for the things of real life such as names, places or faces. On at least one occasion he failed to recognize the host of a party he had attended the previous evening, even insisting that they had never met when the man addressed him while on one of his walks.

Dodgson worried incessantly about the quality of air and temperature in his rooms and protected himself against drafts under the doors despite wearing no overcoat while outside. He would move about from room to room to check the system he devised to keep all room temperatures equal. [21] He kept detailed records of his letters, maintaining copies and cross-indices by subject for all of the 98,000 or more that he wrote over the course of his lifetime. These letters were written on papers of different size, the precise one chosen beforehand such that both sides were always filled exactly, with no paper wasted. All of the records supporting his ongoing projects were equally well kept. Records of meals served to dinner guests, including the seating arrangement, were maintained in order to avoid repetition in any subsequent invitation. When he traveled, he counted out all of the money that would be needed for train fare, porters, cabs, and other needs, and kept each exact anticipated amount in a separate portion of his money-holder. His luggage was all tied in a specific way and the contents were categorized and wrapped meticulously in paper. His publishers were instructed on precisely how any packages to be sent to him should be tied, down to the specific knots to be used.

All of these activities reflect obsessive-compulsive personality characteristics. Such activities involve the repetition of minute, often meaningless, tasks whose effect is to keep the psyche busy and distracted from anxieties. They are all signs of the extreme perfectionistic anal personality attempting to maintain a visible external order to hide the inner chaos and its potential explosiveness. Metaphorically, "anal" behavior represents unconscious efforts to keep the bowel contents as representative of the dirtiness felt to be inside the distressed self from being released for the world to see. Lacking order on the inside, the self maintains the image of order in externally visible behavior. [22] Such activities are also often considered constructive substitutes (sublimations) which replace the manipulating activities of wished-for masturbatory activities. In effect, they provide another, more "acceptable" way to self-soothe. Given the explosiveness we have already seen in Dodgson's writing these activities could protect him from putting the fantasized acts into practice or create in a partially intended way an unassailable image which would prevent any such accusations from being believed. For, in addition to these images of perfect self-control, Dodgson was by every account without exception a perfect gentleman, always seen as returning every social obligation, and extremely generous to the point of giving more than he ever received.

In his dealings with adults Dodgson could be shy, distant, obviously preoccupied, pompous, pedantic, witty, sometimes cutting, but most often withdrawn. In a group setting, he often offered little more than a question or two and was, therefore, judged boring by many. Mark Twain, on a visit to England, found him the most shy man he had ever met, with the possible exception of Uncle Remus. [23] When asked to present something orally, although reluctant to do so, he proved to be an excellent raconteur and entertainer and was thoroughly enjoyable. He often invited women to dine in his quarters, but he specifically excluded their husbands on the invitation, and generally avoided socialization with men outside of the Common Room shared by the Oxford residents. Within that familiar setting he and Liddon often "held court."

With inhibitions and difficulties using the spoken word, the written word became Dodgson's method of communication, both in the nonsense works we have seen as well as the letters and the nearly two hundred pamphlets he published which presented his own thoughts and opinions. This focus on his own ideas affected the quality of his works in both Mathematics and some of his pamphlets and inventions. These works could have benefitted from awareness and incorporation of the thinking of others and allow him to make them more valuable as contributions to subject development rather than just very clever self-generated creations which were, for all intents, redundant. Having never moved on to master Calculus, Dodgson was unable to write creatively in mathematics. His works reflect just clever presentation.

Perhaps more than for most writers, Dodgson's serious efforts were produced more for his own benefit and enjoyment than for purposes of really impacting the world in which he lived. Based on what we have seen in the nonsense, it is highly likely that the motivation behind his publishing of works in mathematics was to allay possible criticism that he was using the position of don inappropriately by publishing only nonsense for his own financial benefit. These productions also would have satisfied his father (until 1868) as he published in an area of Papa's interest. They also displayed his own cleverness and served for ego gratification. None of these suggested motivations is intended to preclude that they were his best efforts under circumstances in which other preoccupations played such a dominant role in his inner life. Such inner stress tends to blunt truly creative work, except as revenge takes over and places the creative faculties to the task of rage release, a subject well covered by Alice Miller. [24]

While the role of photography as it touches the subject of his child-friends will be covered in the next chapter, the photographic process itself provided an outlet which could satisfy a number of Dodgson's characterological needs. Introduced to the subject by his bachelor uncle Skeffington (Lutwidge), he purchased his first camera in 1856 at age twenty-four. He received permission from the University to set up a studio and dark room in an area above his quarters. This hobby was to become a passion as it provided him with a time-consuming detailed activity. He sometimes complained of not having enough time for his real work, but time for this was always allotted. This hobby gave him access to the children for lengthy periods and in turn produced something tangible for their parents to have in return for allowing them to pose and spend so much time in his company unattended. The quality of his work may also have lessened fears that there might be anything going on of which Mrs. Grundy would disapprove. Photography also gave him access to notables whom he sought unceasingly once he had gained skills in the art. While he avoided any public connection between his publishing identity "Lewis Carroll" and "Dodgson, the Oxford don," except when it suited him in gaining access to the famous, he sought public recognition and approval for his work as a photographer. As a likely substitute for his acknowledged disappointment at his own artistic abilities, photography allowed him to concentrate almost entirely on portraits of "idealized subjects: little girls and famous people" [25] in search of perfect images. He photographed groups later in this career/hobby. A perfectionist in all aspects of his hobby Dodgson would never touch up his negatives, choosing to re-take them if necessary. [26]

The photography and developing process itself served Dodgson's needs for compulsive activity as well as his need to maintain control over his environment, especially the subjects therein. The process of actual photography and the development and print processes that followed were very intricate and complicated. The photographer and materials moved from darkroom to studio and back to darkroom quickly. First, collodian, the developing chemical was poured over the photographic plate, which was then placed in a solution of silver nitrate. Still wet, the plate was brought to the studio, where, after whatever delays ensued in preparing the pose, the picture was taken. The subject was required to remain still for forty-five seconds or longer. Returning immediately to the darkroom, the photographer became developer. He heated, varnished, and dried the plate, thus creating the negative. The process of making prints followed [27]. Dodgson maintained this hobby until 1880 when he suddenly abandoned it. A student of Victorian photography and Dodgson's role in it, Helmut Gernscheim considered Dodgson's talents to be extraordinary, the best amateur of the era, while other critics considered him among the best. [28]

There is much speculation regarding the reasons for his having abandoned something he found so satisfying. Some have attributed it to the introduction of the more modern dry process which he regarded as inferior. However, nothing prevented him from continuing to use the more elaborate method he preferred. Others posit that his later frequent practice of photographing children in the nude caused him to give it up to avoid criticism and curtail unsavory inferences being made. As far as the first issue is concerned perhaps he did not wish to "compete" against a process he saw as inferior but which still produced good results. As to the second, for twenty years already he had risked and withstood the whispers and criticism of his involvement with the young girls; this new criticism does not appear to have been particularly compelling, as he had been photographing nudes on occasion for several years. There occurred however, at about this time, an incident during which he kissed a seventeen year old girl thinking she was younger. This raised the wrath of her mother, who did not accept his apologies. While Dodgson may have withdrawn for fear that his long held practice of kissing his child friends might get him into trouble when combined with the nudity, I suspect that the time demands for the *Sylvie and Bruno* works may have begun to intrude and take priority in his mind. By this time he had already been collecting the material for more than ten years due to the considerable time and intense concentration required to formulate anagrams and doublets. It would not be until 1885 that he would begin assembling the "litter" into a novel and all the while he was very busy with other writing projects. During these next years he was also to publish two books on Euclid, *Rhyme? and Reason?*, *A Tangled Tale*, *Alice's Adventures Underground*, *A Game of Logic*, and the first part of *Curiosa Mathematica*, all done before *Sylvie and Bruno* was finished in 1889.

Having by this time given up teaching Dodgson felt he was too withdrawn from University affairs. In 1882 he sought and was appointed Curator of the Common Room following the term of his friend Vere Bayne. Attacking this responsibility as he did all things, he expended a great deal of time and energy on the details and human interactions involved in trying to please clientele, so much so that he reported that he suffered a migraine type attack in which Common Room ledgers were part of an extended nightmare. In any event the projects in which he was involved were becoming both significant and time consuming. One thing is certain; his abandonment of photography was done for one other reason that has not heretofore been acknowledged: it no longer served his needs as well as did other activities. I believe it is highly unlikely that external forces controlled the abandonment of what had been a consuming hobby.

Dodgson's photographs of his family do deserve an observational comment. There are several reproduced in biographies which include all or most of his sisters. For some reason, whether due to his own conscious efforts to pose them as "ice children," the lengthy stillness required for maintaining the pose (though other subjects don't reflect it), or the extremely inward focus of his sisters, the women appear expressionless. Their eyes are unfocused, each person is staring off into a different area of space, distinctly away from both the camera and each other. On occasion, a child is in the photograph and only that child reflects any expression or animation. This somberness does not appear to be characteristic of other photographs of women taken by Dodgson. Given what we know, it is startling though perhaps coincidental evidence of the family's disconnectedness.

We will return to Dodgson's photographic work with children in the next chapter.

A second activity so essential to Dodgson's life was his attendance and involvement with the theater. It was so important to him that he sought and received special dispensation from Bishop Wilberforce who considered such involvement an "absolute disqualification for Holy Orders." [29] His friend Henry Parry Liddon interceded with the Bishop on his behalf. The favorable decision allowed Dodgson to continue his attendance at the theater and still remain a deacon, forsaking the expected taking of final orders, which he never did take.

From what has been seen so far, a strong inference can be made that if there was any intent at all to follow through with priest's orders, it was a weak one. With his friend Liddon's involvement this inference is strengthened.

Clark alone among the many biographers writes of the extent to which Dodgson embraced the Bohemian life; and it appears she struggled with the inconsistency this represents with other aspects of his public life. She describes how, after completing his first teaching term at Oxford, he and his friends Bayne and Rankin headed off for the Old Hummums bath house in the Covent Garden Piazza in London, a locale with a decidedly questionable past. They stayed several days and made the rounds together. Dodgson found the theater and opera much to his liking. [30] Among other writers, only Ethel Arnold, one of Dodgson's child friends, would comment in her later years how she sensed the incongruity at how Dodgson could reconcile his attachment with the Bohemian life style of theater people with his "rigid evangelism," so rigid that he would never tolerate derision, ridicule, or humor involving the Bible, or any children's story which touched any Biblical reference. [31]   Until 1885 *Bohemianism* referred only to the "anti" and unconventional lifestyle of artists, writers and actors. After that it came to refer to people open to suspicions of leading irregular or immoral lives. This change in meaning no doubt evolved due to the behavioral changes taking place during Dodgson's era.

What is known about that part of London at the time is that whatever else cultural it offered, it was also heavily frequented by both male and female prostitutes who met the demand for "gay" services. Again we are left with no ability to draw definitive conclusions between Dodgson's written imagery and his practices, yet he appears to have placed himself in a position where temptation could either be conquered or conquer him. If he embraced the activities, the opportunities were there to do so in all their varieties. His attendance at the theater was so frequent and his notes on the events constitute a significant portion of the diaries. These comments reflect an astute critical eye applied to all aspects of the productions, though some writers indicate that his tastes were decidedly middle-class. He seemed to particularly enjoy comparing different productions and performers in the same plays. In many ways his comments reflect unfulfilled wishes for both acting and production. Despite his many theater contacts, the Dodgson name is rarely mentioned in works which focus on the history of Victorian theater.

In his later years he introduced many of his child friends to the theater, particularly the various *Alice* productions. Of course this offered him the opportunity to meet and engage many new child friends among the acting families. In addition he found a source of supply for the many costumes in which to pose the children, costumes which he brought back to his quarters, creating an extensive wardrobe for his purposes.

Although his diaries are viewed as reflecting little of his emotional life, it is in the early diaries that we find recorded events which touched him deeply, nearly all experienced in the theater or museums, or with his little girl friends. He would mark many events as "white stone days" or use the Latin phrase "dies notandis." Two examples of some more obscure moments deserve attention; in both cases they make sense only in view of what we have learned about his struggles. On June 22, 1855, he records attending a performance of Shakespeare's *Henry VIII* in which the angelic forms descending during Catherine's dream nearly brought him to tears.

> ... but oh, that exquisite vision of queen Catherine's! I almost held my breath to watch: the illusion is perfect, and I felt as if in a dream all the time it lasted. It was like a delicious reverie, or the most beautiful poetry. This is the true end and object of acting — to raise the mind above itself, and out of its petty cares. Never shall I forget that wonderful evening, that exquisite vision — sunbeams broke in through the roof, and gradually revealed two angel forms, floating in front of the carved work on the ceiling: the column of sunbeams shone down upon the sleeping queen, and gradually down it floated, a troop of angelic forms, transparent, and carrying palm branches in their hands: they waved these over the sleeping queen, and oh! such a sad and solemn grace. So could I fancy (if the thought be not profane) would real angels seem to our mortal vision, though doubtless our conception is poor and mean to the reality. She in an ecstasy raises her arms towards them, and to sweet slow music, they vanish as marvelously as they came. Then the profound silence of the audience burst at once into a rapture of applause; but even that scarcely marred the effect of the beautiful sad waking words of the Queen, `Spirits of peace, where are ye?´ I never enjoyed anything so much in my life before; and never felt so inclined to shed tears at anything fictitious, save perhaps at that poetical gem of Dickens, the death of little Paul. [32]

This theme of being released from torment by angels appears in Dodgson's serious poems and resonated with him here as his own plea for relief from the torments of the Furies. Theater-as-escape could not be better stated or described.

His last sentence in the entry provides another snippet from the diary which provides a vast window into his emotional life. It is so important that I will spend considerable space here exploring it. "Little Paul" is a character from Charles Dickens' less well known but considered by many his best Victorian novel, *Dombey and Son*. It is a story centered on the emerging *laissez faire* economics of the Industrial Revolution and presents Mr. Paul Dombey as a man of commerce who destroys everyone in his path in pursuit of the success and growth of his business. Little Paul, the Dombey's first son born after an only daughter, is arguably the first victim of Papa Dombey's obsession, arguably because Little Paul's mother, Fanny (!) dies immediately following his birth; she is later accused by relatives of having "given up." The essence of the story of Little Paul which leads up to the death scene which resonated with Dodgson is that Paul dies at the age of six though with all the characteristics of an old man. But more of the story is worth re-telling because it parallels so much the story of young Charles and reflects Dickens' insights into perhaps the most essential ingredient in the development of a healthy infant self: the confirming, approving, mirroring-back of the mother's face in response to the gaze of the child. It would be many years before this activity would become part of a systemized theory of child development— Heinz Kohut's Self-psychology.

Mr. Dombey's plans for his son in the business, a concept he cannot separate in his mind, are so strong that on his wife's death-bed this exchange occurs:

> `The house will once again, Mrs. Dombey,´ said Mr. Dombey, `be not only in name but in fact Dombey and Son; Dom-bey and Son!´
>
> ... `He will be christened Paul, my — Mrs. Dombey — of course.´
>
> She feebly echoed, `Of course,´ or rather expressed it by the motion of her lips, and closed her eyes again.
>
> `His father's name, Mrs. Dombey, and his grandfather's! I wish his grandfather were alive this day!´ And again he said `Dom-bey and Son,´ in exactly the same tone as before. [33]

Following his wife's death, Mr. Dombey hires the mother of a large, financially struggling family to be nurse for his son especially and caretaker for Florence, who is about the same age as Fanny Dodgson was when Charles was born. As part of the arrangement, Mr. Dombey requires that Polly live in the Dombey household, forbids her to visit her own family, and also forbids her from forming any emotional attachment with Paul. He alone, Mr. Dombey — as in "Dombey and Son" — is to be the center of the boy's world. Paul's future has been laid out for him while just a baby in the crib, i.e., to join the father in his business as soon as possible. Polly is soon released for visiting her own family.

> Yet, in spite of his early promise, all [Mr. Dombey's] vigilance and care could not make little Paul a thriving boy. Naturally delicate, perhaps, he pined and wasted after the dismissal of his nurse, and, for a long time, seemed but to wait the opportunity of gliding through their hands, and seeking his lost mother. [34]

Paul's childhood was filled with sickness and obstacles to a healthy growth. In the meantime, his father, impatient for him to progress into the business, dismissed every minor malady as just another delay of that goal. Paul was loved by his father, for all the love the latter could give, and was the favored child; Papa would kiss Paul, but shake the hand of his daughter, Florence. At the age of five, Paul, increasing in precocity, pursued his father with questions about the meaning of money. In the exchange he inquires about its inability to give him a Mama or to keep him in health, and wonders about Papa's obvious devotion to its quest. Finally Paul withdraws from his questioning, aware of his father's discomfort with the subject.

Paul begins to contemplate his own death and withdraws into a very close relationship with his sister who is in the process of becoming his surrogate mother. He also begins to withdraw into fantasy. Fearful that Florence is adversely affecting Paul's health and thinking and concerned about his thinness, though this is attributed to his childhood ways, Papa sends Paul away to live with a Mrs. Pipchin, a renowned expert in the most modern child-rearing techniques, a woman Dickens describes as a "child-queller." Her task is to remove any further signs of a child in the five-year-old over the next year. Paul develops into an old and dreary child and becomes preoccupied with learning the message in the sound of the rushing river. Papa, not satisfied with the progress being made, sends Paul to another school with the goal that he should be ahead of all the other six-year olds.

The child begins learning Greek and during the course of studies concludes that all the words of the sages were nothing but words, with no relevance to the world. In the meantime, Papa is ecstatic that the forcing has brought Paul nearer to manhood:

> `This is the way indeed to be Dombey and Son, and have money. You are almost a man already.´
> `Almost,´ returned the child. [35]

Challenging a doctor friend of his father's, Paul asserts that he would rather be a child than a man, and collapses in tears as his wish to remain close to and mothered by his sister becomes visibly evident. Papa separates the two and forbids Floy to visit him so often. School continues for Paul though he and the four other students are often in tears over their lessons. As his mind begins to deteriorate, he becomes categorized as strange — "singular" — by the other boys and struggles without success to be liked and accepted by them for who he is. He begins to suffer from fainting spells; as he escapes into characters seen in the wallpaper of his room, the room itself begins to become distorted. His most ardent desires become a wish to go off and live in the fields with Floy and to have a man to talk with about his interests. Finally, he asks to return home from school and his wish is granted.

As Floy becomes his caretaker Paul sinks into a state of near death. When his father comes to visit, Papa turns away, unable to endure the emotion of the moment. Paul senses Papa's inability to accept the impending loss of the other half of Dombey and Son. Rising as he always has in his efforts to meet his father's needs, Paul calls to him "`Don't be so sorry for me, dear Papa! Indeed I am quite happy!´" [36], a cry the boy makes daily from his bed as his father can no longer approach his dying son. Dickens then puts into Paul's mouth a most fundamental question in Self-psychology: Was I ever mirrored by a mother? Did I ever see the gleam in her eye?

> `Floy, did I ever see Mama?´
> `No, darling, why?´
> `Did I ever see any kind face, like Mama's, looking at me when I was a baby, Floy?´
> He asked, incredulously, as if he had some vision of a face before him.
> `Oh, yes, dear!´
> `Whose, Floy?´
> `Your old nurse's. Often.´

`And where is my old nurse?´ said Paul. `Is she dead too? Floy, are we *all* dead, except you?´

Polly is summoned to see him, as are the rest of his acquaintances and friends for a last good-bye. Paul dies in Floy's arms as they talk of the rushing river and finally he sees the vision of his mother's face accepting him as he is in death and as he never really was in life.

On March 18, 1856, Dodgson records that he attended a performance of Handel's *Messiah*. He described Jenny Lind as singing "with almost a child's delight" [37]; and he was especially touched ("a white stone day") by renditions of "He shall feed His flock like a shepherd", "I know that my Redeemer liveth", and "Why do the nations so furiously rage together?", all of which touch deeply with words and music a longing for redemption, resurrection of a purified body, and a questioning of the pursuit of vanity and institutionalized hypocrisy. His selections are worth reproducing in order to reflect the bases on which he may have personalized them.

> He shall feed His flock like a shepherd: and He shall gather the lambs with His arm, and carry them in His bosom, and gently lead those that are with young. . . . Come unto Him, all ye that labour and are heavy laden, and He will give you rest [used in 1868 in "The Valley of the Shadow of Death"]. . . . Take His yoke upon you, and learn of Him, for He is meek and lowly of heart: and ye shall find rest unto your souls.

> I know that my Redeemer liveth, and that He shall stand at the latter day upon the earth:. . . And though worms destroy this body, yet in my flesh shall I see God. . . . For now is Christ risen from the dead,. . . the first fruits of them that sleep.

> Why do the nations so furiously rage together,. . . why do the people imagine a vain thing? The kings of the earth rise up, and the rulers take counsel together, against the Lord, and against His anointed.

It is at times like these that one struggles with the question of whether the presence and depth of Dodgson's public image was indeed a charade hiding an arrogant bravado or a very thin defense hiding a deep and ever-present inner turmoil.

It was also in the theater that most of his public priggishness manifested itself. He was known to walk out of a stage performance if a male actor took the part of or dressed as a woman [38] but would tolerate women playing men, just as he accepted little girls playing boys. Dodgson's position regarding boys playing girls changed as his letter to Savile Clarke on August 5, 1888, reflects. In the letter he withdraws his earlier suggestion that it be allowed and agrees with Clarke that it would be vulgar. As Anne Clark records, in December 1888, following a performance of *Alice* Dodgson sent à letter of protest to Clarke, who was then, with his permission, producer of the operetta. It seems that the White King (in tights) fell backward onto the stage accidentally, feet toward the audience, who were, in Dodgson's words, "`presented with a view of him which — which I leave to your imagination.´" [39] In the same letter he objected to the Red King having lifted his skirt, claiming that while the exposed tights themselves were not objectionable, that once the skirt is worn, "`... it was *distinctly* indecent to pull it up.´" [40] In 1855, he saw his first ballet, and vowed never to attend another stating that he preferred to see the natural dancing of "cottage children" to the more artificial form of ballet. [41] It was the same position he maintained about girl's attire, as he despised garish colors and crinoline, and used simple dress or peasant costumes in his photography.

Dodgson's responses to things he considered inappropriate in the theater were repeated in other interactions. Just as he wrote to hosts or guests chastising them for speaking irreverently of things sacred and begging them not to do so again when he was present, he wrote letters to the newspapers objecting to such things as W. S. Gilbert's light stage treatment of curates. [42] In 1890, he became entangled in his own letter-writing because of a letter he wrote to *The St. James's Gazette* in which he complained about an Oxford-related masquerade he found profane. He was answered by a reader who criticized his own parody "'Tis the voice of the sluggard" as profane because it referenced the Book of Proverbs. The newspaper identified the writer of Dodgson's letter as "Lewis Carroll." He wrote and begged the editor never to make the connection in print again; but he never wrote another such letter to the *Gazette*. [43] In a moment when he was younger and a little less priggish he wrote a parody of a popular book on etiquette. Later published in *Mischmasch*, under his pseudonym, he offered his alternatives, all of which are quite humorous. They are, however, blatantly suggestive of the themes found in the anagrams we have seen and subject themselves to Doublet conversions. His introduction ends with "... The following examples exhibit a depth of penetration and a fullness of experience rarely met with." There follow two of his suggested alternatives which are particularly suggestive:

> On meat being placed before you, there is no possible objection to your eating it, if so disposed; still, in all such delicate cases, be guided entirely by the conduct of those around you.
>
> As a general rule, do not kick the shins of the opposite gentleman under the table, if personally unacquainted with him: your pleasantry is liable to be misunderstood — a circumstance at all times unpleasant.

What is so "delicate" about eating meat? Is Dodgson implying that if the gentleman is an acquaintance, that the meaning of the kick will not be misunderstood and the consequent circumstances will not be unpleasant? Or is the statement summarized better by the anagram found from the title "Poeta Fit non Nascitur": "*Tap no fit Onanite curs?*"

Dodgson's significant dealings with publishers and artists surrounding the production of his books provide more insights into his character. He stayed intimately involved with all aspects of this production. In his later years he rendered a kind of apology to Macmillan, Inc. for the way he had treated them over the years and commended them for their patience. John Tenniel found him insufferable to work with throughout the *Alice* productions, and told him, perhaps for the sake of diplomacy, that he had lost all talent for such illustration when asked to do additional work. [44] Tenniel warned Harry Furniss that he would not be able to tolerate the interference when he heard Dodgson had engaged him for the *Sylvie and Bruno* works. Furniss told one story of how he blocked the entrance to his studio and threatened to destroy all work in progress if Dodgson insisted on an inspection. Furniss was bluffing; he actually had no work in progress at this time. Later, however, he did repeatedly threaten to quit and this included the time when Dodgson began measuring the square-inch line density of his drawings and compared them to those of Tenniel and Henry Holiday, who did the illustrations for *The Hunting of the Snark*. On the other hand, Dodgson was most generous when compensating his artists.

In what most feel is an exaggerated telling of the story, Furniss does describe in his *Diaries of a Caricaturist* in 1891 that on one occasion Dodgson ordered him not to allow his wife to see any of the contents of the *Sylvie* works. Furniss refused. He further writes that Dodgson even resorted to cutting the manuscript into individually coded strips which required re-assembly by the publishers in order to maintain secrecy. Furniss returned his copy when received that way, and was eventually provided a complete and intact copy. The story is not quite as unbelievable when we consider the content of the works whose secrecy Dodgson no doubt wanted to protect at all costs prior to publication. Dodgson eventually belittled Tenniel's work when compared to that of both Holiday and Furniss, though many *Alice* critics considered the Tenniel illustrations even superior to Dodgson's stories. He was very taken by Furniss's artistic rendering of Sylvie and Bruno, especially the curved thinness of Sylvie's legs. But all was not well between Dodgson and Furniss, as we can see from an anagram found in Chapter XXV in *Sylvie and Bruno Concluded*: *"The funeral baked meats did coldly furnish forth the marriage tables."* While the context for the statement lies in the quickness with which Lady Muriel moved from her marriage feast with Arthur to his supposed death, the statement (as fine an example of visible "construct" as was found) becomes through re-arrangement: *"Harry Furniss called me a harsh, demented tart, but I faked the glib fool."* *Tart* fits well with Furniss's published comments regarding the eccentricities which Dodgson displayed.

As we can see from this portrait of Charles Dodgson, he entered adulthood with a depleted self, not sure how he would achieve the goals of revenge he had set for himself, nor how he would fulfill the requirements of self-support necessary and expected of him. His teaching efforts were very much a failure, though they lasted until 1881; his mathematical publishing was mediocre. The activities of photography, and nearly compulsive theater-going, publishing of his notions and ideas, inventions of gadgets and puzzles, and letter writing, though so time-consuming, had the first effect of pleasing himself, though the pleasure they gave others cannot be denied. These activities, all of which were done obsessively, became self-soothing activities in his efforts to maintain self-cohesion and esteem as well as efforts to achieve recognition. The nonsense works evolved into his means of support as well as avenues for rage release. Throughout it all, he maintained an appearance which was interpreted as eccentricity, but a very acceptable Victorian version of eccentricity, as he maintained all the social requirements of a perfect gentleman.

On January 7, 1856, as Dodgson approached his twenty-fourth birthday, he recorded in his diary rambling reactions to his reading of Charles Kingsley's *Alton Locke*. We can see clearly the depleted self, possessing yearning desires to contribute on a grand scale, limited in the ability to make a commitment to anything without assurances beforehand of success.   The willingness to engage in the external struggle is completely lost in his own inner turmoil.

> [If Kingsley] were but a little more definite, it might stir up many fellow workers in the same good field of social improvement.   Oh that God in His good providence, may make me hereafter such a worker! But, Alas, what are the means? Each has his own nostrum to propound, and in the Babel of voices nothing is done.   I would thankfully spend and be spent so long as I were sure of really effecting something by the sacrifice, and not merely lying down under the wheels of some irresistible Juggernaut.
>
> ... How few seem to care for the only subjects of real interest in life.   — What am I, to say so?   Am I a deep philosopher, or a great genius?   I think neither.   What talents I have, I desire to devote to His service, and may He purify me, and take away my pride and selfishness.   Oh that I might hear `Well done, good and faithful servant!´ [45]

In later years he would criticize his brother Edwin (in an unpublished Diary entry) for choosing the natives of Zanzibar for his missionary work when there was so much to be done in England. But, for him, it would not be until *Sylvie and Bruno Concluded* that he would have his fictional father/adult self, Dr. Arthur Forrester, respond spontaneously and fearlessly to the needs of the river people suffering from a plague, as the kindly doctor nearly lost his life giving aid to the dying with selfless disregard for his own well-being, even to the point of abandoning the bride he had just taken.

Health as the Mirror of the Man

Hopeful that this has been an adequate effort to present examples (from many) of Dodgson's extremely complex character and personality, I now return to the subjects of his stammering and migraine. For what we think we know of Dodgson's enormous internal conflict is reinforced by the knowledge we have about the somatic release of conflict evidenced by the presence of these two conditions.

Dr. Oliver Sacks has devoted much of his medical practice to the treatment and study of migraine. Early on in his research he found that the broad array of symptoms could last for just moments and included distortions in speech, perception, thoughts and emotions, thus touching nearly all areas of neurology. However, it was not until Sacks began looking into the emotional lives of his patients that he was able to provide effective treatment. [46] Historical thinking on the subject had included a humoral theory which hypothesized that humors built up in the digestive tract, causing constipation and subsequent symptoms of migraine. Treatment included the use of laxatives and the maintenance of a sparse diet. [47] A second theory points to sympathetic causes and posits that there exists an unconscious communication between parts of the body so that distress which really exists in a number of internal organs settles in the head with headaches, vertigo, depression, despair, madness, and nightmares. [48]

In the nineteenth century studies of migraine proliferated and studies in mid-century pointed to "heredity `taint´" and masturbation, which fit in nicely with the perception of the latter as the road to insanity. Edward Liveing's Victorian study *On Megrim, Sick-Headache and Some Allied Disorders*, published in 1873, described migraine as "nerve storms" which could affect an endless variety of bodily functions. Later studies built on this and assigned "faints, vagal attacks, vertigo, and sleep disorders" to the list of symptoms, linking the illness to epilepsy. [49] Also identified were "moving fortifications," jagged half or full circular images which would block or distort a portion of the vision of one eye. Dodgson reported that he experienced this kind of vision problem; and it is a classical symptom of migraine. [50] In addition, symptoms include the following sensed experiences, all of which were experienced by Dodgson. These include changes in perception (enlargement or contraction), zoom vision, speech disorders, states of double or multiple consciousness, at times with feelings of *déjà vu* or *jamais vu*, or in states of dreaminess, nightmarish, trance or delirium. [51]

While many physicians and sufferers continue to seek physiological causes and treatments, most recent studies have sought psychosomatic causes, with a "migraine personality" identified though not accepted by all practitioners. Sacks himself does not see such a typical personality as universal among sufferers. The personality characteristics most often seen, however, reflect ambition, success orientation, perfection, rigidity, orderliness, cautiousness, and emotional constipation, with breakdowns taking a somatic form. In her 1937 studies Fromm-Reichmann arrived at a clear-cut conclusion:

> Migraine. . . is a physical expression of unconscious hostility against consciously beloved persons. . . [which reflect] ambivalence and repressed hostility. [52]

In Dodgson's case, extreme love/hate has been identified as existing toward his parents; his relationship and attitude toward his siblings, who constituted his family after the death of his father, and the true nature of his relationships with his child-friends are reviewed in the following chapter.

Supporting the concept of the "migraine personality" and the condition of the typical sufferer, Dr. Roy Mathew in his 1981 work *Treatment of Migraine*, added the following susceptibilities: a tenseness in response to anxiety; inability to handle anger, usually suppressing it; a preoccupation with achievement; the maintenance of:

> . . . superficial interpersonal relationships, sexual maladjustment, and obsessive preoccupation with moral and ethical issues, in general, [a person more neurotic than nonsufferers]. [53]

Turning to Dodgson's stuttering, Dr. Dominick Barbara's 1982 work *The Psychodynamics of Stuttering* and the 1977 work *Stuttering: the Disorder of Many Theories* by Gerald Jonas, himself a stutterer, are particularly useful. Barbara identifies the coercive, overprotective, engulfing parent, preoccupied with perfectionistic "shoulds" in all things, including speech, as one of the causes of stuttering. The child attempts to please both parents through speech as well as other behavior. [54] This describes the scenario already identified in Self-psychology in which the mother or both parents use the child as a selfobject; the child then responds by creating a false self that is alienated from the true self, so that even speech seems externally controlled. Stuttering may also be precipitated for the emotionally handicapped child by a traumatic event such as an illness, frightening experience (accident or operation), or the coercive efforts to convert the child from left to right-handedness, or brought about by tension and worry in the home, gang violence, or by the child being caught in a shameful act such as masturbation. [55] The effort to accomplish a left-hand/right-hand switch was seen in the 1920's as causing psychic confusion over motor control of the most finely tuned motor skill, speech, which requires enormous left/right coordination of the muscular structures in the head, jaws, and neck. [56] Hesitation brought on by psychic uncertainty emerges and a vicious cycle between parent and the child's speech ensues. [57] In efforts to restore the self, rebelliousness sets in and is particularly marked by a stubbornness and hypersensitivity to coercive control by the parent. The emerging rage is held in behavioral check and thus somatized in a deepening if not worsening stutter. Unable to respond to either inner or outer requirements, self hate emerges as failures to achieve the expected perfection begin to cause the creation of excuses which assign blame outside the self. [58]. Feelings of uniqueness, intellectualization, and a general turning inward, combined with a withdrawal from the loathed self occurs and alienation becomes the core of the personality. An inner futility grows into an absence of hope and goals and feelings that life is slipping away, with nothing fulfilled.

> The handicap reaches into the lives of its victims and leaves a trail of suffering, sorrow, waste, and destruction. [59]

The stutterer, with no feeling for "self" can find feeling only in compulsive activities and "relentless drives." [60] Memory for names, places and faces is lost. The stutterer feels impersonal, ". . . that he is just one big bluff and lives in constant dread of being exposed," with life governed by pride [61] rather than the goals and values that should comprise the self-directed individual.

Stutterers become "constant blockers" in nearly all other areas of their lives. In retaliation and an attempt to defend the self, the external world becomes the imagined enemy. That the individual strikes back in retaliation for his own hurt is seen as fully justified. The means for doing this become a kind of "magic" and is typified by such things as placing the hand in front of the mouth while speaking, positioning oneself carefully in pre-established locations in reference to others before speaking, special body movements performed while speaking, or calling on the help of a friend to be present to fill in gaps in conversation. [62] Men usually choose a woman as the friend, a surrogate for the magical mother who was always present and ready to help. The stutterer scans his audience constantly, searching for approval. [63] Another ritual involves the process of planning word avoidance, a task which requires enormous psychic energy to foresee in the speaking situation the approach of likely troublesome words. Dodgson used this latter ritual extensively; and it apparently worked adequately for him in later life.

Words, both written and spoken, gain "omnipotent significance." The self focus of the stutterer causes him to objectify and depersonalize the audience; thus he creates no real audience but himself. Words become the only means of communication for "feelings, opinions, and attitudes." With speech distorted, all communication becomes distorted. [64]

The child whose efforts at speech, however imperfect, are not accepted by the parent, but are subject to constant correction develops feelings of failure in this important mastery function, the communication of ideas and feelings. Belittlement only adds to the injury.

> Confused and embarrassed by his apparent failure to control his speech apparatus, the child eventually accepts the notion that there is something deeply wrong with him. [65]

Stuttering reflects the effort not to fail in speech, but is symptomatic of a more pervasive and general fear of failure in all things, with such fear a product and symptom of the poorly developed, alienated self.

In both these brief summaries of migraine and stuttering it is possible to see manifestations of nearly all the psychological and somatic symptoms in Dodgson's life experiences, i.e., internal emotional conflict incapable of external behavioral or therapeutically reconciling (verbal) expression turned against the body until it is manifested in visible behavior and somatic distress.

CHAPTER 11

FAMILY AND FRIENDS

The people in Charles Dodgson's life comprised a fairly small circle at any one time although his total number of social acquaintances became quite large. There were family of brothers and sisters, aunts and uncles, and gradually several nieces and nephews. There were the few close adult male friends with whom he associated from the Oxford community, the few child friends he was able to keep when they became adults, and the Victorian notables such as the Rosetti and Tennyson families along with others whom he met through his photography, theater, and interest in the arts. Finally, there were the very many young girls, well over two hundred, whose friendship he cultivated throughout his adult life. It must be said that except for some few acknowledgements regarding Dodgson's eccentricities, the testimony of these people, especially the children, is universally positive, so positive that it is difficult to describe it as anything but adoration. (This research finding became a constantly recurring cause for doubt in the production of this work.) Yet from what we have already seen, there are numerous cracks in the looking-glass which were kept from the awareness of most. If there is a place still left in Dodgson's life for genuine love, without the accompanying hate, this aspect of his life is where we should find it. This chapter explores the quality of these relationships, beginning with his siblings, then to his adult male friends, a brief stop with Tennyson, and then his child friends. This is followed by a summary of the insights gained from these relationships with Dodgson's sexuality.

Family

Dodgson's brothers and sisters can be described as having held him in awe; and they were extremely protective of him following the latter's death. He stepped in and took over their father's position at the time of his death in 1868, when he stayed for weeks until all of them were properly housed, and oversaw the acquisition of "The Chestnuts" at Guildford in which those that remained unmarried could live. The diaries reflect Dodgson's fervent prayer for guidance and help in being a comfort to his family during the period of mourning. He gave generously of his time; they, in turn, maintained a room in the house for him to accommodate his frequent visits. He provided advice throughout their lives, and managed, as it were, some of their affairs with the outside world. As they acknowledged later, he also provided a life of comfort for them from the royalties of his books, both during his life and through the estate left entirely to his family.

Upon the death of Charles, for some reason that remains unidentified, most likely to protect him from being unfairly treated by others in biographies they might write and perhaps also to gain from the benefit of his notoriety as the unmarried sisters appear to have had no other income, his family participated actively with Mary's son Stuart Collingwood to produce a biography of their own within a year. To insure their complete control in that process they reportedly looked over Collingwood's shoulder as they gave him access to the diaries, which were then stored away unceremoniously upon completion, the already mentioned volumes finally lost. As part of the spirit of the centennial of Dodgson's birth planned for 1932 his heirs worked diligently with Roger Green to locate and publish them. With continued protectiveness they used razor blades to cut out the few pages containing material they did not wish him to see while they crossed out other entries in pencil. These sections reportedly containing private family matters; but there was at least some in-text editing done because a page from the period when Dodgson's relationship with the Liddell family soured was excised and the preceding page summarily concluded in someone else's hand. Green successfully negotiated the inclusion of some of the crossed-out material before he was finished, there even being a message to the family in the margin regarding his wish to include an anecdote they had designated for exclusion. The most striking feature I found in examining the original manuscripts against the edited and published version was the number of what appear to be sincere, heart-rending pleas to God, in which Dodgson begged for deliverance from a "hardness of heart," unnamed activities, and habits which were haunting his life, pleas which peaked during the years in which the *Alice* works were being produced (conscious that two volumes prior to this were missing), then gradually disappeared.

It seems that Mary was his favorite among his brothers and sisters. Throughout his schooling he communicated with her in long letters and their length became a subject of amusement within the family. These letters reflect that he shared much detail from his activities and interests, but nothing about what we know was occurring in his inner life or the events that led to these changes. In his later years he wrote her letters on religious subjects, responded to her concerns about faith with long treatises reflecting his own thinking, or comforted her at the time of deaths within the family. As nearly all of the siblings suffered from the same stammer as Charles did, he helped in numerous ways to provide them with speech training though these were generally unsuccessful efforts.

Coincidental with all of this so obvious "good feeling," we know now that Charles' hidden self was secretly laying the groundwork for the eventual destruction of the family name. He was purposively contriving to create the greatest possible shame in the Victorian society of a family with such historic ties to the Anglican Church by writing sexually erotic material with explicit allusions to his relish of the activities he described. The basis for his feelings toward his siblings, which can only be described as contempt even if they resulted from an overflow of unbridled rage directed elsewhere, goes beyond sibling rivalry, though it may have started there. His sisters had the sexuality he wished for himself; there was that envy. He may have seen himself as abused or excessively controlled by the older ones who most likely had responsibility for him in the large family. He loathed babies throughout his life and this may reflect his great resentment of the "oldest brother" role he had to play with the younger children. He did however protect his brothers from the Rugby experience when he recommended a gentler school for them. He most likely identified the experience he went through as a Victorian and family expectation for male children, but from which his sisters were protected by gender. As sexuality became the basis for both his suffering and rage expression, those whose innocence was saved by their accident of birth would become hated for their good fortune. Role resentment may have existed in every act of generosity he performed for them; and this is compounded by the fact that he as oldest brother had to provide for them throughout his life. This represented an adult role he felt very inadequate for at the beginning, which found relief somewhat by the income derived from the sale of his books. The presence of his sisters, with ways that no doubt reflected greatly the continued presence of his mother, either in imitation or as he saw the damage done them, also, became constant reminders of the task he had taken on, refuelers of the hate which drove him on.

In examining Dodgson's works, writers have often commented on the twelve chapters in each of the *Alice* works reflect the size of his family. Indeed they may have, with each individual receiving a privately dedicated expression of rage. As we look at the earlier works, knowing that he had already begun both his anagrams and Doublet creation as the precocious adolescent in *Useful and Instructive Poetry*, we can see the violence in the early poem "Brother and Sister" in which the brother attempts to make a stew out of his sister and is stopped only by the hired cook who ended the plot when she withheld a pan. The whole theme of making "stew" may have been a deceptive screen for the moral: "Never stew your sister." For a simple re-working produces *"Never wet your sisters,"* a possible early appearance of the recurring themes of "tea" and urination. "The Two Brothers," written at age twenty-two is another poem with a violent theme. In this poem one brother uses the other for fish-bait at the end of his fishing pole. This poem contains many possible Doublet conversions and ends with the brother abandoning his fishing, leaving the "bait" in the water, while a sister asks when he will return:

> "When chub is good for human food,
>   And that will never be!"
> She turned herself right round about,
>   And her heart brake into three,
> Said, "One of the two [brothers] will be wet through and through,
>   And t'other'll be late for his tea!"

In addition to "chub" allowing for a favorite doublet conversion, the allusion to the possibility of *either* brother being "wet through and through" when only one was in the water relates to an earlier verse:

> Many words brought the wind of "cruel" and "kind,"
>   And that "man suffers more than the brute":
> Each several word with patience he heard,
>   And answered with wisdom to boot.

With quotes and quote placement as clues, both "cruel" and "kind" (i.e., *"cur led kin)* brother led his kin into an anagrammatic trap. "Man suffers more than the brute" re-works to *"He, men, suffer thorn, masturbate."* The nature of the Fury thorn appears again and identifies masturbation as worse a problem for man than animals in the original statement.

In Chapter IV of *Through the Looking-Glass*, the nonsense poem "The Walrus and the Carpenter" reflects another violent theme of oral aggression, as both characters devour a bevy of oysters without any, even pretended feeling. In addition to the aphrodisiacal allusions in the eating of oysters, by Doublet conversion, oyster becomes sister (ouster, muster, mister).

In Chapter III of *Sylvie and Bruno Concluded*, Dodgson pursued the question of the legitimacy of inherited wealth which has been derived fraudulently.

> `. . . If you could trace [aristocratic wealth] back, from owner to owner, though you might begin with several legitimate steps, such as gift, or bequeathing by will, or "value received," you would soon reach an owner who had no moral right to it, but had got it by fraud or other crimes; and of course his successors in the line would have no better right to it than *he* had.´
>
> `No doubt, no doubt,´ Arthur replied. `But surely that involves the logical fallacy of *proving too much*? It is *quite* as applicable to *material* wealth, as it is to *money*. If we once begin to go back beyond the fact that the *present* owner of certain property came by it honestly, and to ask whether any previous owner, in past ages, got it by fraud, would *any* property be secure?´
>
> After a minute's thought, [the narrator] felt obliged to admit the truth of this.

Lennon notes that when Dodgson drew up his will on November 4, 1871, he stipulated that his entire estate should be divided equally among his siblings. In contrast to Collingwood's description of Dodgson as generous, helping family and friends, often secretly [1], his banker saw him as "extravagant" because his estate totalled just a little more than £4,004. [2] What he did leave, for the benefit of the family, was the stream of royalties deriving from material wealth, including a logical defense for their receiving it within one of the works. The extent to which the bequeath of his property represented for him a bequeath of contempt in ill-gotten wealth which would reach beyond the grave seems a distinct possibility. The other places to which his considerable income may have exceeded his acknowledged generosity are discussed below.

Again reflective of a more positive feeling toward his brothers, in late April, 1887, Charles wrote a letter to his brother Wilfred in which he complemented the parenting skills of Wilfred's wife, Alice. On a week-end visit to their home he had noticed and appreciated the particularly fine behavior and manners shown by the children. What he found of special significance was the presence of youthful spirits which had not been broken. [3] Dodgson recognized that parenting accomplishment as unique and worthy of praise. There was most likely a bitter-sweet feeling as he thought about his own family.

Perhaps the most telling evidence of the inner feelings Charles had for his sisters is reflected in a brief letter written on January 13, 1870, to Mary following the birth of her first child, Stuart Dodgson Collingwood, who would become his biographer. Stuart was his first nephew and Charles would soon become his Godfather, as he acceded to Mary's request two weeks later, finally overcoming a reluctance which had emerged after many other acceptances. It is a most troubling letter and one which reflects the depth of Dodgson's use of bitter sarcasm veiled in the facade of the loving brother. Consisting of just two short exclamations directed to her, he wishes that God will bless her newborn, that she will be to her son what their mother was to him, followed by the assertion that he could not express a more appropriate wish, and ending the letter with the usual affectionate closing. [4]

On March 3, 1896, shortly before he died, Dodgson offered to write a Preface for a children's book addressed to tiny boys written (in words no longer than four letters so that they could read it unassisted) by his niece Elizabeth Georgina Wilcox, the title of which was *The Lost Plum Cake*. In writing it he made complimentary remarks about the author and made a plea that parents provide "Sunday treats" such as this book as a diversion for their children to use during church services, especially sermons, to prevent their later losing interest in attending church. Dodgson was no doubt aware of the anagram formed from "Sunday treats:" "*Stay nude, rats!*." He further wrote:

> [It is good not to be writing one's own Introduction.]
> . . . since, however sweet the "blowing of one's own trumpet"
> may sound to the enraptured trumpeter, it is apt to pall on
> other ears.

The "pall" is due, not to just the egotistical "blowing of one's own trumpet," but to the sound produced by the "*of bowel trumpet now in song*." Cohen [5] references two suggestions that Dodgson also wrote Chapter 11 of the Wilcox work, which, upon examination, appears true for the word-use Cohen gives as well as the thematic affinity with the scenes that close *Sylvie and Bruno Concluded*, his last "official" work.

The conclusion from this section is that there is clear evidence that Dodgson's inner world reflected a raging hatred toward family members behind the so much good he also did for them and on their behalf. The maintenance of this loving facade toward siblings he saw often may very well have contributed to the continuing migraine attacks he experienced.

Male Friends

Biographers list a number of men among Dodgson's adult friends, most of them in the early Oxford and post-Oxford days. Edward Sampson, sixteen years his junior, was a fellow lecturer at Oxford. Henry Barclay attended Oxford with Dodgson, before going to teach at the grammar school level. Robinson Duckworth, an Oxford friend, accompanied Dodgson with the Liddell children on the famous river trip on which the original *Alice* adventures were "spawned." Dodgson included him in the work as the "Duck;" and he autographed Duckworth's personal copy of *Alice's Adventures Underground* "The Duck from the Dodo 9 June 1887". [6] Did Dodgson omit the word *to* at the beginning because it would spoil the anagram "*The Dodo fuck'd mother.*" followed by the date, and if so, was Duckworth "in" on the hidden message?

William Ranken was also an Oxford friend and became the subject of Dodgson's poem "A Valentine;" this was sent to Ranken ostensibly in response to his complaints that Dodgson's attentions seemed to last only when he visited. It was later published with modifications in *Phantasmagoria and Other Poems*. Green quotes from the *Nonesuch Omnibus*, pp. 775-776, and reflects a more personalized and most likely earlier version than is available in other sources. This rendition indicates clearly that the "lover" is from Radley (the school where Ranken taught), and includes the lines "And if he be an Oxford Don, /Or `Jonson's learned sock be on´...." [7] This latter line, presented as a quoted phrase seems clearly to be an anagram for "*So clean or jerk on dons' bones!*" Perhaps Dodgson's coded angry message, so familiar to us today, was not intended to be understood by its recipient, or was one well understood between the two friends. We shall see this method of rage expression occur again in response to a friend not as accepting of Dodgson as he expected and wished.

Dodgson's two closest friends, as already mentioned in earlier material, were Thomas Vere Bayne and Henry Parry Liddon. Bayne was a lifelong friend from childhood and Dodgson's diary manuscripts reflect that he included visits to Bayne's mother when he visited London, often taking her to art museums. Bayne's diary mentions on numerous occasions his taking long walks with Dodgson, though Dodgson's recordings of such events are scant. Considered an amiable if uncreative fellow who served as an archivist at Christ Church and who also avoided publicity and did not preach, though a clergyman, Bayne's most notable contribution to the Oxford community seems to be his service as Steward of the Common Room for fifteen years preceding Dodgson's ten years of service, followed by writing a biography of his mentor, Dean Liddell, following his death. An examination of his diaries at Christ Church, Oxford, reflect a much closer social relationship with the Liddell family, including the children, than do Dodgson's. Bayne appears to have been far less irascible and grating than Dodgson was and never alienated the Dean or his wife as did Dodgson. Although not directly critical of Bayne, Dodgson wrote several humorous comments in an article entitled "Twelve Months in a Curatorship," as he found on his assumption of the duties a considerable overstock of wines and liquors, the best of which is:

> ... one curious phenomenon I wish to call attention to. The consumption of Madeira (B) has been, during the past year, zero.... After careful calculation, I estimate that, if this rate of consumption be steadily maintained, our present stock will last us an infinite number of years. And although there may be something monotonous and dreary in the prospect of such vast cycles spent in drinking second-class Madeira, we may yet cheer ourselves with the thought of how economically it can be done.... [8]

The most curious historical fact regarding Vere Bayne was revealed following his death when it was announced that he left an estate of £138,000 [9], with no visible source of that wealth. Already suspecting strongly that he participated with Dodgson in anagram and Doublet creation in Dodgson's works, it is certainly possible that Dodgson paid him for his work from his royalties, an income Bayne kept secret and saved rather than draw suspicion by spending it. There are, however, two other possible explanations. The first is reflected in unpublished material from Dodgson's diaries. After he took over the Common Room curatorship, Dodgson discovered that Bayne had failed for some time to notify new students that the stipend to be given the curator was optional, and not part of the mandatory fees, and had been collecting it from the unwitting for some time. He criticized Bayne (in the diary, at least) for the dishonest practice, vowed in his new position to disclose the fee as optional, and also reflected Bayne's apparent admission that it was the reduction in "receipts" that had caused him to wish to resign. A second possible source of wealth might have been the result of an arrangement with the Common Room liquor supplier which produced the overstocked inventory.

Indicative of the closeness that existed and most likely some sharing of their emotional lives, Bayne did report in his own diary on March 6, 1888, that he and Dodgson had gone through a "Slough of Despond" that day, no doubt a part of a review of their waste of life's opportunities. After Bayne's own death, the following verse from Percy's "Winifreda" (Reliques), was found written in Dodgson's hand:

> And when, with envy Time, transported
> Shall think to rob us of our joys,
> You'll in your girls again be courted,
> And I'll go wooing in my boys.

My interpretation of the presence of this verse is that between Dodgson and Bayne there existed pederast interests of a heterosexual and homosexual nature, with regrets expressed that access to children would be declining as they aged. This and the other circumstantial evidence of collusion helps explain the presence of the types of imagery in the anagrammatic themes.

Comments have already been made regarding Liddon's authorship of the final title of *Through the Looking-Glass*, with strong suspicions of his awareness of the anagrammatic theme. However it appears that in general Liddon kept more distance between himself and Dodgson (in fact, Bayne's diaries reflect that he and Liddon were quite close and travelled to Europe together on several summer vacations, while Dodgson headed for the beach). Dodgson and Liddon did travel to Russia together from mid-July to mid-September, 1867; Liddon made the trip an official one, representing the Church of England to the Russian Church. He recorded in his own diary:

`July 15. —Dodgson was overcome by the beauty of Cologne Cathedral. I found him leaning against the rails of the Choir, and sobbing like a child. When the verger came to show us over the chapels, he got out of the way. He said that he could not bear the harsh voice of the man in the presence of so much beauty.´ [10]

This is one of very few recorded incidents during which Dodgson appears to have lost emotional control; and it is also the kind of incident which reflects such release of otherwise denied true inner feelings that the intensity of Dodgson's inner struggle becomes plausible. It would be after his trip that the prayers in his diary began to be less frequent, after an emotional peak before the trip.

Although friends, Liddon and Dodgson had some strenuous disagreements. On July 28, 1867, Liddon's diary reflects a long argument after Church with ellipsis points (. . .) in John O. Johnston's biography *The Life and Letters of Henry Parry Liddon* leaving the subject of the argument undetermined if indeed Liddon identified it. [11] Later letters reflect their significantly different views regarding church ritual (Liddon was somewhat more "Romanized"), and Eternal Punishment. On the latter subject Liddon took the early position that though the teaching of the Church was a mystery, it must be believed, a position quite different from that taken by Dodgson. Liddon argued that the gift of moral freedom left us with "awful liabilities, as well as with its inconceivable capacities for good." [12] In later years, however, he moved more toward the position of there being a saving process possible during the life that followed death.

Liddon himself seems to have had some problems with his family, especially his mother, as indicated in Johnston's descriptions of his early priesthood days. [13] In 1848 when he considered taking the vow never to marry, Liddon became alienated from his family. For some unknown reason, the young man's mother was worried about the depth of her son's life and commitment as she advised him:

> `You may be a good scholar, a good Churchman, and yet not
> a good Christian. You must conquer self.´ [14]

The notion of "conquering self" is a typical Victorian position and is especially difficult if the self has not been enabled and was already depleted at Liddon's young age. In the days preceding his mother's death in 1849, he records in detail the attention he paid when accompanying her to Church for the last time and her nearly final words to him:

> `She kissed me and said, "Good-bye, Henry; I know that you
> have stood temptation. I have no fear for you.´

What had happened to assuage her fears is not known. Seventeen years later, Liddon recalled the words, again, for reasons not known.

`How often do I think of her words during the last Oxford vacation that I spent with her! — "You may become a great scholar, but will you become a true Christian?"´

Liddon's diary records "`delightful´ walks, and bathing." Johnston indicates both were done with intimate friends in the country.   Other activities included music and talks.   Some inconsistencies in Liddon's life are encountered when his attitude toward the theatre is explored.   Recall that it was Liddon who interceded for Dodgson with Bishop Wilberforce when he recommended that attendance at the theater should not exclude one from the studentship or deaconate, even if it did exclude Dodgson's taking priest's orders.   In a letter dated May 15, 1879, and whose contents are in regard to the proposed formation of a church and stage guild, Liddon (referencing a communication from Dodgson) writes:

> Certainly we must all of us agree that if the Stage could be enlisted in the cause of Religion and Morality, or even so influenced as not to oppose that cause, it would be an immense gain to the Church of Christ and to mankind at large.
> But at the risk of seeming faint-hearted, I must avow my belief that this happy result is quite impossible; and that, while there always have been, are, and always will be, excellent people who devote their lives to dramatic representation, the Stage, as a whole, is and will be against us. It may be that the conditions of dramatic representation make this inevitable — human nature being, upon the average, what it actually is.
> Speaking for myself, there is no form of entertainment which I should so entirely enjoy, as good acting. *But I have never been inside a theatre since I took Orders in 1852, and I do not mean to go into one, please God, while I live* [my italics]. [15]

Liddon then goes on to indicate the example that the clergy must keep in order to be influential with the brethren.   In a letter dated September 10 on the same subject he writes:

> . . . In what you say about Greek life I quite agree.   It was elegant and detestable.   When the Renaissance tried to revive it in mid-Christiandom, the church looked hard at it.   She smiled on it in Leo X, but she would have none of it

before the sixteenth century had closed. It was the paganism of Italian Renaissance-life which gave its main strength to the Reformation Movement in the south of Europe. Only think of what a gospel Mr. J. Addington Symonds's would be! [16]

Given the adamant tone of the letters and particularly the statement regarding his own attendance at theatrical presentations, one would conclude that his memory on the matter was certain. Yet Dodgson's diaries contain (at least) three entries which indicate that he and Liddon went to the theater together: January 22, 1858; July 20, 1863; April 10, 1867 (with Wilfred); and possibly a fourth on July 3, 1865, when Dodgson reports he saw Ellen Terry at the Olympic after his having called on and walked with Liddon earlier in the day. The discrepancy is unexplainable, but if we can believe Dodgson's diary, may easily be interpreted as representing an insight into another aspect of Liddon's character. Alternatively, it raises the question of the extent to which Dodgson's diaries may have been at least partly constructs written for biographers. Their evenings together may have been in the London theater district, but not included attendance at a theatrical performance. Or they may have been in areas of London which were centers of prostitution, for they existed for every taste and budget between the West and East ends, either about a mile and a half or less distant in either direction from the Covent Garden and theater district which Dodgson frequented and which carried its own reputation.

Another suggestion that Liddon may also have lived a life in contrast to the successful and celibate clerical career as supporter of Dr. Pusey and the Oxford Movement and in his later years writer of a four volume biography of his mentor, lies an unpublished entry in Dodgson's diary. While there are several which indicate that Liddon traveled on a number of occasions in the company of a particular woman, this one, a list of guests at Guildford, is entered in a way which suggests Dodgson perceived them as a couple.

Dodgson also recorded on November 13, 1862, that he began writing down the original *Alice* story following a walk with Liddon. The two of them may have hatched the idea of using the nonsense in the children's stories as their vehicle for rage expression. On Liddon's death in 1890 Dodgson noted that he had lost a good friend, and England a good Churchman.

Just as hidden material is incorporated in Dodgson's nonsense works, serious poems, and family communications, it also exists in the articles he wrote within the Oxford community. A few examples will suffice. The title of the previously mentioned article "Twelve Months in a Curatorship" written in 1884 contains a subtitle "By One Who Has Tried It." While both refer to Dodgson's service as Curator of the Common Room, the subtitle also answers to the anagram formed from the title: "*Worship at an evil mother's cunt.*" This imagery is considerably more explicit and angry than the examples which appear in more typical Victorian pornography, including *Cythera's Hymnal*, where the expression usually reflects worshiping at a (woman's) "shrine." In his first paragraph he likens his year of service to and highlights "Five Years in Penal Servitude," whose re-working yields: "*Fit a very vile arse, nude penis!*," which personifies the penis as self. This is followed by the experience being like "Six months on a treadmill," which becomes, among others: "*I'd not thrill mamas on sex.*"

Dodgson's parody "The Blank Cheque A Fable" written in 1874 to criticize the "blank check" philosophy regarding the planning of changes at Oxford, is filled with double meanings in a domestic story of "blank check" vacation planning within a family. The title itself is an anagram, as are two phrases in an opening quotation, one of which means "going mad", the other "bein' incurable." The opening paragraph describes "five o'clock tea" as deriving from "`rude forefathers,`" and as being a specific (i.e., treatment for) "`all the ills that flesh is heir to.`" "Five-o'clock tea" converts to "*Eat of evil cock*" or "*of vile cock tea.*" The chief character in the story is "Mr. DeCiel", a phonetic cryptogram for "Mr. D. C. L." or C. L. D. "Harry" is playing with a cat and the mother says:

> `Harry-Parry Ridy-Pidy Coachy-Poachy!`. . . `Harry's very fond of Pussy, he is, but he mustn't tease it, he mustn't!`. . . And the boys tumbled out of the room again,. . . shouting `Let's have a Chase in the Hall! [17]

"Harry Parry" has been identified as Henry Parry Liddon by other writers. *Pussy* was Victorian slang for a girl or woman, also an effeminate, finicky, old-maidish boy or man, and also a homosexual dating from 1583 (OED). And we have here, perhaps, an early extension of *puss*, a valid Victorian alternative slang for *cunt*, but a meaning that would not be valid until the late 19th Century. "Let's have a Chase in the Hall" re-works to "*Chaste have sale in the hall!*" with other alternatives, also. There appears to be no end to the games played with the Oxford community. Nearly all titles of presumably serious articles that have been republished allow for anagrammatic reconstruction. And nearly all of them contain passages which allude with sly humor to the material hidden in the title.

Alfred Lord Tennyson

Dodgson maintained a close relationship with the family of Alfred Lord Tennyson (also known for his own erotic imagery) for a period until things soured between the two. Photography was an early and primary basis for the relationship, in addition to the connection through poetry. It is in reference to poetry that we find an entry in Dodgson's diary written on September 22, 1857. Dodgson records that he questioned Tennyson on the meaning of two passages from his poem "Maud" which had always puzzled him. [15] The first reads:

> `two men somewhere
> Drinking, and talking of me:
> "Well, if it prove a girl, my boy
> Will have plenty, so let it be".´

While Tennyson indicated that it referred to a match being arranged between two fathers and Maud, I suspect Dodgson's puzzlement was founded in either pederast imagery or ambiguity regarding sexual identity. The second verse described the poet:

> `Dowered with the hate of hate, the scorn of scorn,
> The love of love.´

Tennyson told Dodgson it might take any meaning, but he wrote it to mean "`The hate of the quality hate, etc.,´" essentially the essence of the most intense hatred. The line in question is not from "Maud," but is from Tennyson's "The Poet," written in 1830. Perhaps Dodgson personalized more than the lines referenced, as the poem begins:

> The poet in a golden clime was born,
>   With golden stars above;
> Dower'd with the hate of hate, the scorn of scorn,
>   The love of love.
>
> He saw thro' life and death, thro' good and ill,
>   He saw thro' his own soul. . . . [19]

It describes quite accurately Dodgson's inner world of both intense love and hate toward parents, family, and nearly everyone with whom he came in contact. One may only wonder if this diary entry was left for biographers.

Chapter II of *Through the Looking-Glass* represents a virtual dedication to Tennyson as it mentions all of the flowers which Tennyson used in "Maud" with the exception of the passion flower. When Dodgson learned that the name of this flower was a reference to Christ's Passion, he changed to a less sacred reference by choosing a tiger lily, which preserved meter. While he and Tennyson had not officially had their falling out over Dodgson's possession of a copy of an unpublished work by Tennyson, this Chapter entitled "Garden of Live Flowers" is so filled with anagrams it would be better named "Garden of Evil Flowers," with *flowers* used as a verb.

Child Friends

It can be said without exception that the recollections of Dodgson's child-friends reflect nothing but pure delight experienced during their many hours spent with him, as they either played games with mathematics, puzzles, or words, posed for photographs in or out of costume, watched the magical photo-development process, read the Bible together while receiving gently rendered correction, or listened to the many stories he created for them at their urging and insistence. He was a Pied Piper and a favorite uncle all rolled into one, a man who carried a little black doctor's type bag filled with pins and gadgets to facilitate his efforts to engage the attention and affection of any young girls he met at the beach or on the train. In his personal dealings with them, he spoke constantly of his wishes to keep even the appearance of impropriety from coming within the view and criticism of "Mrs. Grundy," the fictional ever-present Victorian judge of propriety. Even when he photographed the children in the nude, he made great efforts, not only to insure parental approval, but to insure comfort on the part of the child. He would cease the activity with any child who gave the least evidence of discomfort. From everything I have found, it is clear that biographers have universally concluded that in this regressed childhood state he found his greatest happiness and delight. I believe that the loss of his stammer in the presence of the children is a significant piece of evidence of the comfort he experienced with them as well as a more sinister explanation: the amount of control he had over them, enough to lose all fear of discovery as a fraud.

With this very brief summary of the essence of the historical descriptions of what Dodgson meant to the children, we can move on to a more complete analysis of what they meant to him, already fully aware that it was into these children's hands that he placed his children's books, and on their (as he described it) "innocent minds" that he developed and practiced the integration of nonsense and erotic themes. For there is no better an example of the concept of using others to soothe the distressed self than Dodgson's involvement with these little girls. And while his justification of the morality of this involvement is left to the next chapter, any judgmental feelings toward the depth of deviousness and ruthlessness of his rage-driven perversions can be mitigated only by the historical fact that the children he touched do not appear to have emerged adversely affected by the contact.

While a number of sources and examples support the presentation, there is a single source which reflects all aspects of the self that Dodgson presented to his child friends. This is the brief adoring article by Ethel Arnold, granddaughter of Dr. Arnold from Rugby, in her "Reminiscences of Lewis Carroll" published in *The Atlantic Monthly* in 1929. Her description of their first meeting when she was five and he was thirty-eight typifies the relationship children had with him. She describes how a small bevy of girls out for a walk encountered the figure of Dodgson approaching and determined to make a barrier so that he could not pass. On seeing it, he made a mock charge at the group, umbrella raised. When he reached them there was mass confusion as all of the girls tried to grasp and cling to him. Before they could realize what had happened, two of the shyest, one of them Ethel, had been taken by the hand and were thoroughly caught up in the chattering and laughing group as they all joined in walking along with him. [20]

Following descriptions of the delight and wonderment at the magical things she could find in the cupboards in his rooms, her own amazement at the photographing and development process, and her categorization that Dodgson's childhood and schooling was "ordinary," Arnold presents samples of his letters to her. One contains a postscript which, when coupled with what we now know, perhaps clarifies that his public detestation of boys was real.

> `There is a baby boy there to be admired __ about two years old I think, and in this matter you will be of *incalculable* service to me, and relieve me of all responsibility as to saying the proper thing when animals of that kind are offered for inspection.´ [21]

In addition to the emphasized word being an anagram for "*Clue: can I ball?*," perhaps the "service" he sought, this is one of a number of negative references to boys, another being the ending of a letter to a girl friend:

`My best love to yourself — to your Mother kindest regards
— to your small, fat, impertinent, ignorant brother my
hatred´ [22]

Quoting an unidentified source, Lennon writes that he told the father
of one of his child friends "`As a salmon would be on a gravel path, so
should I be in a boys' school.´" [23] The intended allusion may have
been to his difficult experiences teaching boys, which would have been
the death of him, but in its full imagery should include the writhing
and spasmodic thrashing that would precede the fish's death. Another
letter to Beatrice Hatch reads:

`I wish you all success with your little boys — to me they are
not an attractive race of beings (as a boy, I was simply
detestable). . .!´ [24]

These and other references further confirm the "boy" to "pig"
conversion in *Alice's Adventures in Wonderland*.

One letter written to Arnold when she was eighteen reflects the
turn Dodgson's otherwise thoroughly entertaining and lovely sounding
letters could take when a little girl did not respond as he wished. It
reflects that the tool of rage so evident in everything else he wrote
— the anagram — emerged as well in letters written to these children
under his own name, with this example very mild and veiled in
presentation if not in imagery. In it, he chastises Ethel's sister ("with
my love, which I send *most* reluctantly," a phrase that sets the trap)
for her "utterly heartless behavior" in his rooms the prior day, though
he declines explicitly to describe it to Ethel, who was not present. His
promised retribution would be to withhold some "cool lemonade" on
some future day when she is nearly fainting from thirst.

`. . . This I will uncork, and pour it foaming into a large
tumbler, and then, after putting the tumbler well within her
reach, *she shall have the satisfaction of seeing me drink it
myself* — not a drop of it shall reach *her* lips!´ [25]

He then goes on with a semi-nonsense play on words.

I am convinced from many other allusions that Dodgson's public
school experience included numerous indignities — better yet, assaults
— involving urine as well as semen and feces. Among these are his
nonsensical but aggressive pouring and drinking of ink as a means of
retribution — with *ink* submitting to a Doublet conversion to *tea*, the

slang word for *urine*. There are numerous references, particularly in the *Sylvie* books, to five o'clock tea, by then an English custom. Dodgson's retribution here would not be with the withholding of cool foaming [sic!] lemonade, but with her watching him drink cool "*demon ale*," another anagrammatic code word for urine, and be herself unable to drink and enjoy any of it. In the chapter entitled "Looking-Glass Insects" in *Through the Looking-Glass*, the Bread-and-butter fly will, and often does, die due to the unavailability of "weak tea with cream in it", except for the word *weak*, Victorian slang for semen mixed with urine. "Bread-and-butter" is Victorian slang for the position of a couple's body during sexual intercourse.

Except for support received from such occurrences in other letters the conclusion drawn from this letter alone that Dodgson played the same games with the children is weak. John Pudney cites a manifestation of Dodgson's loneliness as a bachelor in a letter to his child-friend Agnes Hull (identified by Cohen as written to the same Ethel Arnol dated February 24, 1885), now nearly sixteen and having expressed in her letter to him a wish to reduce their open demonstrations of affection. Dodgson responded by telling her that she might wish to be less affectionate, but that his right to continue to demonstrate his feelings was also legitimate.

> `. . . And of course you mustn't think of *writing* a bit more than you *feel*: no, no, *truth* above all things! (Cheers — Ten minutes allowed for refreshment.). . . .´ [26]

He then went on with a semi-nonsensical conversation with himself on having a last kiss, ending with:

> `"You are right, Common Sense. . . I'll go & call on other young ladies. . ."´

Having urged his friend to write true feelings, Dodgson took ten minutes to refresh himself by performing mental masturbation that the creation of erotic literature, especially pornography, can represent as Khan describes (quoting Jean Paul Sartre) "`The onanist wants to take hold of the word as an object.´" [27] Dodgson left his letter writing, as it were, performed word manipulation to restore his self-esteem, and returned with a rage-based phrase construct beginning "Cheers. . ." — an anagram for (among others) "*She treats, dorm fellow! Semen in her cunt, free!*" After releasing his anger in secret, he resigned himself to losing a child-friend, and ended the letter as usual with "Yours always affectionately,. . ."

An oft quoted phrase used by Dodgson to describe the failures of his child relationships to pass into puberty and adolescence was that these young girls:

> `... get shipwrecked at the critical point "where the stream and river meet,´ [sic!] and the child-friends, once so affectionate, become uninteresting acquaintances, whom I have no wish to set eyes on again.´ [28] [Lennon's *sic*! and brackets]

Dodgson coined this phrase in a letter to Isabel Standen on August 4, 1885. [29] Lennon is the only writer to acknowledge however briefly the physical implications of the six-word phrase, with which Dodgson himself was more explicit in the derived anagram in which he acknowledged the emergence of adolescence and his feelings about the abandonment it entailed: "*Ream, whet, treat her semen drive!*"

In a letter to Agnes Hull dated November 26, 1869, Dodgson was angered when she told him she was affectionate only because he was taking her to the Lyceum, implying a *quid pro quo*. He accused her of "cat" behavior:

> `... I don't care a bit for such affection. Do *you* care for the affection of a cat, that only purrs and rubs itself against you as long as it thinks there is cream in the cupboard?´ [30]

In a letter dated April 1, 1889, Dodgson responded to Mary Brown twenty years after they had first met, having received two Christmas cards and flowers from her over a two year period in which he had not responded. He apologized, but indicated (as he usually did) that he had no use for presents. In an otherwise friendly sounding letter he wrote:

> `... My memory of you, as a little girl who sat on my knee (a performance you may have totally forgotten by now)... and yours of me — well, of not quite such an old "lean and slippered pantaloon" as I have now become!... Whether our characters have not become, by this time, hopelessly discordant, is an open question!´ [31]

The "lean and slippered pantaloon" or "*dapper, anal don — spell `O-n-a-n-i-t-e´*" is most likely the basis of the possible character discordance suggested.

In 1888, Girls Latin School in Boston, Massachusetts, already having sought and received Dodgson's permission to use the name "Jabberwock" for their literary publication and his encouragement as they embarked on their new venture, published some material from George Washington's diary which he found offensive. He wrote them his objection; and the editors apologized. Dodgson then wrote a letter on May 17 suggesting that in view of the "Black Draught" he had sent them previously, he should provide a "Lump of Sugar," which he did in the form of his poem "A Lesson in Latin" on the subject of *amare* (to love) which he enclosed. His anger still raging, the criticism, or "Black Draught" (*"Bad luck th' rag"*), continued, not accompanied by a "Lump of Sugar," but produced by the ale as *"foul rump gas."* The poem on love which he enclosed contains the baleful cry: "Amare! Bitter One!". This is an anagram for "*O, me! Bare tit near!*" In 1856 he recorded in his diary for his own amusement the naivete displayed by a writer who attributed a "spiritual motivation" to a late-night excursion and return which Nathanial Hawthorne had observed George Washington take on horseback past his house.

Jabberwock later published a limerick about a Deacon in Lynn (Massachusetts) who lived in sin and denied it angrily when confronted [32]. Dodgson cancelled his subscription, professing deep disappointment at their making light of the confession of sin. It must have been too close.

When one of Dodgson's favorite children, Isa(belle) Bowman, came to tell him she was to marry, he became so angry he snatched a bouquet of roses from her waist and threw them out the window, shouting: "`You know I can't stand flowers.´" [33]   His perceived abandonment by this, his perhaps most favored child friend, must have been momentarily devastating. Green writes that he had calmed down by the following day. Another unpublished diary entry tells of his efforts to induce the Liddell children to learn new games, but reflects his disgust at their insistence that he retell the "interminable" story of Alice, a story he had barely just written out. For what is believed to be this his most favored friend, he considered writing a poem in her honor, using her middle name in its proposed title — "Life's Pleasance" — an anagram for "*Place lines! Safe!*". I suspect Ellen Terry was in fact his best child-become-adult friend, as she was in the theater, by any measure a fine actress both as a child and an adult, maintained her friendship longer and was a source of access to many other children.

While these letter examples represent only a minute sample of the total number of letters he wrote to his child friends, most of which are just delightful, they do demonstrate clearly that these children served as selfobjects for Dodgson. They were there to satisfy his needs. Any who failed to do so particularly by any actions he construed to be abandonment, were subject to an expression of the rage that waited for an outlet, with words containing erotic themes written in secret his preferred mode.

Conclusions

There are a number of interpretations and conclusions to be made from Dodgson's relationships with these children, many of which conflict significantly with biographers and writers. Others confirm suspicions held by those relatively few who have always seen a hostility in his works. My formulation is somewhat different and offered as an alternative to these hostility-supporting interpretations.

Without reviewing the arguments presented by others, I suggest that the disclosures we have seen allow us to reject out of hand any assertions that Dodgson "loved" any of these girls in a way which could have led to marriage, as has been speculated for some time about Alice Liddell and Ellen Terry. If there exists evidence to suggest marriage was in his plans, it certainly would not have been based on a "love affair" of the idealized quality posited or imagined. However, it could have been based, as some marriages are, on the nearly pathological need of one or both parties to possess another as a necessary adjunct to the meeting of emotional needs. In such a marriage each party serves, not to complement in a healthy way, but to fill badly unfilled emotional needs of the self and other with an underlying fragility subject to annihilation of the self should rejection or abandonment occur. Such a marriage would have repeated the dynamics in Dodgson's relationship with his mother.

In his Preface to *Alice's Adventures Under Ground*, Dodgson wrote of the effect experienced by anyone who has ever loved a child as:

> . . . the awe that falls on one in the presence of a spirit fresh from GOD'S hands, on whom no shadow of sin, and but the outermost fringe of the shadow of sorrow, has yet fallen: he will have felt the bitter contrast between the haunting selfishness that spoils his best deeds and the life that is but an overflowing love. . .

Within this statement we can see both sides of Dodgson's use of children, his awe at their innocence and his awareness of his own abusiveness. He used the children to develop his rage expression and then used that expression directly against them on occasion in secret. He was committing a kind of psychological non-violent and impotent rape of virgin children. His awe was directed not only to their innocence but also to his ability to carry on his assault outside their awareness while he was fully aware of what he meant by what he said. What purposes did this serve in Dodgson's efforts to maintain a self?

These little girls served as transitional objects for his mother, just as other things did (see Appendix 2). This is the same theme of which Grotjahn wrote as he described Alice and all the little girls as representative of phallus. This interpretation is supported by the theme of "Jabberwocky" as it is interpreted within the context of sexual perversions. These girls were subject to being loved and loathed, manipulated and abused, kissed and cuddled, to satisfy his efforts to restore a self that was unfortunately consumed in hate. They were transitional objects which reflected an incomplete and unsuccessful effort to separate emotionally from mother, overwhelmed instead by his innocent efforts to adapt to meet her selfobject need for him. The experience at public school was felt as complete abandonment by the one he adored and felt adored by, and was the event which triggered the expression of what was already present. His rage driven perversions, not just sexual, which had to exceed societal proscriptions (a necessary ingredient in perverse practices [34]) were thus directed to the use of girls as mother-surrogates to develop the means of rage expression, not always, but whenever he required it. These children also satisfied his deep hatred for what the girls were and had which he wished for himself, to be the girl he could not be. And, more positively, the girls provided an emotionally safe place to which he could regress: back to his own pre-pubertal years which is very much where his emotional life was stuck.

The photographing of little girls, posing them in costume as well as various states of undress, represented an effort to find the perfect image he wished for himself and never found, a search nearly as consuming as the rage. I do not believe this "viewing" which photography provided met Dodgson's need for oral gratification in the prurient sense of his dwelling on them in a carnal way of using the eyes, as Greenacre suggests. I also do not believe he was masturbating in secret in their presence, as does occur in many similar situations, if for no other reason than the enormous emotional risks involved in his being caught and forever losing access to their very much-needed presence. Again, unpublished diary entries reflect extreme loneliness when he arrived at the beach a few days before other families arrived and had to endure just a few days alone without the presence of any children.

Dodgson's interest in them was never heterosexually carnal or aimed at consummating anything physically explicit. The kissing and cuddling was aimed at nothing other than his adoring and being adored by his mother-surrogates just as he felt she had adored him in the pre-school days. His rage re-emerged when they grew up and abandoned him. Reinforcing the rage was the fact that their abandonment of him occurred at just about the age when his feelings of abandonment occurred or reached their greatest intensity. Yet, continuously and beyond their awareness, he penetrated them repeatedly. For he used them to test his hidden material, to feed it to them and validate appropriate childhood responses to the nonsense, and in general fine tune his skills. He presented the works to them, wrote poems to them, and personally autographed their copies.

In contrast to his hate and contempt for them, Dodgson provided them with what was to them a close adult relationship who accepted them for what they were, as several have attested. This was an experience he did not have. He was to them what he wanted for himself at their age. So he was both offering and receiving confirming images of himself, and of himself as the wished-for little girl. I believe further evidence of this "pursuit of inner image" is best reflected in Dodgson's work with Harry Furniss in the development of the illustrations in *Sylvie and Bruno*. As time was running out on his life Dodgson became intimately involved in every aspect of the creation of the physical image of Sylvie, moreso than Bruno. With great urgency he instructed Furniss to travel all around the geographic area in search of perfect models. He provided him with the names and resident locations of a little girl with a perfect nose, another with perfect legs, or perfect eyes, or ears. (In fact, Furniss said he used his daughter as his model.)

Dodgson even indicated in working with his artist/friend Gertrude Thompson, who provided him a milieu in which he had access to girls willing to pose undressed and drew the nude fairies used in *Three Sunsets*, that he was not sure if the perfect human form would ever be observable or capable of being drawn in this life. Dodgson sought for another physical self-image all of his life, as he repeated his mother's lack of acceptance by refusing to accept his own physical image. In photography, his early and later efforts to draw the human form, and in his intrusive involvement with his artists, a search for the pre-pubescent female form was in a way all-consuming.

Sylvie and Bruno

Fairies: from *Three Sunsets*

The loss of stammer in the presence of the girls appears to derive from several factors which provided mutual support. In his play with them he regressed to the most comfortable time in his life. They adored him, and raised his self-esteem. But most of all, the extent to which he was in control, and able to do as he wished without risk, provided him with the confidence which caused the fear of his disclosure as a fraud to disappear. For, with the good and loving image he continually set and reinforced, if any of the children (or their parents) "found" any of the deviant material, he could always scold them, and, by manipulation, move himself back into their good graces, restoring the relationship he was for them. If they persisted in their criticism, he could terminate the relationship.

I believe his professed hatred for boys was not only a rejection of his own sexuality, but, at least in the Oxford community, a defense against his more natural sexually explicit impulses. Had these been practiced, they would have presented a far greater risk of his being exposed by Mrs. Grundy. For what he could do in secret and impotently with the girls, he might do in the open potently with boys, with perhaps a disastrous impact on his security. If he did indeed involve himself with physical homosexual acts as an adult, it was with boys or homosexual men in London, both readily available, or with boys or male friends on his very long, nearly daily country walks. While there is no evidence beyond anagrammatic suggestions and assertions that any such activities actually took place, the nature of the material does not preclude the inclusion of animals in his sexual perversions. Domesticated animals such as sheep and goats, long used in rural environments as sexual objects, were certainly available along the countryside paths.

Within a theoretical framework which distinguishes sexual perversions and homosexuality as two different situations, I believe Dodgson was a homosexual. The primary evidence for this lies in the search for a confirming feminine image. How that orientation would have manifested itself alone in a society which accepted it is not known because that struggle for acceptance continues. Some portion of his erotic imagery speaks to the need for homosexual activity within a homosexual relationship. Compounding the total picture are the perversions and the activities engaged in to restore the self which also extended well beyond all acceptable societal bounds. To imply that all of Dodgson's activities were or are reflective of stereotypical homosexual behavior or behavior for which the homosexual community seeks societal approval today would be grossly unfair to the sincere members of that community.

This concludes, perhaps inappropriately briefly, a most important facet of the Dodgson personality and character. As one would expect in a person so consumed by rage, the quality of Dodgson's closest relationships reflects the depth and breadth of the inner conflicts which were in complete control of his emotional life. What remains to be done is an examination of his religious struggles, the extent to which even these reflected rage, and how he attempted to reconcile all of this with his Christian upbringing, which taught fear of an avenging God more than the promise of Christian redemption.

CHAPTER 12

RELIGIOUS STRUGGLES

The last aspect of Dodgson's inner world to be explored is the role that religion and religious beliefs played in bringing him through life. This will help fill out the portrait of rage as it affected and was in turn affected by this aspect of his struggle. Not unlike other areas explored, we are presented with enormous contradictions. These can lead us to conclude (perhaps judgmentally) that we are dealing with an amoral man, whose religious presentations and protestations were all merely a facade; or, we can view them as evidence of moral struggle by a man consumed by rage yet haunted to the point of terror by fears and doubts that his course of behavior might lead to Divine retribution. In the following analysis I attempt to avoid argumentation on religious truth and the objective nature of morality and moral behavior. Instead, I shall continue on the basis of a framework which attributes both behavior and its motivation to the survival, cohesion, and enhancement needs of the self, a psychological concept more in tune with an existential view of man than the deterministic position of the usual Freudian (and Victorian) framework. This chapter focuses primarily on two areas: the use of material of a religious nature as a manifestation of rage directed to Dodgson's father, and his publicly presented struggles with the notions of suffering, "Heaven" and "Eternal Punishment." I shall also attempt to draw a conclusion regarding the true nature of his beliefs.

While the side of Dodgson presented thus far has very much escaped biographers, there is much evidence that he did many good and charitable works which would and did cause beneficiaries to see him as living what his Church would have considered a model Christian life, based on the religious culture in which he and they lived. He brought great joy and comfort to many, particularly in his mid and late adult life. His diary entry for December 10, 1895, notes a unique experience in his forty years of attending chapel; he was the only person there, unaware that the dean had suspended the holding of daily services.   This suggests he was in frequent, if not daily, attendance, an inference supported by other entries which comment on such events.

Just as we have already seen the presence of Dodgson's public denunciation of things sexually suggestive, there were also numerous verbal and written remonstrances he directed to adults who in any way made light of or profaned the Bible or things of a religious nature, very much following the example set by his father. There are many letters, some of a religious nature, a number of which are so touching that one would conclude that they could have been written only by someone who had experienced or was still suffering great pain. They offer encouragement and comfort to recipients in the face of their own suffering. No matter the form his personal beliefs and behaviors took, he publicly endorsed conformity with the accepted moral and ethical codes of the day. When he helped others the variations from Victorian harshness that his religious discourses took were to reduce worry, encourage best effort, and reduce feelings of guilt.

A letter to Mrs. William Greet, playwright sister-in-law of Ben Greet, a theater manager in London, dated April 7, 1894, provides a good example of Dodgson's publicly professed attitude toward religious things.   Offended by one of her plays and unsure of her religious beliefs he wrote with what was and would be seen as heartfelt sincerity of his concern that the theatrical jesting on things sacred had provided ". . . nothing but real *pain*: to *me*, I can assure you, it gave *great* pain. . ." while it only encouraged those who would laugh the louder at the profane use of ". . . the names of God, and of Jesus Christ." [1]

On April 13 he answered in turn to her response that she meant no irreverence but rather meant to have the material reflect on parental neglect in the children's education. He reiterated the ". . . pain felt by people who are trying to live in the spirit of their daily prayer "`Hallowed be Thy Name´. . ." while he claimed that such jesting only gives

> . . . pain to good and reverent people (and the *more* reverent the people the *greater* the pain), at hearing holy things profaned.
>
> They give pleasure, a harmful, often a sinful pleasure to those who love to `make a mock at sin,´ [Proverbs XIV 9] and to turn sacred things into ridicule. . . . [2]

Curiously and uncharacteristically, both letters were signed "Lewis Carroll."

Rage at Papa

Cynicism is the most bitter defense used by the alienated and degraded self as it attempts to restore self-esteem by pushing its own self-contempt out onto others. Cynicism creates a feeling of superiority in order to restore a feeling of adequacy. We have seen it in play already; but it is in the religious sphere, where one would least expect it, that it reaches its peak. Having also searched everywhere for a rage one should expect Dodgson would have directed to his father, it is here that it is to be found. Playing the Dodgson game, just as *love* is in *gloves*, *hate* is in *father*. If sexual perversions and the manipulation of children would be his attack directed primarily to his mother, the use of things holy for disclosure as well as profanation would be the means of attack on his father. Despite the fact that it is necessary to identify the depths of his rage, it was with great reluctance that I began the process of searching for anagrams in the biblical and religious or religious "sounding" quotations used by Dodgson in his writings. But I do not believe there is any other way to demonstrate the depth of his feelings and the extent to which he used his writings to show the meaninglessness of words, even sacred words, than to proceed.

But before returning to the Greet letter quoted above, realizing that he had been "put down" by Mrs. Greet and fully expecting to find a secret counter-attack, just as we found in letters his child-friends, let us move to the *Sylvie and Bruno* books, both of which were developed primarily after the death of Papa. Biographers and critics of the *Sylvie* works have long panned the lengthy moralizing and preaching in the Prefaces of both, but especially the *Concluded* Preface and text, as the work of a tired nonsense-writer turning without inspiration to life-ending tasks. Quoting from the Preface to *Sylvie and Bruno*, following Dodgson's expressed wishes to write a child's Bible, we find the inspiration. I have included this lengthy quotation in order to present what I interpret as the elaborate cynicism of the piece. All italics are Dodgson's except those in brackets.

> ... Secondly, a book of pieces selected from the Bible... to be committed to memory... [for several uses], and, best of all, when illness, while incapacitating us for reading or any other occupation condemns us to lie awake through many weary silent hours: at such a time how keenly one may

realise the truth of David's rapturous cry `*O how sweet are thy words unto my throat: yea, sweeter than honey unto my mouth!*´

This italicized phrase does not appear to submit to anagrammatic re-working, but does submit to word substitution using Doublet conversions.   Given the oral/genital imagery already seen in abundance, the conversion of *words* to *cocks* and *honey* to *semen* or *urine*, the imagery we have come to expect is maintained. Continuing the Preface after he also suggests producing books of inspiring passages from books other than the Bible and an expurgated version of Shakespeare for girls:

> If it be needful to apologize to any one for the new departure I have taken in this story — by introducing, along with what will, I hope, prove to be acceptable nonsense for children, some of the graver thoughts of human life — it must be to one who has learned the Art of keeping such thoughts wholly at a distance in hours of mirth and careless ease. To him such a mixture will seem, no doubt, ill-judged and repulsive. And that such an Art *exists* [*It's sex!*] I do not dispute: with youth, good health, and sufficient money, it seems quite possible to lead, for years together, a life of unmixed gaiety — with the exception of one solemn fact, with which we are liable to be confronted at *any* moment, even in the midst of the most brilliant company or the most sparkling entertainment. A man may fix his own times for admitting serious thought, for attending public worship, for prayer, for reading the Bible: all such matters he can defer to that `convenient season,´ which is so apt never to occur at all: but he cannot defer, for one single moment, the necessity of attending to a message, which may come before he has finished reading this page, `*this night shall thy soul be required of thee.*´

"Convenient season" submits to several anagrams: "*A convent! See no sin.*," "*A convent? See son in,*" "*On incest? Save none!*," etc.

There are also several anagrams from the final italicized phrase which implores that one be prepared at any moment to meet his Maker:

> "*The queer don is healthy! He stirs! Big, hot, full!*"
> "*The queer filth — this night ode — shall be yours!*"
> "*O, he first hated queer boy lust, his night hell.*"

"I fight the sin. Request he holdeth your balls."
"To ball, she requireth the hefty in loud sighs." ,etc.

Continuing the Preface:

> The ever-present sense of this grim possibility has been, in all ages [Dodgson's footnote: `At the moment, when I had written these words, there was a knock at the door, and a telegram was brought me, announcing the sudden death of a dear friend.´], an incubus that men have striven to shake off. Few more interesting subjects of enquiry could be found, by a student of history, than the various weapons that have been used against this shadowy foe. Saddest of all must have been the thoughts of those who saw indeed an *existence* [*entice sex!*] beyond the grave, but an existence far more terrible than annihilation — an existence as filmy, impalpable, all but invisible spectres, drifting about, through endless ages, in a world of shadows, with nothing to do, nothing to hope for, nothing to love!. . .
>
> We go to entertainments, such as the theatre — I say `we´, for I also go to the play, whenever I get a chance of seeing a really good one — and keep at arm's length, if possible, the thought that we may not return alive. Yet how do you know — dear friend, whose patience has carried you through this garrulous preface — that it may not be *your* lot, when mirth is fastest and most furious, to feel the sharp pang, or the deadly faintness, which heralds the final crisis — to see, with vague wonder, anxious friends bending over you — to hear their troubled whispers — perhaps yourself to shape the question, with trembling lips, `Is it serious?´, and to be told `Yes: the end is near´ (and oh, how different all Life will look when those words are said! — how do you know, I say, that all this may not happen to *you* this night?
>
> And *dare* you, knowing this, say to yourself `Well, perhaps it *is* an immoral play: perhaps the situations *are* a little too "risky", the dialogue a little too strong, the "business" a little too suggestive. I don't say that conscience is *quite* easy: but the piece is so clever, I must see it this once! I'll begin a stricter life to-morrow.´ *To-morrow, and to-morrow, and to-morrow!*
>
> . . . Let me pause for a moment to say that I believe this thought, of the possibility of death — if calmly realised, and steadily faced — would be one of the best possible tests as to

our going to any scene of amusement being right or wrong. If the thought of sudden death acquires, for *you*, a special horror when imagined as happening in a *theatre*, then be very sure the theatre is harmful for *you*, however harmless it may be for others; and that *you* are incurring a deadly peril in going. Be sure the safest rule is that we should not dare to *live* in any scene in which we dare not *die*.

But, once realise what the true object *is* in life — that it is *not* pleasure, *not* knowledge, *not* even fame itself, "that last infirmity of noble minds" — but that it *is* the development of *character*, the rising to a higher, nobler, purer standard, the building-up of the perfect *Man* — and then, so long as we feel that this is going on, and will (we trust) go on for evermore, death has for us no terror; it is not a shadow, but a light; not an end, but a beginning!

[Apologizing for his treatment of the British passion for "Sport"] . . . But I am not entirely without sympathy for *genuine* "sport" [*Urine! Sponge 't!*]: I can heartily admire the courage of the man who, with severe bodily toil, and at the risk of his life, hunts down some `man-eating´ [*man-teaing*] tiger: and I can heartily sympathize with him when he exhults in the glorious excitement of the chase and the hand-to-hand struggle with the monster brought to bay. But I can but look with deep wonder and sorrow on the hunter who, at his ease and in safety, can find pleasure in what involves, for some defenceless creature, wild terror and a death of agony: deeper, if the hunter be one who has pledged himself to preach to men the Religion of universal Love: deepest of all, if it be one of those *"tender and delicate"* [*Dean! Detect liar den!*, etc.] beings, whose very name serves as a symbol of Love — *"thy love to me was wonderful, passing the love of women"* ["*Few fellow dons give phony love to mouth man's wet arse*," with two more variations] — whose mission here is surely to help and comfort all that are in pain or sorrow!

> *"Farewell, farewell! but this I tell*
> *To thee, thou Wedding-Guest!*
> *He prayest well, who loveth well*
> *Both man and bird and beast.*
>
> *He prayest best, who loveth best*
> *All things both great and small;*

> *For the dear God who loveth us,*
> *He made and loveth all."*
>
> [Dodgson's italics]

Dodgson's Preface ends with that verse segment which is given new meaning from the anagrammatic material.

Quoting briefly from the Preface to *Sylvie and Bruno Concluded,* Dodgson criticizes some of the new rituals in church services, then continues:

> As an instance of the dangers, for the Clergy themselves, introduced by this new movement, let me mention the fact that, according to *my* experience, Clergymen of this school are *specially* apt to retail [sic] comic anecdotes, in which the most sacred names and words — sometimes actual texts from the Bible — are used as themes for jesting. Many such things are repeated as having been originally said by *children,* whose utter ignorance of evil must no doubt acquit *them,* in the sight of God, of all blame [cf. the argument in the letter to Mrs. Greet]; but it must be otherwise for those who *consciously* use such innocent utterances as material for their unholy mirth.
>
> Let me add, however, *most* earnestly, that I fully believe that this profanity is, in many cases, *un*conscious: the "environment" [*Net no vermin!*] . . . makes all the difference between man and man; and I rejoice to think that many of these profane stories — which I find so painful to listen to, and should feel it a sin to repeat — give to *their* ears no pain, and to *their* consciences no shock; and that *they* can utter, not less sincerely than myself, the two prayers, `Hallowed be Thy Name,´ and `from hardness of heart, and contempt of Thy Word and Commandment, Good Lord, deliver us!´ To which I would desire to add, for their sake and for my own, Keble's beautiful petition, `help us, this and every day, To live more nearly as we pray!´ It is, in fact, for its *conse-quences* — for the grave dangers, both to speaker and to hearer, which it involves — rather than for what it is *in itself* [*It's elfin!*], that I mourn over this clerical habit of profanity in social talk. To the *believing* [*evil being*] hearer it brings the danger of loss of reverence for holy things, by the mere act of listening to, and enjoying, such jests; and also the temptation to retail them for the amusement of others. To the *unbelieving* [*I beg, evil nun!*] hearer it brings a welcome

confirmation of his theory that religion is a fable, in the spectacle of its accredited champions thus betraying their trust. And to the speaker himself it must surely bring the danger of *loss of faith* [*O, filth of ass!*]. For surely such jests, if uttered with no consciousness of harm, must necessarily be also uttered with no consciousness, at the moment, of the *reality* [*irately*] of God, as a *living being* [*Begin living!*], who hears all we say. And he, who allows himself the habit of thus uttering holy words, with no thought of their meaning, is but too likely to find that, for him, God has become a myth, and heaven a poetic fancy — that, for him, the light of life is gone, and that he is at heart an atheist, lost in ` *a darkness that may be felt´* [*That may be felt as "snarked."* This is a return to the annihilation theme of the poem.]

. . . and I think that, among them [those who read this Preface], some will be found ready to sympathise with the views I have put forwards, and ready to help, with their prayers and their example, the revival, in Society, of the waning spirit of reverence.
Christmas, 1893.

"From a hardness of heart, and contempt of Thy Word and Commandment, Good Lord, deliver us" allows for an anagram with several different word placements, all of which revive the Orestes theme. I present only one which seems to reflect the conflict and torment supported by other anagrams. *"I hated pederast thorn, a worst fury. Don't condemn! A command from God saved don from Hell!"*

"Help us this and every day to live more nearly as we pray" allows for an important anagram: *"Today I slay ye, mother! Sway viper! Hurl a venereal spend!"* *Spend* is a Victorian-appropriate noun for released semen. This anagram returns us to the viper-mother-penis-transitional object, and the masturbatory theme of "Jabberwocky."

Finally, and perhaps more disturbing to many due to its familiarity, we have "Hallowed be Thy name." This phrase from the Lord's Prayer, appears twice over two pages in the Preface to *Sylvie and Bruno*, and again years later in the letter already quoted to Mrs. Greet (along with an angry ` *make a mock at sin´* — *It's a knock, Mama!*, *knock* a valid word for *ridicule*). This prayer segment solves to (at least) the following anagrams:

At hallowed hymen be! (a return to the "shrine" theme.)

Hell? Name thy bad woe!
O, why hate men? Bed all!
O why bed all men? Hate!
Lay, bathe held women.
Beat hallowed hymen!
Bleed, healthy woman! (reflecting a Victorian pre-
occupation with menstruation in its pornography)
Why done? He blameth a. . .
Ah, they allow men bed.
Why men balled? Hate!
Howl! They blame dean!
Only we had the blame.
Had we the blame only?
Both he, we, damn ye all!
                etc.

For purposes of completeness, all of the Biblical or quasi-biblical verses chosen by Dodgson for use in these works have been examined for anagrammatic re-working with the last presented below. In Chapter XIX of *Sylvie and Bruno Concluded*, as Sylvie and Bruno sang the Fairy Duet, overwhelming the narrator/listener with a feeling of peacefulness:,

... there fell on me a sense of awe that was almost terror
— some such feeling as Moses must have had when he heard
the words `Put off thy shoes from thy feet, for the place
whereon thou standest is holy ground.´ ... while their voices
rang together in exquisite harmony as they sang: —

`For I think it is Love,*
For I feel it is Love,
For I'm sure it is nothing but Love!
[Dodgson's italics]

The verse attributed to Moses becomes: "*To soften the gritty souls of the shy pederast clan whom Fury houndeth, offer hope!* — a theme eloquently presented by J. A. Symonds in *A Problem in Greek Ethics*, privately published in 1883, but well worth re-printing today. It is the plea for gays today, and for all those alienated in society for being different and rejected.

Strangely and coincidentally, just as Dodgson had published a pamphlet stating his views opposing the practice of vivisection as far worse than hunting just prior to the publication of *The Hunting of the*

Snark, he published an article "The Stage and the Spirit of Reverence" in *The Theatre* in June, 1888, just prior to the appearance of *Sylvie and Bruno*. Its themes include the irreverent treatment of Biblical passages, jesting and parody of both good and evil spirits, the ability of words that are harmless in one society to have quite another meaning in another, and the suggestion that the most deliberate and blameworthy use of profane language occurs, not on the stage, but "in fashionable Society and popular Literature." There is criticism of Gilbert's placement of the words "Damn me!" in the mouths of children in *H. M. S. Pinafore*. The article ends with touching suggestions for the writing of a play based on the parable of the Prodigal Son. Just as with the article on vivisection, this article appears to be an effort to establish a distraction for his work which is forthcoming.

Let us return for a moment to Dodgson's poem "The Valley of the Shadow of Death," written in 1860 when he was twenty-eight. I used it in Chapter 8 to support conclusions about the likely manifestation of deep emotion on his part as he reflected on a most difficult part of his life. Rather than re-write that portion of the chapter, I have chosen to leave it there to demonstrate the difficulty in drawing anything serious from his work even as we re-examine the single verse which draws on Biblical material, a familiar verse, but coincidentally one which also brought to a resounding conclusion a sermon published by his father seven years earlier on the subject of the evil receiving Holy Communion.

> I could not see for blinding tears,
>   The Glories of the west:
> A heavenly music filled mine ears,
>   A heavenly peace my breast.
> `Come unto Me, come unto Me —
> All ye that labour, unto Me —
> Ye heavy-laden, come to Me —
>   And I will give you rest.´

If we examine the first two lines of the verse, we can see by the presence of the colon that they preface the six lines that follow. And while the line "The Glories of the west" is lyrical and rhyming, it really has no particular relevance. Perhaps the "blinding tears" refer to the convulsive laughter produced or suppressed from the anagrams formed from that lyrical line: *"Let few host the orgies"* or *"We left the hog stories,"* or *"Go, test the whore's life!"* And the word *come* takes on a quite different meaning as it fits in with the other themes which imply the experience of both "rapturous" and temporarily self-soothing passive sexual activities.

What we have seen is the carefully calculated preparation of rage expression, Dodgson's intellectual faculties totally focused in this service. In what appears to be a defiance of the Deity in whose belief he was raised, he chose a method which would attack in secret all that his father stood for. Yet he buried it in expressed sentiments which were in total conformity with what his father taught. The themes themselves suggest internal struggle, anger, guilt, shame, and, perhaps more than ever, Dodgson's compulsively repetitious efforts to master the oral/anal/genital trauma experienced at Richmond and Rugby.

Eternal Punishment

In order to understand Dodgson's attitudes toward the concept of "eternal punishment," it is important to be aware of the position taken by his Church. Drawing from the writings of Henry Parry Liddon, his friend, but also a visible supporter of Dr. Pusey's brand of Anglican thought, we can gain a view of not only the Church's position, but perhaps fundamental differences between the two.

Liddon writes in 1874:

> ... Although we may rightly shrink from saying that any given individual is certainly so unfaithful to light and grace as to incur the eternal loss of God, we do know that many are so. God knows who they are.
>
> It is impossible — for me at least — to doubt that this awful doctrine is a part of Divine Revelation. But does it really present a difficulty different in kind from that of the greatest of all difficulties — the origin of the existence of evil?
>
> How many of us have, perhaps, dared sometimes to think, `if I were an almighty and perfectly good being, I never would have allowed evil to exist at all´!
>
> ... We can only say that in giving the great gift of moral freedom, God gave it to immortal beings, with all its awful liabilities, as well as with its inconceivable capacities for good. . . . [3]

Later in 1878, we have:

... Of course, the Revealed doctrine is an unspeakably awful one; the imagination recoils from it. But it is revealed; and there is no more to be said. ... [4]

Others who wrote on the subject included Dr. Frederic William Farrar, Dean of Canterbury, who in the publication of his sermons on *Eternal Hope* wrote this description of the Church's teaching and his disagreement with its position regarding:

1. the physical torments, the material agonies... of Eternal Punishment;
2. the supposition of its necessarily endless duration for all who incur it;
3. the opinion that it is thus incurred by the vast mass of mankind; and
4. that it is a doom passed irreversibly at the moment of death on all who die in a state of sin. [5]

Farrar's work encouraged a more merciful view of God, a position publicly refuted by Dr. Pusey, though later eased. Farrar's position was that he would prefer to die as a beast without any soul than even think that a place for eternal punishment could exist. Many of Dodgson's communications on the subject reflect similar argument and presentation as that which appears in Rev. Farrar's work.

If there is a summary of Dodgson's conflicted attitude toward God it is depicted in the two anagrams formed from the signature "C. L. Dodgson" that he used in most of his letters, even those to family members. These are: *C. L. D., God-Son* and *C. L. D., no gods.* At times he reveals a sense of connectedness or chosenness, as in the Orestes theme, where whatever he did he considered a command from God which left him totally blameless for his actions and only further driven in defiance of the thorny prick of the Fury torment to accomplish the appointed task. On the other hand, there are at times a total defiance of the notion of the existence of any deity, based on what he perceived to be the unjust infliction of a lifetime of tortuous pain at a time when he was still in a state of childlike innocence. Dodgson endured a lifetime of struggle with the notions of "good" and "evil," with both played out in the reality of his life.

What were his true, innermost feelings? This is perhaps the hardest of all the questions to answer. For in his pursuit of this ultimate question Dodgson combined two very sophisticated psychological defenses to ward off anxiety and find ultimate peace. The first of these is intellectualization, the process of analyzing a problem intellectually, in total isolation of the feelings generated by the anxiety. In this pursuit, his understanding of the principles of logic served him well. The second self-preserving psychological defense is rationalization, the process of hiding the real meaning of things to oneself by the invention of plausible and acceptable explanations. Rationalization creates self-justification to restore self-esteem. In Dodgson's treatment of the question of "Eternal Punishment," he used both defenses which held together by emotions that intruded at key points of logical discourse to create the desired outcomes. Even in this, however, the game-playing continued.

Before proceeding to an examination of Dodgson's writings on the subject, a brief explanation of the notion "sophistical reasoning" is in order. The Sophists were Greek philosophers from about 500 B. C. who provided guidelines for successful living. Their reasoning became characterized by the presence of a fallacy, not intended as deceit, within their long logical arguments intended to defend their behavioral position. Dodgson's use of lengthy logical argument to support his own positions founded in anxiety appear sophistical in nature, as they contain unstated assumptions drawn from *felt* states to support his otherwise rigorously derived conclusions. Given what we have seen elsewhere, one could infer that some of these fallacies were introduced deceitfully to demonstrate his own intellectual superiority; others may have been introduced accidentally to support his own pre-conceived conclusions, the only conclusions which could rescue his self-cohesion. Sophistical arguments are often used to prove the absurdity of alternative positions, screened by the mere volume of words, assumptions, and interim conclusions.

In an examination of the last example from his writings in his paper entitled "`Eternal Punishment´," written in 1895 and published in *The Lewis Carroll Picture Book* in 1899, the scheme described is clearly revealed. This article was the first of what he hoped would be an extended pursuit of the subject but the task was interrupted by his death. The statement of the problem to be solved is placed at the beginning of the article:

> `I believe that God is perfectly good. Yet I seem compelled to believe that He will inflict Eternal Punishment on certain human beings, in circumstances which would make it, according to the voice of my conscience, unjust, and therefore wrong´ [6]

After a long and circuitous argument which reflects the constant intrusion of the intuitive acceptability or rejection of certain notions,

Dodgson establishes four possible positions one can take and his own conclusion:

> Any one of these four views may be held, without violating the laws of logical reasoning.
> Here ends my present task: since my object has been, throughout, *not* to indicate one course rather than another, but to help the Reader to see clearly *what* the possible courses are, and *what* he is virtually accepting, or denying, in choosing any *one* of them. [7]

Which of the four does Dodgson seem to embrace? The secret lies in the title of the paper, which he uncharacteristically enclosed in quotation marks; "`Eternal Punishment.`" I believe this is an anagram for "*Pen neutral shit, men!*," which is exactly what a lengthy, sophistical argument often does, due to its inherent imbedded fallacies.

In Dodgson's letter to his sister Elizabeth dated November 25, 1894, he explores the notion of "free will," the ever-present possibility that a sinner will repent, and the likely injustice of anything like the "Eternal Punishment" taught by his Church. An examination of the underlying communication with "Lizzie" reveals more than the argument presented. Dodgson opens his discussion with:

> Many people talk on *this* subject, just as if the phrase `I believe in the doctrine of eternal punishment´ had *one* meaning, and one *only*, and that everybody knew what that one meaning was. [8]

He proceeds to suggest "it" (the statement) has at least three meanings, all quite different. (In the Dodgson trap, "it" could mean the phrase itself or its contents.) After a long logical presentation he assures Lizzie that the meaning of the statement has indeed taken on three quite different meanings.

There *are* "at least" three meanings to the phrase "I believe in the doctrine of Eternal Punishment" beyond those acknowledged by Dodgson. [Note that he uses the same conditional as I came to use in solving anagrams. One could wonder if this relates to the mysterious "Rule of Three" which appears throughout his works, introduced in the *Snark*.] One is "*I'd be proven insane if I let the lion meet her cunt.*" The second is: "*I believe the Fathers condemn penile nutrition.*" No doubt Dodgson could argue "sophistically" that any two of the three meanings could be held simultaneously, but not all three. This is the very approach he used with his sister in the open communication of the letter. He ended with the suggestion: ". . . I'd better `make hay while the sun shines´!" From this we derive "at least:" "*Aha! Why shun the menses I like?*" or "*Why, she sins like thee, Ma, a Hun!*"

In Lizzie's response to the above letter she took offense at his sending him an "argument." In return he revealed a little more about his beliefs by identifying himself as a member of the "Broad Church," which he indicated believed that (1) the God worshipped in the Church is perfectly good, and (2) that except in the case of a being "*continuing in sin*" (Dodgson's italics) it would be wrong to suffer eternal punishment on any being. [9] (He had already acknowledged that he was less than fully "High Church" in a letter in 1882 [10] to an unidentified recipient.) To Dodgson, High Church members (including his brother Edwin) accept (1), reject (2) and believe a third: that God is capable of inflicting eternal punishment even if the being has ". . . *ceased to sin*" (Dodgson's italics). This was a position he could not accept. He ends the letter with a rather impassioned expression of hope that God will not condemn any of His beings whom He has given free will on the basis that there is always the chance that such a being in rebellion will eventually repent. [10] In an earlier letter to Mary Brown dated June 28, 1889, in which he explored the same issues in addition to the Biblical meaning of "Hell," he allowed that even the Devil should be granted the possibility of repenting and of being forgiven, a distinctly different position than that taken by his Church. [11]

Dodgson resumed preaching occasionally in 1890 after a long hiatus. His diary entries in 1896 and 1897 reflect two such occasions. What is particularly interesting are the subjects he chose for his sermons, as they must have been difficult to develop and sustain in front of the large congregations he reports were present. On December 6, 1896, he spoke for "eighteen minutes" on "*Mark ix, 24,*" whose theme is "`Lord, I believe: help Thou mine unbelief.´" [12] On March 7, 1897, he preached for forty-five minutes on

Job, xxxviii, 28: And unto man he said, `The fear of the Lord, that is wisdom´, and the prayer in the Litany, `Give us an heart to love and dread thee.´ [13]

In attempting to summarize any position which Dodgson may have held himself, one is challenged by his apparent ability to take any position at any time, one in the clear, one hidden. In many of his letters on the subject he incorporates anagrams with the usual sexual imagery. I shall, however, attempt to list the elements which seem to have had meaning to him, without attempting to tie them together in a

logical system. I suggest these beliefs provided for him a level of
comfort in his anxiety. But they also reflect the distance he kept from
the Anglican Church as he rejected all thoughts of a vengeful,
punishing God, and accepted only the image of a loving and forgiving
God. In the final analysis, however, Dodgson's belief in God seems to
have been qualified by the pervasive conditional "If He exists." I have
concluded this despite his extensive logical presentations in letters on
agnosticism. For, I don't believe he ever truly reconciled for himself
the fairness of the life he had been dealt by the loving God he sought.
His numerous writings on the subject represent efforts to accomplish
that reconcilement by "talking" his doubts through. These writings
reflect a continuing struggle to achieve some level of understanding,
even if he denied the effort so often in the facade of arrogance and
cynicism.   I believe these positions, which derive from recorded
conversations with children particularly and from his letters to invalids
on suffering, reflect the essence of his religious thinking:

> God is perfect and chose to create beings, including men, who
> have free-will, i.e., the ability to choose between good
> and evil. In so exercising that ability (*regardless of
> which is chosen*), men are acting in accordance with the
> will of God. "I am human; therefore, I am saved."

> Children are born in a state of Original Goodness. Sin is
> introduced externally by the environment.

> Spirits external to man exist. These include both good and evil
> spirits and angels, both of whom influence the behavior
> of men, for good and bad.

> God causes even the innocent to suffer as a means of building
> character in preparation for their role in the world to
> come. In this, they imitate the life of Christ, who,
> Himself, suffered as part of a self-perfecting and
> redemptive process. Those who suffer and conform
> their behavior to the suffering which God has chosen to
> give them, emulate Christ.

> Heaven consists of a number of "planes" or levels of perfection,
> which reflect higher and higher levels of worthiness for
> eternal reward. Souls move up from level to level
> toward eventual perfection as they come to repent for
> their sins. The final resting place of Heaven or Hell is
> not established upon death, but after a long process
> during which the soul has the opportunity of repentance
> still open to it.

Life is but the smallest moment of time in the total temporal opportunity to repent. Sins committed in life are always subject to a change in heart by the sinner and repentance later in life or after death.

Hell means "for a long time," not "for an infinite period."

Doing the best one can is all that one can do. Things done for motives that are both selfish and/or unselfish will be rewarded on the basis of the happiness they provide others, not on the basis of their motivations.

Nothing in our behavior can add to the redemptive act of Christ. In fact, the behavior of the worst sinner *enhances* the miracle of Christ's redemptive act.

As Dodgson came closer to the end of his life, my sense is that most of the struggles with the incompleteness of the above positions were reconciled with one final conclusion, still conditioned by "If God exists:"

Jesus Christ alone is the source of redemption. It is *only* by belief in and attachment to Jesus Christ as Redeemer that Eternal Life will be gained.

On May 23, 1897, less than a year before his death, Dodgson copied the following lines, written by Margaret Fuller Ossoli, ostensibly for the benefit of his friend Hettie Rowell.

Let me but gather from the earth one full-grown fragrant flower:
Within my bosom let it bloom through its one blooming hour:
Within my bosom let it die, and to its latest breath
My own shall answer `Having lived, I shrink not now from death.´
It is this niggard halfness that turns my heart to stone;
'Tis the cup seen, not tasted, that makes the infant moan;
For once let me press firm my lips upon the moment's brow;
For once let me distinctly feel `I am all happy now;´
And Love shall seal a blessing upon that moment's brow. [14]

As we come to the end of this religious discussion and of the life of Charles Dodgson, we arrive at his death itself on January 14, 1898. Can we learn about the nature and depths of his beliefs as he lay on his deathbed, about to confront that uncertainty, the ". . . land of the great departed. . . the silent land" [15], as he called it? A few days before he died, Dodgson asked one of his sisters to read to him the words of a favorite hymn whose verses end in the words ". . . Thy will be done." [16] I believe it is the following hymn written in the middle of the 19th Century:

My Jesus, As Thou Wilt!

My Jesus as Thou wilt!
O may Thy will be mine!
Into Thy hand of love
I would my all resign.
Through sorrow or through joy,
Conduct me as Thine own;
And help me still to say,
"My Lord, Thy will be done."

My Jesus, as Thou wilt!
Though seen through many a tear,
Let not my star of hope
Grow dim or disappear.
Since Thou on earth hast wept,
And sorrowed oft alone,
If I must weep with Thee,
My Lord, Thy will be done.

My Jesus, as Thou wilt!
All shall be well for me;
Each changing future scent
I gladly trust with Thee.
Straight to my home above
I travel calmly on,
And sing, in life or death,
"My Lord, Thy will be done."   Amen. [17]

Or, did Dodgson, with a self totally destroyed, remain a cynic to the end, and play the role of believer for the benefit of his sister? Was he fully aware that there are "at least" three anagrams formed from the hymn's refrain? "*Ill done, why bet?*;" "*Bed with lonely*;" and "*Beeth wild only.*"

We began with an enigma. We end with an enigma. But perhaps we know a great deal more about the man and the difficult struggles with which he coped during his lifetime. May he rest in peace as we attempt to benefit from the many insights his life and works can continue to provide us.

PART IV

CONCLUSION

CHAPTER 13

CONTEMPORARY RELEVANCE

If I have been successful in meeting you through this book, you are uneasy, maybe even upset, perhaps in a way which you cannot quite identify. Hopefully what I have touched is your own anger.

Charles Dodgson wrote about hypocrisy: the obscene distortion and cynical violation of principles and values we claim to honor and revere. He showed us in his works that words, even the most revered words, have no meaning except that which we give them in the way we live our lives. And he showed us in his life the effects hypocrisy has on our lives and the lives of the children who learn its tolerance from us. His literature may never again be the place to which we can escape in search of relief from our own pain or as a hideaway from the suffering of others.

I invite those who find this story belonging to another age and another time to reconsider the relevance which the issues raised have for us today. For 150 years later we are no less an alienating society than that faced by Dodgson. For whether it be gays, blacks, women, the homeless, the unskilled, mentally ill or retarded, we tolerate an environment of alienation, of rejection. And perhaps most of all, we provide precious little value to children as children. Until we include rather than exclude, share rather than take, accept rather than deny, face rather than avoid, clarify rather than confuse, and act rather than observe, there will be Charles Dodgson's all around us. Like him they will be victims of a self-destroying childhood, callously indifferent to a hypocritical society. Their goal in life will be to survive, with escape so often the means to be chosen.

And it is escape that is the means chosen; for escape into other worlds — be they media-created or drug created — is increasingly the coping mechanism of choice for larger and larger segments of our society. We know that this is true when we see that the exploitation and treatment of alienation have become the largest growth industries in a society which embraces and rewards highly the most obscene distortion and perversion of fundamental principles of honesty, fairness, and justice.

APPENDICES

APPENDIX 1

RAGE

While the main body of this work has explored the life of rage of a single individual little has really been said about rage and how it differs from anger. Rage represents a qualitatively different affective expression than anger. The purpose of this appendix is to explore how it is different, how it develops and how it manifests itself. I have drawn heavily on the works of Alice Miller, and Heinz Kohut. For ease of reference, even though it may aggravate some, third person references to "child" use the word *he*; I have rejected the use of *it* because such use disconfirms the child as a person.

There are two fundamental tasks which must take place during the psychological development of the child, both of which involve the emotions more than the intellect. The first of these is the neutralization of aggression; the second involves the separation and individuation of the self from the primary caregivers. Both reflect the child becoming an individual who exercises control over himself.

True to the Victorian and pre-Victorian tradition which viewed the child as steeped in Original Sin, the "beast to be tamed", Freud deemed aggression to be a fundamental instinct. Man was born with aggressive tendencies; the developmental (and therefore parental) task was to tame these tendencies. Within the framework of Self-psychology, which prefers to view the child as living on the "Original Goodness" end of the moral continuum, aggression is deemed to be a defensive response to a disorganized internal world, triggered by the emotions, not the intellect, and expressed in an effort to preserve the self from the felt presence of an external or internal threat. [1]

As one expression of aggression, anger is directed to people as people, usually is limited in scope to a single specific issue and can be dissipated in some sort of resolution in a short period of time. Rage, on the other hand, is not directed to people as people, but to people as things, as objects which are necessary to one's self-esteem, to selfobjects. When directed to people, rage de-personifies the target; rage is blinded to the humanity and human failings of the person. [2] It is not of limited scope, tends to be felt throughout the body as generalized although the underlying issue may be specific, and is not readily dissipated.

Rage reflects an internal state filled with built-up anger as would result from continual dis-confirmation of the self by those expected to be confirming selfobjects. Rage seeks retribution for continued wrongs and is triggered when actual or symbolic repetitions of the original wrongs persist, repetitions of being overpowered, of giving in, of being denied or frustrated, of being victimized, of being rejected for what one is. Rage goes beyond anger in that it seeks destruction — annihilation — of the object at which it is directed. Rage cannot be satisfied until that destruction is accomplished; yet rarely is in fact satisfied even when the target is destroyed. For most often, the current target is only a substitute or representation of the original perpetrator of the wrong.

Captain Ahab's pursuit of Moby Dick was a rage-based act of revenge, rage at the whale having taken his leg and at its ability to avoid capture. It was no longer a source of oil and other commercial products, but had become personified as the destroyer of Ahab's very self. Only its total destruction would satisfy the Captain; and he would risk himself and all his crew in the pursuit of his lonely, driven task. Like we have seen with Charles Dodgson, Ahab saw himself allied with God in his pursuit, with belief or unbelief, of confirmation or dis-confirmation, in the balance with success or failure. .

Using an even simpler experience, the amateur carpenter who bends a nail with a hammer may strike out at the nail in frustration, personifying it, attributing to it evil intent aimed at destroying his self-esteem. In the process of destroying this enemy or bringing it under his domination, he may also damage the surrounding area as he flails with rage at this object-become-selfobject destroyer of his self.

A primary developmental task, then, is for the child to learn techniques for experiencing, dissipating, and neutralizing aggressive feelings in a way which maintains self-esteem and restores calm to the threatened self. It is the skill of self-soothing. It is not just the skill of controlling anger, which often means in our society a repression of and denial of the "unacceptable" feelings under a mistaken belief that bad feelings are sinful, a notion often taught to children who do not even know yet what feelings are and how to neutralize them as an alternative to aggressive action. For it is this denial, this false control, this failure to experience and neutralize, which forms the seeds of rage.

The second developmental task which *the child* must accomplish is the two-fold one of individuation and separation from the adult caregivers. The emphasis is appropriately on *the child*, for the parents cannot do it; they can only create the environment in which it can take place. Or, they can inhibit it. Individuation is accomplished as the new person begins to realize that he is physically separate from and different from his caregivers; it is accomplished successfully when the child and parents can accept the differences and accomodate them within a self-nurturing environment. Separation occurs when the child can tolerate distance and function successfully away from the physical and felt or spiritual presence of the parents. Individuation begins to take place as the infant begins to realize that there is a "me" and a "not me" __ that the me and the caregiver are not one body, even though it may seem that way. Separation takes place in two stages, the first as the toddler begins to push the parent away or begins to crawl, then walk, then run from the parent, to venture out into the strange new world. He can be observed as being uncertain at first, always returning for reassurance, then venturing off again, further and further away. It takes place again during and following adolescence as the emerging adult repeats the process with much more independence and what may appear to be rejection of parents even as it is very much an effort to confirm the self. The quality of the second separation is very much conditioned by the quality of the first, influenced by the adaptations that both parents and child have made in the interim.

Inhibition of the separation and individuation process takes place when the parent transfers or projects his or her unreasonable fears onto the child, or, like Mr. Dombey and the Red King, views the emerging child as an extension of himself or his dreams and overpowers him with expectations. It occurs when a mother views her child as her "thing creation," her primary source of amusement or joy, or the vehicle for reflecting her qualities as a person and mother out to the world. In such cases, the child becomes a selfobject for the parents who mold *it* to be what they want, with the nature and needs of the child partially, if not totally, ignored.

From the moment of birth the neonate is beginning to adapt to his environment and relationships, continuing the process begun in the womb. Already conditioned by genetic factors, the nurturing or destructive chemistry of the pre-natal experience, even touches of transferred anxiety from a mother steeped in conflict, the child emerges with a most rudimentary intellect and a very highly developed sensing system. This ability to sense the environment, which he can barely see and certainly cannot understand, is the mechanism for experiencing and learning survival techniques in the home. In these first days and weeks the infant does not know what causes comfort or discomfort, what soothes or aggravates. All he knows is that "I feel" and the feeling is comforting or it is not. When a mother (or primary caregiver) soothes the hunger, relieves the discomfort of elimination products, touches, coos, talks, or sings __ all of which comprise the fundamentally important act of mirroring and confirming the wonder of the child ⸺ he does not know that it is not some part of *him* that is active and approving his emerging self.   Mother is his earliest selfobject, that "part of me without which I cannot exist" that "me who approves of me."

The way in which this selfobject acts will have a fundamental effect on the development of the felt or emotional life of the child. Repetitions of the same or similar experiences, good or bad, will create an emotional "imprint" which will "set" the pattern of child's emotional repetoire until he experiences (if he ever does) powerful corrections to his earliest learning. Safety and security are most fundamental to the newborn and are learned in a non-hostile environment where prompt and sustained confirming attention is paid to the infant, where his sensing mechanisms ⸺ sucking, touching, hearing, seeing, smelling, are not assaulted, where new experiences are accompanied by the soothing presence of the familiar and approving.

Failure to provide such an environment encourages adaptation, certainly an eventual ingredient for growth; but at this stage an adaptatation to hostility directed to the self.   This will cause an adaptation of the self during its creation stage, not its maturation stage, and will represent an adaptation to outside forces before the internal forces are even understood or experienced.   A primary adaptation will be to assuage fears of abandonment; the child will accept whatever the parent demands as a living requirement in the home, however unreasonable, however abusive. For the young child, this *is* the world. And without his parents the future is felt to be most uncertain. The earliest seeds of rage are laid in this period, awaiting expression when the child or adult finally realizes in a conscious or felt awareness that he was betrayed during a time when he was most vulnerable and totally dependent on his selfobjects/parents, when he was not accepted for who and what he was, when he realizes that perhaps he was there for them, and that they were not there for him.

Alice Miller verbalizes for the "perfect", "gifted" child the feelings of dis-confirmation awaiting later realization:

> `What would have happened if I had appeared before you, bad, ugly, angry, jealous, lazy, dirty, smelly? Where would your love have been then? And I was all these things as well. Does this mean that it was not really me whom you loved, but only what I pretended to be? The well-behaved, reliable, empathic, understanding, and convenient child, who in fact was never a child at all? What became of my childhood? Have I not been cheated out of it? I can never

return to it. I can never make up for it. From the beginning
I have been a little adult. My abilities — were they simply
misused [by you for your benefit]?´ [3]

As the child grows he becomes more verbal and more able to use
language to process events, his emotional reactions and communicate
his needs and feelings. This is a period during which he needs to look
to parents whom he can idealize, who will not only show him in their
lives how these things are done but also which of the many conflicting
values evidenced in the environment are capable of being embraced
and cherished as his own. Again the influence of the parent is critical,
not in what is taught, but what is lived. Parents who create an
environment in which feelings are stifled, where bad feelings such as
anger are denied, go unprocessed, are not verbalized, are not
experienced and soothed, teach by the example of being looked up to
woefully inadequate tools for managing uncomfortable feelings and
aggression.
    Here also is where the tolerance for hypocrisy is learned. And, as
the child moves to adolescence with what has been by now a lifetime
heavily weighted by dis-confirmation of the real "me" by others and
self-adaptation to the point where the real "me" is impotent, or totally
lost, the ingredients for an explosion of what in many ways is infantile
rage, but now in the powerful body and mind of a near-adult are
present. For what may become realized, with or without a traumatic
event, is that the self is filled with emptiness, that the self is not
prepared to enter the adult world, and that the earliest fears of
abandonment are about to take place. The source of rage is the sense
of helplessness which comes from the inability to control the outside
world the way the narcissistically damaged person (heretofore always
under the control of others) wishes he could control himself. The
associated feelings are not those of guilt, but of emptiness,
helplessness and unbearable shame. [4]
    Parenting styles can be abusive in far more than the recognized
ways of assaultive physical abuse. For in its essence, coercion is at the
bottom of abuse in the parent/child relationship, a relationship based
on power. And coercion, or a bending of the will, can be done with a
moment of violence, with sustained violence, or in the most subtle
suggestions or implications that the child will not be loved, will be
abandoned, or, with complicity between parents and God in a total
mis-application of the Fourth Commandment, rejected even by God.
Punishments which far exceed the understanding of justice held by the
child foster the plotting for revenge and for ways to perform the act in
the future so as to avoid the punishment, a plotting of ways to get

back at the parent/monster who uses power to destroy the exploring "me."

The intellectual growth of the child may proceed splendidly, even precociously, as *this* becomes the source of parental approval. Intellectual pursuits may be the child's defensive way to escape the emotional pain of the parental assault. They may be accompanied by escape into fantasy, to be followed later by more adult means of escape. Such children often come to feel loved not for who they are, but for how they reflect on the parents. This well developed intellectual capacity may, as we saw in Dodgson's case, become the very tool used in rage expression. In the meantime, the child becomes passive to the parents, lonely, lonely within the home and within the self, and alienated, confirmed only by further, perhaps compulsive, pursuit of the recognition which is forthcoming in further destruction of self.

If the injury or repeated injury is seen as coming from caregivers wrapped in "claims of love and material indulgence" [5], the child or adolescent internalizes the belief that his rage is unjustified. Consequently, he turns it inward, wracked with guilt on the one hand (Dodgson's Furies) yet demanding of an expression on the other. In such cases the mode of expression is also inwardly focused, seen in suicide, such bodily abuses as eating disorders, or in self-directed sexual perversions [see Appendix 2].

Heinz Kohut [6] states that the severest form of aggression occurs when psychic conflict emerges between the "grandiose self" (that part of "me" seeking confirmation as "wonderful," "powerful," etc.) and the image of the earliest powerful selfobject (the one who should have supported grandiose self development in mirroring and confirmation). And it is most destructive, not when reflected in wild behavior, but when done with meticulous planning, the wish to destroy closely tied with an absolute belief in their own greatness and their *devotion* to the early all-powerful selfobject. Revenge which becomes an all consuming compulsion is a characteristic of narcissistic rage (deriving from destruction of a positive view of the self). It is particularly dangerous because, despite being totally in the control of the underlying out-of-control emotion, intellectual prowess is sharpened. All the normal controls over reason come under its control. Plotting and rationalizing of the planned activity become the intellect's all-consuming function. Rage, a most pernicious psychic affliction, is filled with spite, may strike out in vengeful acts or may be evidenced in "a cunningly plotted vendetta." [7]

APPENDIX 2

PERVERSIONS

The purpose of this Appendix is to provide additional insights into the subject of perversions from the framework of Self-psychology. Charles Dodgson used the placement of clue-laden but hidden explicit Victorian pornography within his writing, and appears to have been fully aware of much of the motivation and meaning behind that effort, anticipating much of what clinicians have painstakenly drawn from their patients. Much of this material comes from Alice Miller's several works and Masud Khan's focused work *Alienation in Perversions*.

Reflective of common usage if not what would appear to be considerable private practice, the 1989 Edition of the *Oxford English Dictionary* defines *perversion* as disordered sexual behavior which seeks satisfaction through avenues other than heterosexual intercourse. In 1948 the definition refers to the landmark Kinsey studies of the 1940's:

> unnatural acts, acts contrary to nature, bestial, abominable, and detestable... [English common law is] committed to the doctrine that no sexual activity is justifiable unless its objective is procreation.

In 1892, *perversion* referred to an "inversion" of the sexual feelings, i. e., a passion for a person of the same sex, with awareness of its morbid nature.

I prefer to provide a broader, perhaps more clinical definition that remains true to the theoretical framework in which I have written and which focuses on underlying conscious or unconcious motivation. Perversions are sexual behaviors which are a manifestation of a fundamental disorder of the self. More specifically, they are sexual behaviors whose primary purpose are restoration of the self (self-soothing) and which looks on the object of sexual stimulation as a selfobject (to be used and abused as an object, not a person). In this framework heterosexual behavior including intercourse would be perverse if one partner did not consent, a condition which implicitly includes adult/child sexual behavior as perverse. This definition does not categorize homosexual activities as perverse *per se*.

Left unexplored here but certainly running throughout this work and Dodgson's battle with the meaning of words is the notion that society chooses to define its perversions. For within the same definitional framework, the pursuit of greed, the accepted "engine" of our economic system, could very well be considered a "perverse" activity as it often reflects self-restorative efforts by its participants, efforts which all too often de-personalize other system participants. Yet it is handsomely rewarded.

Perversions as Expressions of Rage

We have already seen that the pursuit of revenge is a rage response which involves repetitive and compulsive plotting, planning, and aggression taken against an outside objectified person or personified object as a way of maintaining a sense of self-cohesion. Perversions are sexually oriented behaviors driven by the same underlying mental processes and states. "What we see in perversions is unconscious, introjected contempt." [1] Such activities represent a re-enactment of the early parental rejecting experience, accompanied by the *felt* presence of the mother [2] who rejected the child's true self, either with subtlety or with physical or sexual abuse committed or tolerated.

Compulsively driven orgasm experienced in masturbation or with a fetish or another person requires this felt rejecting presence to accomplish its goal of self-restoration. [3]   Those suffering from perversions bear the early rejection of the mother, with continuing felt rejection by the self or others as her surrogate an essential ingredient for the perversion to provide a satisfying relief of self.

A second essential ingredient to perverse acts is actual or potential social disapproval. The acts performed must be those which violate individual or community moral, legal, or social beliefs, standards, or customs. If they do not, the potential for re-enacted rejection is lost; the behavior, though still of a perverse nature no longer satisfies, and is no longer perverse for the person. Approval by "observers" would require that the compulsive expression be changed. Implied or actual permission to perform the activity would destroy the ever-present horrified eyes and image of the rejecting mother. [4] We see the rage response of the child now in the adult, who, once rejected and impotent, becomes potent and creates a scene which would disgust the "observing" mother-image far more than the original activity which caused rejection. Out of this feeling of retribution comes a momentary sense of feeling to replace the emptiness, a momentary soothing of the self and a most likely out-of-awareness feeling of satisfaction that the mother's disgust has been kept intact.

In his many years of clinical experience Masud Khan [5] found that chldren who engaged in perversions after reaching adulthood had been very much loved by their mothers, with fathers present but not experienced fully as persons by the child. Physical body care was lavished on the infant and child but was impersonal in nature, efficient but not done in a way that met other selfobject needs of total acceptance and nurturance. It may have been done promptly and correctly in all ways, but it was done impersonally, as just another in a series of caretaking tasks; it was not felt as part of a you/me relationship.

> The child was treated as her `thing creation´ rather than as an emergent growing person in his or her own right. [6]

The mother/child relationship was one of *idolization*, not *idealization*; it exploited the infant's earliest instincts and thought processes for her own purposes. In becoming an object of idolization, he has become a thing, an "it." The child becomes her selfobject and feels something very special about itself, but not about its own personhood. Learning to tolerate this feeling of early splitting of the self the child changes its behavior in order to maintain the relationship with its mother as her special created "thing." As he models her behavior, he too begins to imitate and internalize her idolizing attitude, with the created false self becoming an idolized "it" self.

Khan also finds that such children have usually experienced a sudden separation during the Oedipal phase (normally about age 3) — delayed from its appropriate time one or two years by the strong mutual attachment. And, this separation is initiated by the mother instead of the child as she suddenly realizes that the intensity of their relationship is inappropriate or uncomfortable for her, or, may be drawn away by other children or responsibilities. Felt at this stage more acutely by the child, the task of this first separation is partly and inappropriately completed and experienced with panic and ultimate fear of annihilation. Fearful and alone now but skilled only in idolization of self, the intensity of this idolization increases while accompanied by efforts to keep all evidence of fear hidden from the environment. For if he discloses his fear, his mother may discontinue whatever remnants of idolization remain, or reunification for the wished-for prior relationship will be threatened.

Typically, these children are lacking in the experience of play and the use of transitional objects. For these are children who have always been little adults, little mother's helpers in an emotional as well as a physical sense. They are "astonishingly empathic to their mother's moods" [7] and invest their energies in further augmenting their role as her created-thing. They offer little initiative of their own. Their energies, instead of being used to learn the negotiation of the outside environment, turn inward to focus on the inner idolized self for the sake of self preservation and cohesion in the face of fears.

These children arrive at puberty and adolescence feeling special, innocent, with strong wishes to be outward-focused; but they are inadequate to the task. They have, instead, a total though vague self focus and are depleted and unable to reach beyond themselves to offer anything to others. What had been a subtle sexualization of the relationship with the mother now becomes in puberty and adolescence more overt. Though they feel the same quality of closeness, a secret mutual sharing and support, there is a lack of vitality and commitment. Relationships will reflect a cautious dependency for he has already experienced strong feelings of abandonment once. Accompanying these feelings and mixed in with them are the intense and complex feelings of puberty, and self-created sexual feelings become the preferred means of soothing the anxious or deadened self.

In exploring the use of objects to self-soothe, it is useful here to define and describe the notion of "transitional objects," the purposes they perform and the characteristics they have. The use of transitional objects is an important childhood experience. Such objects may be blankets, pieces of cloth, stuffed animals, or whatever the child chooses. During the time when the child separates from mother, transitional objects provide a bridge or link by being mother-like (a selfobject). Like her, they provide self-soothing assistance when the child is attempting not to turn to mother, yet cannot quite do it alone. So, rather than an unhealthy sign, transitional objects are a healthy sign that separation from mother is being initiated by the child and is taking place. The child is beginning to search beyond mother for other selfobjects as well as beginning to self-soothe. As to characteristics, a transitional object must be chosen by the child and be its exclusive property. It must be able to endure all the loving, cuddling, hating, and aggression directed to it by the child. It must seem to the child to give warmth and comfort, have texture as if it had a reality beyond what is apparent to the adult; it should, therefore, never be changed but left with all its dirt and familiar odors intact. Its fate must be left to the child, who will abandon it when ready, after which it will not be mourned, but will never be forgotten. The child's need for it will just dissipate. What needed external but not-mother assistance becomes internalized and part of the self. [8] The transitional object has all of the characteristics that made up the child's world with mother, including texture, familiar odors, and constant presence; yet it is not-mother.

"All perversions entail a fundamental alienation from self in the person concerned" [9] with sexual activity used in the attempt to identify personhood. The pervert is inconsolable with an insatiable appetite. The ultimate object of idolization, idealization, and narcissistic identification becomes himself as represented by his genitals, a fetish, or another person, all of which become invested in the reparative process of self-soothing. Lacking original transitional objects at the appropriate early stages, these objects become self-soothing transitional objects in puberty, adolescence and adulthood, transitional objects which have now become an integral part of self definition. [10]

> Through its, his, or her readiness to comply it lends itself to be invented [i.e., represent in fantasy whatever is desired or needed], manipulated, used and abused, ravaged and discarded, cherished and idealized, symbiotically identified with and deanimated all at once. [11]

But the perversion will never repair the damage done in self-development by the empathic failures of the mother.

The fact that another person can be and often is the transitional object indicates clearly that these kinds of perversions involve two people with complementary if different deficiencies in self. Each is willing to fulfil the requirements of transitional object for the other. If one party is to be used, the other is to use. There is a partnership in which both are searching for self-cohesion. Consent can only reduce or eliminate external coercion, but the compulsion to participate remains, though it may now be expressed as choice. For those suffering in perversions, never having chosen or experienced a transitional object to facilitate the soothing of separation anxieties, or, having had the transitional object taken away abruptly and inappropriately, the relationship to the object of their perversion is one of choosing, use, and manipulation. The perversion is an effort to re-create what was never experienced with mother-as-selfobject, or with a transitional object. But dissipation rarely occurs, even if the object is changed, perhaps constantly, as the chosen object-as-person refuses to submit or cooperate. There is a repetitively compulsive quality to the activity, [12] which is more willed than desired, and reflects, therefore, one of the characteristics of rage. It may be masochistic, where the eroticized enjoyment is derived from one part of the split-off self viewing another part of the self suffering on the basis of activities performed in the felt presence of the initial cause and real target of rage [13], but the self becomes the surrogate target.

When the object of the perversion is a person, the mutuality of sharing lessens feelings of shame and guilt around participation in the activity. This bolsters the self-esteem by partially "undoing" the damage done to the self by the parents by providing pleasure to another person. The activity keeps the pervert from collapsing to a psychotic state of guilt and despair. While communication may take place and be minimally better than the poor communication which took place with the mother despite the overly intimate connectedness, the relationship is shallow, with the mutually shared perversion the primary link. [14]

Miller suspects that the worst cases of pedophilia do not derive from sexual origins, but from issues of power and powerlessness. [15] Rape is increasingly viewed not as sexual in nature, but as a sexualized rage response to a sense of powerlessness and is a misplaced effort to restore a severely damaged self-esteem. The rapist aims his rage at a person who brings back feelings deriving from original relationships or who is perceived as accepting the long wished-for acceptance of sexual performance. The perversions with children reflect worse damage to the self in that they represent a total inability to interact with an adult on any level, even one of violence.

Turning to a different perversion, while the erotic imagery found in Dodgson's works is not quite pornographic, in that it lacks the quality of being sustained, it does contain characteristics of pornography and therefore should be mentioned as another form of rage expression. Khan writes that pornography makes words omnipotent, is filled with "faked climaxes and orgasms," which provide excitement, but which are totally devoid of any inter-personal relationship. Its cultural acceptance is an indication of the individual's and society's inability to create fulfilling experiences from personal effort and involvement. [16] There is no essential difference in goals between the written image or the visual imagery of the motion picture or stage presentation of pornographic material. The goal of pornographic orgastic pleasure is nothing but the release of rage. While the rage is transformed into a pleasurable activity, the rage remains and is not successfully neutralized. It remains intact as no processing of insight or emotional re-working of the earlier depriving experiences has taken place. Quoting Gorer, Khan indicates that the enjoyment of pornography is private because it does not involve a shared experience but rather is enjoyed in isolation and is invariably an imaginative foreplay to masturbation.

> ... Pornography is little more than masturbation writ large, or, in Sartre's postulate, `*the onanist wants to take hold of the word as an object* [Khan's italics].´

Caught in an activity devoid of emotion, driven by compulsion, the addicted reader/accomplice loses the ability to grow in interpersonal relationships. Rather than freeing the individual as is claimed, it further entraps him as it reinforces his own self as being his chosen object of sexual pleasure. [17]

Lastly we have the sexualized rage response which can emerge from the experience of being sexually abused. While often, especially in families wrapped as expressions of love and received that way by the abused child, physical sexual abuse will begin to produce rage in the victim when a realization of the full scope of the manipulation and violation that has been done comes to awareness. Children who are prematurely exposed to erotic material and imagery by caregivers and others also suffer from sexual abuse, but they may never come to realise it, whatever the impact it may have on future relationships. For, in order for rage to develop, even a rudimentary awareness of the violation of self must exist. It may also be seen in behavior which reflects an attempt to master the trauma by repetition of the act or substitute acts rather than emotional working through. In these situations, these people reflect a failure of earlier childhood selfobjects to be available for them to help process the trauma. Based on those or other non-empathic experiences they feel they have no one to turn to in their pain, and, as they have learned to do, will assume all responsibility for their own care of self. By not trusting parent-like selfobjects to provide self functions in times of need, they have lost the ability to choose helpers who represent images of those that failed. Self-soothing can take the veiled form of an effort to master what was originally traumatic. Rage may be directed to the perpetrators or those who are seen by the victim as responsible for providing protection. It may involve either random promiscuity or prostitution, or participation in a twosome using sexual behavior rather than relationship to maintain self-cohesion. Or, reflecting the intergenerational pattern of incest or sexual abuse by others, victims may abuse their own children or other children in what reflects a rage response directed at their own "parenthood" or a compulsion to inflict their own feelings of debased-self onto children as selfobject substitutes for their own selves.

Perversions, then, can take many forms. Above all, they must go beyond what the individual or culture deems acceptable. The human psyche is extremely creative in its ability to create new perversions, with cultural limits being the starting point. Returning to the opening comments, sexual activities, be they masochistic, homosexual, heterosexual, or bestial, when pursued compulsively to fill a void in the self, reflect a rage response to the failure of early caregivers to provide what was expected and deserved — acceptance of the body-self in its totality.

APPENDIX 3

HOMOSEXUALITY

The purpose of this Appendix is to present in summary form some historical theories and attitudes regarding homosexuality, particularly those faced by Charles Dodgson in the mid to late 19th century. It also includes current thinking and the relationship of homosexuality with the framework of Self-psychology.

Homosexuality is an affective or emotional state whereby persons of the same sex are sexually or erotically attracted to one another. Although generally applied to males, as a technical term it applies to females as well, despite the fact that nearly all historical discussion is male-based. (Here, too, the secondary and inferior position of women is reflected.) Homosexual behavior, which must be separated from orientation, consists of activities done with or to the partner in order to achieve the desired sexual satisfaction. Such behaviors must, by physical endowment, involve activities other than heterosexual intercourse, and preclude one of the primary functions of heterosexual intercourse, that of procreation. Separate and important issues within the homosexual relationship as it applies to the discussion of perversions are the extent to which a non-sexual relationship exists between partners so oriented and the bases on which sexual activity takes place.

The study of homosexuality has been plagued by two historical realities. Firstly, the fact that much of the early writings which described Western homosexual behavior are in ancient Greek and Latin texts creates the need for translation. These texts often reflect the attitudes of the translator himself or of the time in which he was writing. Given the pre-Renaissance educational and political structures of Western societies, this means that such thinking was heavily influenced by Christian moral and political thinking as represented by the Roman Catholic Church. These attitudes created translations that either hid references to homosexual behavior entirely, or caused writers to translate allusions as being indirect. To accomplish this translators would accompany them with denials that the writer really meant what was implied. [1] Secondly, when homosexual behaviors are subject to violent attacks against those involved, a situation which began in the 12th century and is still occurring, the stresses experienced by homosexuals from these causes inhibit the ability to isolate in studies what is psychologically stress-caused versus what is "natural" behavior.

The term *homosexuality* is a late 19th century term, introduced by John Addington Symonds in 1891 in his work *A Problem in Modern Ethics* which was published six years before the *Oxford English Dictionary* recognizes the word's appearance. (20) It was then expanded on by Havelock Ellis in his 1898 text *Sexual Inversion*. Ellis considered homosexuality to be an internal state rather than just an externally manifested behavior, a notion that had just begun to emerge in mid-Victorian times.

The attitudes of the early Greek writers as well as Greek society is significant to our discussion, not only because the English public schoolboy and especially the students at Rugby were steeped in it, but because the Greek tradition which accepted homosexuality culturally, even if it did not consider it desirable, is very much being resurrected today. The Greeks considered erotic sexual behavior between younger boys or men and older mentors as a way to provide valuable learning experiences in the educational systems. Such activity was also seen as a way to promote a more thorough bonding between soldiers in the military.   Such bonding would enhance motivation to fight, with survival of the beloved other providing additional motivation to insure survival of self. Within the context of the Self-psychology framework, the military and mentor relationships appear to have been non-compulsive in nature, thus not making the relationships based primarily on sexual expression, and, therefore, in general, not perverse.

The presence of homosexual love appears frequently in the Greek classics along with a variety of more pleasure-seeking behavioral expressions. They receive a full defense in Plato's *Symposium* in the speeches of Phaedrus, from which the word *Uranian*, based on the god Uranus, is derived. *Urning* became a 19th century corruption of Uranian. In the *Symposium*, love between men and boys is described as "heavenly," with heterosexual passion described as "vulgar." (43) A distinction was made between the purity of homosexual love versus heterosexual "passion." Plato considered homosexuality fundamental within the notion of democracy and indicated that any laws that inhibited homosexual relationships by calling them shameful reflected evil, despotism, or cowardice on the part of legislators, rulers, or citizens respectively. (51) Drawing from Aristotle's *Nicomachean Ethics*, Boswell writes that although Aristotle may have viewed homosexuality as "quirky", he "... apparently considered a homosexual disposition perfectly `natural´" (49), arguing that it was not a moral issue; just as one would not judge feminine sexual behavior as unnatural because women experience intercourse passively one should not imply that others so disposed to be passive are immoral. Neither does he consider those who conquer such wished-for behavior as moral. [2] *Passive* is a term which references those who receive or are penetrated, either orally, anally, or vaginally. It has nothing to do with the degree of coercion or desire to participate.   It is the opposite of *active* which refers to the penetrator.   Thus, for Aristotle, anal penetration of a woman was not considered immoral behavior; it was appropriate passive sexual behavior.

In Roman culture, there was serious punishment for the rape of minors, (21) with "strangulation and burning" the punishment for rape of a man by a man. (22) On the whole, discussion of sexuality of any type was not a Roman pre-occupation. Love developed after marriage, was not a pre-condition to it; nor did marital love demand monogamous sexual union. Evidence of this is found in a letter from Augustus to Antony who suggested that despite his being married it did not matter where or with whom one "put it in" in order to receive sexual release. (23) A non-coercive homosexual relationship could exist between two adults or an adult and a young boy, with the word pederasty coming to imply either situation.   (In his discussion of pederasty, Boswell cites a work by Roman writer Pseudo-Lucian entitled *Affairs of the Heart*. (24) Recall *Diseases of the Heart*, the book being read by Dr. Arthur Forrester in *Sylvie and Bruno*.)

There existed contradictory evaluations of homosexuality within the early Church.   Clement interpreted Plato to have been in opposition to homosexual relationships and considered Plato to have been inspired by Holy Scripture. Theodoret of Cyrus (4th to 5th century), on the other hand, contradicted Clement as he interpreted and endorsed Plato's position as having considered such relationships as "happy on earth and blessed in heaven." (25) Theodoret concluded that on the basis of their love, homosexuals were heaven bound, mostly lead blessed and shining lives, and should not be burdened by laws that required them to live in shame and hiding.   In general, however, the reverence of Middle Age thinkers for the classical writers and traditions served to keep the subject from discussion. (26)

Indicative of the problem of those like myself dependent on others for the translations, we can find contradictory views within the same tradition.   Boswell writes that Thomas Aquinas viewed homosexuality as natural; but in his *Summa Theologica* he did not speculate on what its "end" might be. For Aquinas, as with Aristotle, "ends" or "purposes" very much determined what was "natural" and, therefore, moral. Aquinas reflected a caution regarding the prejudices of his time, and failed to take a strong position (327).

> In the end Aquinas admits more or less frankly that his categorization of homosexual acts as `unnatural´ is a concession to popular sentiment and parlance. [3]

On the other hand, Ronald Bayer [4] writes that Aquinas condemned homosexual practices as pleasure driven rather than procreation driven, not based on reason, and therefore lustful and sinful. If he did take this position, Aquinas certainly would have been in harmony with the Emperor Justinian, who in 538 AD clearly spoke against homosexuality as contrary to nature. With that, I leave readers with some sense of the confusion that exists in current studies.

In any case, attitudes against homosexual behavior began taking a negative turn. Beginning in the later period of the Byzantine era, which is approximately set as 1200 AD, castration was defined as the punishment for those caught in "acts against nature." For the first time terror became a part of the life of the homosexual. [5] This was an era when the Church became increasingly involved in controlling behavior and demanding conformity, perhaps in some part due to its felt need to create differentiation from outside "heretical" beliefs. Prior to that, there was either ambivalence, acceptance, or reluctant tolerance of homosexual behavior. (333-334)

In England, taking the issue over from its historical ownership by the Catholic Church, then the Anglican Church, Henry VIII removed sodomy from church jurisdiction to that of the state. He declared the vice of buggery (sodomy) to be a felony that was subject to the death penalty. This penalty was finally removed in 1861, at which time it was reduced to life imprisonment, a sanction that remained unchanged for more than a century. [6] In England the rate of executions by hanging increased from one or two per decade in the last half of the 18th century to one or two per year from 1805 to 1835 (159) though executions for other capital crimes decreased drastically. (16) In the face of this attitude, Kinsey, when estimating that ten per cent of a population is homosexual, concluded that there must have been 400,000 adult gay males in England in 1811, and 30,000 of that number residing in London. (16)

Homosexual activity was tolerated and very much a part of the public school environment although its presence generated instant reaction when publicly exposed and discussed. [7] Newspaper reports nevertheless indicate that street crowds numbering as many as 5,000 and involving fifty constables were known to assemble in sodomy cases with beatings of offenders often undertaken. In 1895, Oscar Wilde was attacked by crowds on his way to prison after his conviction for performing homosexual acts. In essence, Wilde was punished for being caught at what was known to be a secretly widespread practice. [8] In comments referring to the public school system as he experienced it well toward the end of the 19th century C. S. Lewis described pederasty as often the only outlet for rebellion within a demanding structure. (107) What is clear is that there was a fundamental hypocrisy between what the adult/parent world espoused as acceptable, moral behavior and what it tolerated. The victims of that hypocrisy were the children whose participation was coerced by physical means or by peer pressure. For, they were either physically and psychically abused or hardened with cynicism toward the conditions fellow students had to endure in a fundamentally brutal environment.

Turning now to the evolution of theories regarding the etiology of homosexuality, we find such studies modern, as the ancient writers did not see it as abnormal, and, therefore not of interest for great study. [9]   Historical attributions of causality for homosexuality include the following: it exists from birth; it results from seduction by an adult to the gay life and thus is a coerced or learned behavior; it results from too strong or too weak a parent with usually mother dominant; it results from excessive dependence on peer modeling; it is caused by excessively strong or weak sexual drives; an inability to attract or persistent rejection by members of the opposite sex is experienced; the homosexual is an individual at a lower stage of evolutionary development; homosexuality is an expression of rebellion against society; lastly, it represents a reaction to one or more traumatic events. [10]

In 1825, the practice of homosexual acts was seen as freely willed. This freely willed selection of a vice therefore represented a form of mental illness. It was not until the late 1800's that two schools of thought emerged and scientific investigation began. One study posited that homosexuality was an acquired characteristic; but the more accepted position was that it was inborn and the result of heredity. Paul Moreau of France, argued that

> ... homosexuality was the outgrowth of both an inherited `constitutional weakness´ and environmental forces. Given an inborn predisposition to perversion, a `hereditary taint,´ factors ranging from puberty and climate to masturbation could precipitate the manifestation of homosexuality. In a

state midway between reason and madness, those afflicted
were in constant danger of becoming insane.... [11]

In his monumental 1896 work on sexual deviance entitled
Psychopathia Sexualis Richard von Krafft-Ebing attempted to
document a history of mental illness in the family — insanity, epilepsy,
hysteria, convulsions, alcoholism, and physical disorders — in those
who developed as a result of their life experiences, some form of sexual
pathology. (20)

Cesar Lombroso, a nineteenth century Italian, argued that
homosexuals were at a lower level of human development, as
evidenced by their animal-like behavior, and could not, therefore, be
held responsible for their condition. He argued that they should not
be punished, even though he argued that they should be placed in
asylums to protect the public from danger. In the 1860's, anticipating
Havelock Ellis and his *Sexual Inversion*, Karl Ulrichs argued that
homosexuality represented the presence, within a normal male body,
of a brain developed in such a way as to house a female soul, and was,
therefore, inborn. (20-21)

Freud argued that men, born with both heterosexual and
homosexual characteristics became excessively attached to their own
genitals, and were unable to move on to attachment to women as
sexual objects. Later, as his thinking evolved, Freud linked
homosexuality with a failure to successfully complete the pre-Oedipal
task of separation and individuation; the son thus remained fused with
the mother. From this partial identification with the mother, the
homosexual then wishes to be the passive partner in sex with a male.
Another Freudian explanation was that an excessive rejection of the
son by the father in the Oedipal stage took place, in to the excessive
mother/son attachment. This rejection imprinted a fear of castration
should any heterosexual acts take place involving the son. (24) In
contrast to earlier theories which pointed to innate origins, Freud
pointed to internal disturbances in sexual development caused by the
environmental factors of relationships with parents during the Oedipal
phase. Seeking a partner like himself due to narcissistic forces and
still fearing castration by his father due to his lingering identification
with his mother, the son cannot tolerate a partner who does not have
the revered and feared male sexual organ.

Freud's theories held sway until the 1940's when Irving Bieber
and Sandor Rado rejected his theory of a sexual phobia based on fear
of parental responses. Bieber argued that heterosexuality was normal,
while homosexuality was an adaptive response to extremely pathologic
relationships between parent(s) and child. Overly close and

affectionate mothers inhibited the development of maleness; they encouraged feminine behavior (and identity) and discouraged male behavior, sometimes with hostility. A mother might do this by creating competitiveness between the child's relationship with her and his father, forcing a choice on the child's part, even as she presents a subtle seduction by favoring the son over the spouse. Some mothers prevent peer modeling with other boys which creates excessive attachment to her, which in turn thwarts the development of independent and autonomous action. Many boys feel that their fathers are hostile or distant, lack affection, and otherwise fail to provide male modeling behavior. Neither do they provide insights into how to separate from the mother. In this view, homosexuality represented a search for the father-love never felt from other males. [12] In short, Bieber attributed homosexuality to the presence of an excessive attachment to and from a mother who was dominant in the spousal relationship, an excessively strong partner paired with an excessively weak one.

In the late 1960's, Charles Socarides also identified the problem as pre-Oedipal, linked with the inability to separate, but argued that homosexuality resulted from a fear of either separation experienced as abandonment or engulfment and loss of self which would result from an intimate relationship with any other woman than mother. He found homosexuality an adaptive behavior hiding enormous feelings of rage. He found that homosexuals often manifested what are believed to be other rage-based conditions such as obsessions, compulsions, and depression. Believing it to be a serious mental illness based on its association with the early separation phase, Socarides argued that helping the homosexual to accept and adjust to his orientation only worsened his condition, making it less likely that normal sexuality would ever emerge. [13]

Reflective of the confusion as well as cyclical and circular nature of the thinking, the most recent work by Evelyn Hooker in the 1950's and 1960's mirrors that done by Alfred Kinsey in the 1940's and Havelock Ellis in the late 19th century. The aspect of Hooker's work that reflects their findings is that homosexuality is widespread enough to treat it as a legitimate alternative condition. All three argued that much of the observed pathology among homosexuals, such as paranoia (vague or specific unfounded fears), reflected more the fears of societal rejection and retribution than "disease", and that until those environmental influences could be isolated, the claim that homosexuals are fundamentally mal-adjusted could not be supported. (29-43) They argued that social struggle to achieve freedom from the terrible effects of societal rejection was the healing tool, not the treatment of homosexuality as a mental illness. (53)   In conformity with that argument, in the mid 1980's the American Psychiatric Association removed homosexuality from its official list of mental diseases. [14] However, it left open appropriate categories of sexual dysfunction which allow those who seek treatment for anxieties resulting from their sexual orientation to receive it.

Even though none of the theories of etiology are derived from members of the Self-psychology school, it is easy to see that many of the elements identified as causing perversions are represented in these theories.   There are at least two issues worthy of note.   If early rejecting parental attitudes and repetitive failures in providing selfobject needs of mirrored acceptance and idealization during early childhood do in fact cause or contribute to the formation of the male or female homosexual as they do in the creation of perversions, then the curative factor is acceptance of the homosexual as he or she is.   This acceptance is most needed from the parents, if available.   Acceptance will likely do nothing to change the orientation of an adult, but it will be part of a reparative process that enables the individual to enhance self-esteem and cohesion.   Secondly, we should not ignore the great psychic confusion and pain which leads to the inability of children and adults, heterosexual and homosexual, to form sound and mature relationships as such victims pursue instead self-inhibiting, compulsive, destructive sexual activities in efforts to restore the self.   As J. A. Symonds said in his work, and Dodgson in his, "offer hope" to those whose selves are and continue to be rejected by others as well as themselves.

NOTES

CHAPTER 1

1. A. O. J. Cockshut, *Truth to Life: The Art of Biography in the Nineteenth Century.*
2. *Letters.* Morton N. Cohen, editor, *The Letters of Lewis Carroll*, 107.

CHAPTER 2

1. Robert D. Sutherland. *Language and Lewis Carroll*, 170-171.
2. Derek Hudson, *Life of Lewis Carroll*, 214.
3. *Diaries.* Roger L. Green, ed., *The Diaries of Lewis Carroll*, 277.
4. Sutherland, 23.
5. Ronald Pearsall, *The Worm in the Bud: The World of Victorian Sexuality*, 458.
6. George Rowell, *The Victorian Theatre 1792-1914: A Survey*, 57.
7. Andrew Parkin, *Collected Plays of Dion Boucicault*, 7.
8. Arthur Evans, *The God of Ecstasy*, 3.
9. Ibid., 34.
10. Eric Partridge, *A Dictionary of Slang and Unconventional English.*
11. Author unknown. *1811 Dictionary of the Vulgar Tongue.*

12. Steven Marcus, *The Other Victorians: A Study of Sexuality and Pornography in Mid-Nineteenth-Century England*, 105.
13. John Boswell, *Christianity, Social Tolerance, and Homosexuality*, Chapters 1, 2.
14. Vern L. Bullough, *Homosexuality: A History*, 2.
15. Boswell, 1980, 43.
16. Bullough, 6.
17. *Cythera's Hymnal.*

CHAPTER 3

1. Anne Clark, *Lewis Carroll: A Biography*, 253.
2. 1811 Dictionary.
3. Stuart Dodgson Collingwood, *The Life and Letters of Lewis Carroll*, 139.
4. *Letters*, 236.
5. Phyllis Greenacre, *Swift and Carroll: A Psychoanalytic Study of Two Lives*, 197.
6. *Diaries*, 458.
7. Clark, 130.
8. Ibid., 170.
9. Hudson, 310.
10. Clark, 164.
11. *Letters*, 711.
12. *Diaries*, 474.
13. Green, 1982, 6.
14. Richard Kelly, *Lewis Carroll*, Chapter 2.
15. Lewis Carroll, *Useful and Instructive Poetry*, 44.
16. Ibid.

17. Ibid., 8.
18. *Diaries*, 76-77.

CHAPTER 4

1. Martin Grotjahn, "About the Symbolization of Alice's Adventures in Wonderland," 32-41. Another short article entitled "Ferdinand the Bull" describes a story whose message to the hearing or reading child is clearly to remain childlike, to avoid growing up and the risks of adulthood, i.e. the theme of symbolic castration.
2. Francis Huxley, *The Raven and the Writing Desk*, 181-182.
3. Green, 1982, 250.
4. Bullough, 106.
5. Marcus, Chapter 1.
6. Lewis Carroll, *The Wasp in a Wig*, 3. From the Introduction by Martin Gardner.
7. Ibid., 11.
8. Ibid., 14.
9. Daniel Kirk, *Charles Dodgson Semeiotician*, 57.
10. Greenacre, 1955, 194.

CHAPTER 5

1. Belle Moses, *Lewis Carroll: In Wonderland and At Home*, 214-215.
2. John Fisher, *Magic and Lewis Carroll*, 131.
3. Ibid., 132.
4. Florence B. Lennon, *Victoria Through the Looking-Glass*, 116. This is a very insightful work, often dismissed as failing to understand the Victorian era.
5. Greenacre, Grotjahn and others.
6. Greenacre, 1955, 240.
7. Martin Gardner, Introduction to *The Hunting of the Snark: An Agony in Eight Fits*, 23.
8. *Diaries*, 435.
9. Collingwood, 152.
10. *Diaries*, 316.
11. Collingwood, 152-153.
12. There are several alternative anagrams from this line. The one chosen reflects the blame placement consistent throughout the work.

   "Re a foul, thin, brutalised male."
   "Mother failed; I turn, abuse all."
   "I failed all, turn, abuse Mother."
   "Mother beat us; ruined, all fail."
   "The more brutal, dual life a sin."
   "Brutal the dues in a moral life." etc.

CHAPTER 6

1. Clark, 12.
2. Hudson, 56.
3. Langford Reed, *The Life of Lewis Carroll*. 21.
4. Hudson, 21.

5. Alice Miller, *The Drama of the Gifted Child*. See also her *Thou Shalt Not Be Aware: Society's Betrayal of the Child*, and *For Your Own Good: Hidden Cruelty in Child-Rearing and the Roots of Violence*, which focuses on Adolf Hitler as a rage-driven adult based on early childhood experiences of severe and unrelenting physical and psychic abuse at the hands of his father. All are very readable works.
6. Hudson, 28.
7. Janice Delaney, et al., *The Curse: A Cultural History of Menstruation*, 20, 46.
8. Alice Miller, *Thou Shalt Not Be Aware*, 218.
9. Jan B. Gordon, "The *Alice* Books and the Metaphors of Victorian Childhood," 101.
10. Greenacre, 1955, 208.
11. Howard R. Wolf, "British Fathers and Sons, 1773-1913: From Filial Submissiveness to Creativity," 53-70.
12. Miller, 1984, 218-219.
13. Greenacre, 1955, 208.
14. Clark, 12.
15. Ibid.
16. Ibid.
17. Collingwood, 11.
18. Clark, 12, 16.
19. *Letters*, 3.
20. Greenacre, 1955, 205.
21. Collingwood, 13.
22. Ibid., 12-13.
23. Clark, 16.
24. Ibid.
25. Miller, 1984, 158.

26. Clark, 56.
27. Ibid., 34-35.
28. Francis Menella Dodgson, publisher of Lewis Carroll's, *Useful and Instructive Poetry*, 15.
29. Ibid., 38.

CHAPTER 7

1. Hudson, 22.
2. Ibid., 24.
3. Clark, 25-27.
4. Collingwood, 8.
5. Florence B. Lennon, "Escape Through the Looking-Glass," 68.
6. Hudson, 23.
7. Greenacre, 1955, 121.
8. Hudson, 28-29.
9. Clark, 23.
10. Hudson, 25.
11. Clark, 22.
12. Collingwood, 54-55.
13. *Letters*, 4.
14. Ibid.
15. Reed, 46.
16. Collingwood, 131-132.
17. Hudson, 22.
18. Clark, 20.
19. Ibid., 65.
20. From an examination of the facial profiles reproduced in Collingwood, 13.
21. Hudson, 56.
22. Ibid., 26.
23. Collingwood, 13-14.
24. Ibid., 8.
25. Hudson, 25.
26. Kirk, 66.

CHAPTER 8

1. John Pudney, *Lewis Carroll and His World*. 12.
2. Clark, 31-38.
3. Pearsall, 553.
4. Lytton Strachey, *Eminent Victorians*, 212 ff.
5. Ibid., 211.
6. Ibid.
7. Clark, 42.
8. Strachey, 212.
9. Ibid.
10. *Letters*, 5.
11. Strachey, 217.
12. Thomas Hughes, *Tom Brown's Schooldays*, 118.
13. Moses, 24.
14. Hughes, 118.
15. Ibid., 140.
16. Moses, 25.
17. Hughes, 171.
18. Clark, 41.
19. Hughes, 182.
20. Ibid.
21. H. Montgomery Hyde, *The Love That Dared Not Speak Its Name: A Candid History of Homosexuality in Britain*, 110.
22. Ibid., 111.
23. Collingwood, 21-23.
24. Hudson, 45-46.
25. Collingwood, 23.
26. Ibid., 30.
27. Clark, 40.
28. Collingwood, 30-31.
29. Clark, 46.
30. Collingwood, 24-25.
31. Hudson, 48.
32. Ibid., 49.
33. Clark, 43.
34. Hudson, 43.
35. Greenacre, 1955, 130.

36. Emily Bronte, *Wuthering Heights*, 124.
37. Clark, 66.
38. Ibid.
39. Ibid., 74.
40. Hyde, 170.
41. Clark, 77.
42. Hudson, 66.
43. John Addington Symonds, *A Problem in Greek Ethics*, 72.
44. Collingwood, 330.
45. Lennon, 1945(1), 249.

CHAPTER 9

1. Clark, 76.
2. Paul Roche, translator, *The Orestes Plays of Aeschylus*, 79.
3. Reginald S. Copleston, *Aeschylus*, 161.
4. Roche, 116.
5. Edward Tripp, *Crowell's Handbook of Classical Mythology*, 231.
6. Copleston, 167.
7. Roche, 129-130.
8. Ibid., 144-146.
9. Tripp, 231.
10. Roche, 162.
11. Ibid., 186.
12. Rollo May, *Man's Search for Himself*, 1953, 127.
13. Ibid., 129.
14. Tripp, 231.
15. Copleston, 156.
16. Ibid., xvii.
17. Lennon, 1945(1), 121.
18. Sidney Halpern, "The Mother-killer," 71-74. This is a very insightful, if brief article, which demonstrates

the universality of the theme across several cultures.

19. See especially Appendix 2, also Heinz Kohut's "Thoughts on Narcissism and Narcissistic Rage" on the intensity with which rage can overtake the entire self, such that all aspects of self become eroticized, consumed with the plotting and planning of revenge. See Masud Khan's *Alienation in Perversions* and Miller's *For Your Own Good* for discussion of sexual activities (involving either one's own body or another as surrogate) as efforts to self-soothe. Khan, though not a member of the Self-psychology school, provides a considerably more technical discussion which integrates very nicely with Self-psychology. He also provides a good discussion of the role of pornography as an antecedent of masturbation, an effort to self-soothe.

20. Masud Khan, *Alienation in Perversions*, 25 ff.

21. Elizabeth Sewell, *The Field of Nonsense*. This work is filled with insights regarding the presence of Dodgson's inner turmoil as revealed in the nonsense despite her lack of awareness of the hidden self-disclosure beneath the mask.

22. Ibid., 180.
23. Ibid., 169.

CHAPTER 10

1. Clark, 68 ff.
2. Greenacre, 1955, 316-317.
3. *Diaries*, 173.
4. John Skinner, "Lewis Carroll's Adventures in Wonderland," 13.
5. *Letters*, 156.
6. Skinner, 13.
7. Selwyn H. Goodacre, "The Illnesses of Lewis Carroll."
8. Jeffrey Stern, Editor, *Lewis Carroll's Library*.
9. Goodacre.
10. Hudson, 284.
11. Dominick A. Barbara, M.D., *The Psychodynamics of Stuttering.* 12. Clark, 258.
13. Stern.
14. *Letters*, 579
15. Stern, Lot 538.
16. Marcus, Chapter 1.
17. Ibid., 3.
18. Ibid., 31.
19. Ibid., 16.
20. Ibid., 21.
21. Phyllis Greenacre, *Emotional Growth: Psychoanalytic Studies of the Gifted and a Great Variety of Other Individuals*, Vol. 2, 323.
22. See John Skinner, *op cit.* and Paul Schilder, "Psychoanalytic Remarks on ALICE IN WONDERLAND."
23. Greenacre, 1971, 316. Van Wyck Brooks' 1933 work *The Ordeal of Mark Twain*

reviews Mark Twain's traumatic childhood experiences with his mother and father — another such child who escaped into a different world until he discovered himself on the Mississippi river-boats.

24. Miller, 1981.

25. Greenacre, 1955, 146.

26. Ibid., 211, footnote.

27. Clark 93-94. Dodgson's lengthy and humorous poem "Hiawatha's Photographing" describes the process in detail. The *Diaries* contains previously unpublished verse which describes the collodian process.

28. Helmut Gernscheim, *Lewis Carroll, Photographer*.

29. Collingwood, 74.

30 Clark, 85.

31. Ethel Arnold, "Reminiscences of Lewis Carroll," 785.

32. Collingwood, 60-61.

33. Charles Dickens, *Dombey and Son*, 12.

34. Ibid., 103.

35. Ibid., 158.

36. Ibid., 240.

37. *Diaries*, 81.

38. Ibid., 525.

39. Mary Breasted, "Collection of Lewis Carroll Moves on to N.Y.U. Library," 49 ff.

40. Ibid.

41. Hudson, 90.

42. Edmund Wilson, "C. L. Dodgson: the Poet Logician," 199.

43. *Diaries*, 481.

44. Collingwood, 146.

45. *Diaries*, 71-72.

46. Oliver Sacks, M.D., *Migraine: Understanding a Common Disorder*, xvii.

47. Ibid., 2-3.

48. Ibid., 3-6.

49. Ibid., 7.

50. Ibid., 65.

51. Ibid., 84.

52. Ibid., 179.

53. Roy J. Mathew, *Treatment of Migraine*, 57.

54. Barbara, 16-17.

55. Ibid., 17-18.

56. Gerard Jonas, *Stuttering: the Disorder of Many Theories*, 24.

57. Barbara, 22.

58. Ibid., 30-31.

59. Ibid., 34.

60. Ibid., 36.

61. Ibid., 39. Chapter 4 is devoted to the alienation of self suffered by the stutterer. Dodgson's stutter, while lifelong, was less severe than some of what Barbara describes; but the underlying issues are the same.

62. Ibid., 46-64.

63. Ibid., 64

64. Ibid., 67

65. Jonas, 31.

CHAPTER 11

1. Clark, 261.

2. Ibid., 262.

3. *Diaries*, 450.

4. *Letters*, 146.

5. Ibid., 1083, footnote.

6. Ibid., 63, footnote.

7. *Diaries*, 159.
8. Alexander Woolcott, *The Complete Works of Lewis Carroll*, 1178.
9. Clark, 262. Liddon's estate was £47,226.
10. John O. Johnston, *Life and Letters of Henry Parry Liddon*, 100.
11. Ibid., 101.
12. Ibid., 198.
13. Ibid., 8-14.
14. Ibid., 10.
15. Ibid., 282.
16. Ibid., 286.
17. Woolcott, 1173.
18. *Diaries*, 125.
19. Howard F. Lowry, et al., *An Oxford Anthology of English Poetry*, 867.
20. Arnold, 782.
21. Ibid., 787.
22. Skinner, 20-21.
23. Lennon, 1945(1), 211.
24. Ibid.
25. Arnold, 784.
26. Pudney, 102-103.
27. Khan, 221-223.
28. Lennon, 1945(1), 190.
29. *Letters*, 595. Cohen notes Dodgson's substitution of *stream* for *brook* in the original Tennyson line, a substitution not required to maintain the allusion.
30. Ibid., 354-355.
21. Reed, 94.
32. *Letters*, 706.
33. *Diaries*, 518.
34. Khan, 1979. This is an important aspect in sexual perversions as well as those such as greed. For the esteem of a depleted self to be restored in the perversion, the activity must go beyond what is accepted by a specific person, group of people, or society in general.

CHAPTER 12

1. *Letters*, 1012.
2. Ibid., 1018.
3. Johnston, 198.
4. Ibid., 225.
5. Rev. Frederic W. Farrar, *Eternal Hope*, xxiii-xxiv.
6. Green, 1965, 1110.
7. Ibid., 1117.
8. *Letters*, 1040-1043.
9. Ibid., 1044-1045.
10. Ibid., 463.
11. Ibid., 745.
12. *Diaries*, 531.
13. Ibid., 533.
14. Hudson, 307.
15. Collingwood, 310.
16. Hudson, 310.
17. Jane L. Borthwick, trans., "My Jesus, as Thou Wilt!"

APPENDIX 1

1. Michael Basch, "Selfobjects and Selfobject Transference: Theoretical Implications," 33.
2. William Goldstein, "DSM III and the Narcissistic Personality," 8.
3. Miller, 1981, 15.
4. Andrew Morrison, ed., *Essential Papers on Narcissism*, 154-155.

5. Anna Ornstein, "Self-Pathology in Childhood: Developmental and Clinical Considerations, 439.
6. Kohut, 1972, 378-396.
7. Ibid. 396.

APPENDIX 2

1. Miller, 1981, 90.
2. The literature, supported by clinical experience, clearly points to the mother as historically the earliest selfobject.
3. Ibid., 87.
4. Ibid., 88.
5. Masud Khan, *Alienation in Perversions*.
6. Ibid., 12.
7. Ibid., 13.
8. Ibid., 25.
9. Ibid., 16.
10. Ibid., 20.
11. Ibid., 26.
12. Ibid., 26.
13. Ibid., 212.
14. Ibid., 28.
15. Miller, 1984, 123.
16. Ibid., 221-223.
17. Ibid., 224-225.

APPENDIX 3

1. Boswell, 20.
2. Ibid., 30, 49.
3. Ibid., 328.
4. Ronald Bayer, *Homosexuality and American Psychiatry: The Politics of Diagnosis*, 16-17.
5. Boswell, 174.

6. Louis Crompton, *Byron and Greek Love: Homophobia in 19th Century England*, 359.
7. Crompton, 229.
8. Bullough, 110.
9. Boswell, 49.
10. Bullough, 1.
11. Bayer, 18-19.
12. Ibid., 30.
13. Ibid., 35-36.
14. Ibid., 53. Recall Dodgson's play with *nomenclature* — *"no mental cure"*.

WORKS OF LEWIS CARROLL

Alice's Adventures in Wonderland. From Gardner, Martin. 1960. *The Anotated Alice*. New York: New American Library. See also: Green, Roger L., ed. 1982. *Alice's Adventures in Wonderland* and *Through the Looking-Glass*. New York, Oxford University Press.

Alice's Adventures Underground. New York: Dover Publications, Inc. 1965.

A Tangled Tale. from Woolcott, Alexander, ed. 1976. *The Complete Works of Lewis Carroll*. New York: Vintage Books.

Diary Manuscripts of Charles L. Dodgson, courtesy of the British Library, Manuscript Collection.

Pillow Problems. 1958. New York: Dover Publications, Inc.

Sylvie and Bruno. 1988. New York: Dover Publications, Inc.

Sylvie and Bruno Concluded. 1893. London: Macmillan and Co.

Symbolic Logic. 1958. From: *Symbolic Logic* and *The Game of Logic*. New York: Dover Publications, Inc.

The Diaries of Lewis Carroll. Green, Roger L., ed. 1954. New York: Oxford University Press. Referred to as "Diaries."

The Game of Logic. 1958. From: *Symbolic Logic* and *The Game of Logic*. New York: Dover Publications, Inc.

The Hunting of the Snark: An Agony in Eight Fits. Tanis, James and Dooley, John, eds. 1981. *The Hunting of the Snark*. Los Altos: William Kaufman, Inc.

The Letters of Lewis Carroll. Cohen, Morton N., ed. 1979. New York: Oxford University Press. Referred to as "*Letters*."

The Nursery "Alice". 1966. New York: Dover Publications, Inc.

Through the Looking-Glass and What Alice Found There. From Gardner, Martin, ed. 1960. *The Anotated Alice*. New York: New American Library. See also: Green, Roger L., ed. 1982. *Alice's Adventures in Wonderland* and *Through the Looking-Glass*. New York, Oxford University Press.

Useful and Instructive Poetry. 1954. Dodgson, Frances Menella. New York: Macmillan and Co.

The Wasp in a Wig. 1977. Washington: Lewis Carroll Society of North America.

The Works of Lewis Carroll. 1965. Green, Roger Lancelyn., ed. London: Paul Hamlyn, Ltd.

GENERAL BIBLIOGRAPHY

Appel, Alfred, Jr. 1966. "An Interview With Vladimir Nabokov." In *Nabokov -- The Man and His Work*, studies edited by L. S. Dembro. Madison: U. of Wisconsin Press. Nabokov's first work was the translation of *Alice's Adventures in Wonderland* into Russian.

Arnold, Ethel M. 1929. "Reminiscences of Lewis Carroll." *Atlantic Monthly* 143 (June):782-789.

Baker, Howard. 1979. "The Conquering Hero Quits: Narcissistic Factors in Underachievement and Failure." *American Journal of Psychotherapy* 33: 418-427.

Baker, Howard., and Baker, Margaret. 1987. "Heinz Kohut's Self Psychology: an Overview." *The American Journal of Psychiatry* 144 (January):1-9.

Barbara, Dominick A., M.D. 1982. *The Psychodynamics of Stuttering*. Springfield, Illinois: Charles C. Thomas Publisher.

Basch, Michael Franz., M.D. 1984. "Selfobjects and Selfobject Transference: Theoretical Implications." In *Kohut's Legacy: Contributions to Self Psychology*, Paul E. Stepansky and Arnold Goldberg, eds.

Bayer, Ronald. 1981. *Homosexuality and American Psychiatry: The Politics of Diagnosis*. New York: Basic Books, Inc.

Bayne, Thomas Vere. The unpublished diaries of Thomas Vere Bayne, courtesy of Christ Church, Oxford University.

Beaver, Harold. 1976. "Whale or Boojum: an Agony." In *Lewis Carroll Observed*, edited by Edward Guiliano, 111-131. New York: Clarkson N. Potter, Inc. 1976.

Bellow, Gregory, Ph.D. 1986. "Self Psychology and Ego Psychology: a Historical Perspective." *Clinical Social Work Journal* 14, no. 3 (Fall):199-212.

Blake, Kathleen. 1974. *Play, Games, and Sport: The Literary Works of Lewis Carroll*. Ithaca, N. Y.: Cornell University Press.

Borthwick, Jane L., trans. 1854. "My Jesus, As Thou Wilt!" Reprinted in *The Hymnal for Youth*. Westminster Press (Jewett 6.6.6.6.D).

Boswell, John. 1980. *Christianity, Social Tolerance, and Homosexuality*. Chicago: The University of Chicago Press.

Breasted, Mary. 1975. "Collection of Lewis Carroll Moves on to N.Y.U. Library." New York: *The New York Times*, March 19:49.

Bromberg, Philip M. 1986. "The Mirror and the Mask: on Narcissism and Psychoanalytic Growth." In *Essential Papers on Narcissism*, Andrew P. Morrison, M.D., ed.

Bronte, Emily. 1847. *Wuthering Heights*. Reprint, 1959. New York: New American Library of World Literature, Inc.

Brooks, Van Wyck. 1933. *The Ordeal of Mark Twain*. New York: E. P. Dutton & Co.

Bryant, Clifton., PhD. 1982. *Sexual Deviancy and Social Proscription: The Social Context of Carnal Behavior*. New York: Human Sciences Press.

Bullough, Vern L. 1979. *Homosexuality: A History*. New York: New American Library.

Cammaerts, Emile. 1926. *The Poetry of Nonsense*. New York: E. P. Dutton and Company.

Chessick, Richard D. 1983. "Clinical Notes Toward the Understanding and Intensive Psychotherapy of Adult Eating Disorders." *The Annual of Psychoanalysis*, XII/XIII:301-321.

Ciardi, John. 1971. "A Burble Through the Tulgey Wood." In *Aspects of Alice*, edited by Robert Phillips, 253-261. New York: The Vanguard Press, 1971.

Clark, Anne. 1979. *Lewis Carroll: A Biography*. New York: Schocken Books.

Cockshut, A. O. J. 1974. *Truth to Life: The Art of Biography in the Nineteenth Century*. New York: Harcourt Brace Jovanovich.

Cohen, Morton N. 1982. "The Actress and the Don: Ellen Terry and Lewis Carroll." In *Lewis Carroll: A Celebration*, edited by Edward Guiliano, 167-175. New York: Clarkson N. Potter Inc., 1982.

Cohen, Morton N., ed. 1989. *Lewis Carroll Interviews & Recollections*. Iowa City: University of Iowa Press.

Collingwood, Stuart Dodgson. 1898. *The Life and Letters of Lewis Carroll*. London: The Century Company.

Copleston, Reginald S., DD. 1870. *Aeschylus*. Edinburgh and London: William Blackwood and Sons. Reprint. 1880.

Crompton, Louis. 1985. *Byron and Greek Love: Homophobia in 19th Century England*. Berkeley and Los Angeles: University of California Press.

Cythera's Hymnal. 1852. Author unknown; claims publication by Oxford University Press but highly unlikely. Courtesy of British Library Private Collection.

De La Mare, Walter. 1932. *Lewis Carroll*. London: Faber & Faber Limited.

Delaney, Janice., Lupton, Mary Jane., and Toth, Emily. 1988. *The Curse: A Cultural History of Menstruation*. Urbana and Chicago: University of Illinois Press.

Dembro. L. S. 1967. *Nabokov - The Man and His Work*. Madison: U. of Wisconsin Press.

Dickens, Charles. 1848. *Dombey and Son*. New York: New American Library (Signet Classic), 1980.

Dupree, Robert. "She's All My Fancy Painted Him." In *Soaring with the Dodo - Essays on Lewis Carroll's Life and Art*. Washington, D. C.: The Lewis Carroll Society of North America.

Empsom, William. 1971. "Alice in Wonderland: the Child as Swain." In *Aspects of Alice*, edited by Robert Phillips, 344-376. New York: The Vanguard Press, 1971.

Evans, Arthur. 1988. *The God of Ecstasy*. New York: St. Martin's Press.

Farrar, Frederic, Reverend. 1878. *Eternal Hope*. New York: E. P. Dutton.

Fisher, John., ed. 1973. *The Magic of Lewis Carroll*. New York: Bramhall House.

Fraiberg, Selma. 1959. *The Magic Years*. New York: Charles R. Scribner's Sons.

Furniss, Harry. 1924. *Some Victorian Men*. New York: Dodd, Mead and Company.

Gasson, Roy., ed. 1978. *The Illustrated Lewis Carroll*. Poole, England: New Orchard Editions, Ltd.

Gattegno, Jean. 1977. *Lewis Carroll: Fragments of a Looking Glass*. London: George Allen & Unwin.

_____. 1982. "*Sylvie and Bruno*, or the Inside and the Outside." In *Lewis Carroll: A Celebration*, edited by Edward Guiliano, 167-175. New York: Clarkson N. Potter Inc., 1982.

Gayley, Charles Mills. 1939. *The Classic Myths*. New York: John Wiley & Sons.

Gernsheim, Helmut. 1949. *Lewis Carroll, Photographer*. London: Max Parrish.

Goldschmidt, A. M. E. 1971. *Alice in Wonderland* Psychoanalyzed. In *Aspects of Alice*, edited by Robert Phillips, 279-282. New York: The Vanguard Press, 1971.

Goldstein, William N., M.D. 1985. "DSM III and the Narcissistic Personality." *American Journal of Psychotherapy* 39 no. 1 (January):4-16.

Goodacre, Selwyn H. 1972. "The Illnesses of Lewis Carroll." *The Practitioner* August.

_____. "An Unrecognized Lewis Carroll Parody." *Jabberwocky* 5 no. 2.

Gordon, Jan B. 1982. "Lewis Carroll, the *Sylvie and Bruno* Books, and the Nineties: the Tyranny of Textuality." In *Lewis Carroll: A Celebration*, edited by Edward Guiliano, 176-195. New York: Clarkson N. Potter Inc., 1982.

_____. 1971. "The *Alice* Books and the Metaphors of Victorian Childhood." In *Aspects of Alice*, edited by Robert Phillips, 93-113. New York: The Vanguard Press, 1971.

Green, Roger L. 1949. *The Story of Lewis Carroll*. London: Methun and Co., Ltd.

Greenacre, Phyllis., M.D. 1955. *Swift and Carroll: A Psychoanalytic Study of Two Lives*. New York: International Universities Press.

_____. 1971. *Emotional Growth: Psychoanalytic Studies of the Gifted and a Great Variety of Other Individuals*, Vol. 2. New York: International Universities Press, Inc.

_____. 1971. "The Character of Dodgson as Revealed in the Writings of Carroll." In *Aspects of Alice*, edited by Robert Phillips, 316-331. New York: The Vanguard Press, 1971.

Grotjahn, Martin., M.D. 1940. "Ferdinand the Bull." *American Imago* 1: no. 3:33-48

_____. 1947. "About the Symbolization of Alice's Adventures in Wonderland." *American Imago* 4: no. 4:32-41.

Guiliano, Edward., ed. 1976. *Lewis Carroll Observed*. New York: Clarkson N. Potter, Inc.

_____. 1982. "A Time for Humor: Lewis Carroll, Laughter and Despair, and *The Hunting of the Snark*." In *Lewis Carroll: A Celebration*, edited by Edward Guiliano, 123-131. New York: Clarkson N. Potter Inc., 1982.

_____. 1982. "Lewis Carroll in a Changing World: An Interview with Morton N. Cohen." In *Soaring with the Dodo - Essays on Lewis Carroll's Life and Art*. Washington, D. C.: The Lewis Carroll Society of North America.

Guiliano, Edward., and Kincaid, James R., eds. 1982. *Soaring with the Dodo - Essays on Lewis Carroll's Life and Art*. Washington, D. C.: The Lewis Carroll Society of North America.

Halpern, Sidney. 1965. "The Mother-killer." *Psychoanalytic Review* LII, Summer:71-74.

Hencle, Roger B. 1982. "Carroll's Narratives Underground: "Modernism" and Form." In *Lewis Carroll: A Celebration*, edited by Edward Guiliano. New York: Clarkson N. Potter Inc., 1982.

Hicks, Granville. 1967. "All About Vladimir." *SR*, January 7:27-28.

Holmes, Roger W. 1982. "The Philosopher's *Alice in Wonderland*." In *Aspects of Alice*, edited by Robert Phillips, 159-174. New York: The Vanguard Press, 1971.

Hudson, Derek. 1954. *Life of Lewis Carroll*. London: Constable and Company.

Hughes, Thomas. 1857. *Tom Brown's Schooldays*. Reprint 1983. New York: Penguin Books.

Huxley, Francis. 1976. *The Raven and the Writing Desk*. New York: Harper and Row Publishers. A wonderfully entertaining work in search of the meaning of the riddle and many other Carroll mysteries.

Hyde, H. Montgomery. 1970. *The Love That Dared Not Speak Its Name: A Candid History of Homosexuality in Britain*. Boston: Little, Brown and Company.

Johnston, John O. 1904. *Life and Letters of Henry Parry Liddon*. London: Longmans, Green, and Co.

Jonas, Gerard. 1977. *Stuttering: the Disorder of Many Theories*. New York: Farrar, Straus, and Giroux.

Kelly, Richard. 1977. *Lewis Carroll*. Boston: Twayne Publishers.

Khan, M. Masud R. 1979. *Alienation in Perversions*. London: The Hogarth Press and the Institute of Psycho-Analysis.

Kirk, Daniel. 1963. *Charles Dodgson Semeiotician*. Gainesville, Florida: University of Florida Press.

Kohut, Heinz, M.D. 1971. *The Analysis of the Self*. New York: International Universities Press.

_____. 1972. "Thoughts on Narcissism and Narcissistic Rage." *Psychoanalytic Study of the Child* 27:360-400.

_____. 1977. *The Restoration of the Self*. New York: International Universities Press.

_____. 1978. *In Search for the Self*. Edited by P. Ornstein. New York: International Universities Press.

Kohut, Heinz., M.D., and Wolf, Ernest S. 1978. "The Disorders of the Self and Their Treatment: an Outline." *Journal of Psycho-Analysis* 59:413-425.

Lennon, Florence Becker. 1945 (1). *Victoria Through the Looking-Glass*. New York: Simon and Schuster, Inc.

_____. 1945(2). "Escape Through the Looking-glass." In *Aspects of Alice*, edited by Robert Phillips, 66-82. New York: The Vanguard Press, 1971.

Levin, Harry. 1965. "Wonderland Revisited." In *Aspects of Alice*, edited by Robert Phillips, 175-197. New York: The Vanguard Press, 1971.

Lull, Janis. 1982. "The Appliance of Art: the Carroll-Tenniel Collaboration in *Through the Looking-Glass*." In *Lewis Carroll: A Celebration*, edited by Edward Guiliano, 101-111. New York: Clarkson N. Potter Inc., 1982.

Mahler, M., Pine, F., & Bergmann, A. 1975. *The Psychological Birth of the Human Infant*. New York: Basic Books. Margaret Mahler is an early researcher into the psychological development and life of the child.

Marcus, Steven. 1964. *The Other Victorians: A Study of Sexuality and Pornography in Mid-Nineteenth-Century England*. New York: Basic Books, Inc.

Masterson, James F., M.D. 1985. *The Real Self*. New York: Brunner/Mazel Publishers.

Mathew, Roy J., M.D. 1981. *Treatment of Migraine*. New York: SP Medical and Scientific Books.

May, Rollo. 1953. *Man's Search for Himself*. New York: W. W. Norton. Reprint. New York: Dell Publishing, 1973.

McCarthy, James B. 1978. "Narcissism and the Self in Homicidal Adolescents." *The American Journal of Psychoanalysis*, 38:19-29.

Meissner, W. W. 1986. "Narcissistic Personalities and Borderline Conditions: a Differential Diagnosis." In *Essential Papers on Narcissism*. Andrew P. Morrison, M.D. ed.

Meloy, J. Reid. 1986. "Narcissistic Psychopathology and the Clergy." *Pastoral Psychology*, 35, no. 1 (Fall): 50-55.

Miller, Alice. 1979. "Depression and Grandiosity as Related Forms of Narcissistic Disturbances." In *Essential Papers on Narcissism*. Andrew P. Morrison, M.D., ed.

_____. 1981. *The Drama of the Gifted Child*. New York: Basic Books, Inc.

_____. 1983. *For Your Own Good: Hidden Cruelty in Child-Rearing and the Roots of Violence*. New York: Farrar, Straus, Giroux.

_____. 1984. *Thou Shalt Not Be Aware: Society's Betrayal of the Child*. New York: Farrar, Straus, Giroux.

Miller, Edmund. 1976. "The Sylvie and Bruno Books." In *Lewis Carroll Observed*, edited by Edward Guiliano. New York: Clarkson N. Potter, Inc. 1976.

Milner, Florence. "The Poems in *Alice in Wonderland*." In *Aspects of Alice*, edited by Robert Phillips, 245-252. New York: The Vanguard Press, Inc. Article provides originals of the poems parodied by Dodgson.

Monahan, Julian. 1971. *Vladimir Nabokov*. U. of Minnesota Press, no. 96. 1971.

Morrison, Andrew P., M.D., ed. 1986. *Essential Papers on Narcissism*. New York: New York University Press.

_____. 1986. "Shame, Ideal Self, and Narcissism." In *Essential Papers on Narcissism*, Andrew P. Morrison, M.D. ed.

Moses, Belle. 1910. *Lewis Carroll: In Wonderland and At Home*. New York: D. Appleton and Company.

Muslin, Hyman L. 1981. "King Lear: Images of the Self in Old Age." *Journal of Mental Imagery* no. 5, 143-156.

My Secret Life. Late 1800's; publisher unknown. 11 volume, 4200 page "autobiography" of "Walter." Courtesy of the British Library Private Collection.

Nicholson, Barbara L., Ph.D., LICSW. 1989. "Narcissism and Self Psychology," for *Essentials of Self Psychology*, (in press). New York: Jason Aronson Press.

Ornstein, Anna, M.D. 1981. "Self-Pathology in Childhood: Developmental and Clinical Considerations". *Psychiatric Clinics of North America* 4 no. 3: 435-453.

Otten, Terry. 1982. "After Innocence: Alice in the Garden." In *Lewis Carroll: A Celebration*, edited by Edward Guiliano, 50-61. New York: Clarkson N. Potter Inc., 1982.

The Oxford English Dictionary. 1989. Second Edition. Oxford: Clarendon Press.

Partridge, Eric. 1967. *A Dictionary of Slang and Unconventional English*, 6th Edition. New York: Macmillan Co.

Pearsall, Ronald. 1969. *The Worm in the Bud: The World of Victorian Sexuality*. London: Weiodenfeld and Nicolson.

Phillips, Robert., ed. 1971. *Aspects of Alice*. New York: The Vanguard Press, Inc.

Pudney, John. 1976. *Lewis Carroll and His World*. New York: Charles Scribner's Sons.

Rankin, Donald. 1982. "Blessed Rage: Lewis Carroll and the Modern Quest for Order." In *Lewis Carroll: A Celebration* edited by Edward Guiliano, 15-25. New York: Clarkson N. Potter Inc., 1982.

Reed, Langford. 1932. *The Life of Lewis Carroll*. London: W. & G. Foyle. Ltd.

Reade, Brian, ed. 1970. *Sexual Heretics: Male Homosexuality in English Literature 1850-1900*. New York, pp. 158-193.

Roche, Paul., trans. 1962. *The Orestes Plays of Aeschylus*. New York: Mentor Classic, New American Library.

Sacks, Oliver, M.D. 1985. *Migraine: Understanding a Common Disorder*. Berkeley and Los Angeles: University of California Press.

Schilder, Paul. 1938. "Psychoanalytic Remarks on ALICE IN WONDERLAND and Lewis Carroll." In *Aspects of Alice*, edited by Robert Phillips, 283-291. New York: The Vanguard Press, 1971.

Sewell, Elizabeth. 1952. *The Field of Nonsense*. London: Chatto and Windus. Reprint: Norwood Editions, 1977.

_____. 1958. "Lewis Carroll and T.S. Eliot as Nonsense Poets." In *Aspects of Alice*, edited by Robert Phillips, 119-126. New York: The Vanguard Press, 1971.

Skinner, John. 1947. "Lewis Carroll's Adventures in Wonderland." *American Imago* 4: no. 3:3-31.

Stegner, Page. 1966. *Escape into Aesthetics: The Art of Vladimir Nabokov*. New York: Dial Press.

Stepansky, Paul E., and Goldberg, Arnold., Eds. 1984. *Kohut's Legacy: Contributions to Self Psychology*. Hillsdale, New Jersey: The Analytic Press (distributed by Lawrence Erlbaum Associates, Publishers).

Stern, Jeffrey., ed. 1981. *Lewis Carroll's Library*. Washington, D.C.: The Lewis Carroll Society of North America.

Strachey, Lytton. 1918. *Eminent Victorians*. New York and London: G. P. Putnam's Sons.

Sutherland, Robert D. 1970. *Language and Lewis Carroll*. The Hague: Robert D. Mouton and Co., N.V.

Symonds, John Addington. 1896. *A Problem in Greek Ethics Being an Inquiry into the Phenomenon of Sexual Inversion*. London, privately published; Copy 87 of 100, courtesy of the British Library Private Collection.

Tripp, Edward. 1970. *Crowell's Handbook of Classical Mythology*. New York: Thomas Y. Crowell Co.

White, Marjorie Taggart. 1986. "Self Relations, Object Relations, and Pathological Narcissism." In *Essential Papers on Narcissism*. Andrew P. Morrison, M.D., ed.

Williams, Sidney H. 1979. *The Lewis Carroll Handbook*. Update of *The Lewis Carroll Handbook*, by Sidney H. Williams and Falconer Madan, Roger L. Green, ed. Folkstead, England: Dawson.

Wilson, Edmund. 1971. "C. L. Dodgson: the Poet Logician." In *Aspects of Alice*, edited by Robert Phillips, 198-206. New York: The Vanguard Press, 1971.

Winnicott, D. W. 1958. "The Capacity to be Alone." In *The Maturational Process and the Facilitating Environment*, New York: International Universities Press, 1965.

_____. 1956. "The Antisocial Tendency." In *Through Pediatrics to Psycho-analysis*. New York: Basic Books, Inc., 1975.

Wolf, Howard R. 1965. "British Fathers and Sons, 1773-1913: From Filial Submissiveness to Creativity." *Psychoanalytic Review*, LII, Summer 1965.

Wright, Austin., ed. 1961. *Victorian Literature*. New York: Oxford University Press.

1811 Dictionary of the Vulgar Tongue: A Dictionary of Buckish Slang, University Wit and Pickpocket Eloquence. 1971. Chicago: Follet Publishing Co.

INDEX